An Introduction to Philosophical Methods

AN INTRODUCTION TO
PHILOSOPHICAL METHODS

CHRIS DALY

BROADVIEWGUIDES to PHILOSOPHY

LIBRARY AND ARCHIVES CANADA CATALOGUING IN PUBLICATION

Daly, Chris
    An introduction to philosophical methods / Chris Daly.

(Broadview guides to philosophy)
Includes bibliographical references and index.
ISBN 978-1-55111-934-2

    1. Methodology. I. Title. II. Series: Broadview guides to philosophy

B53.D34 2010   101   C2010-903106-7

BROADVIEW PRESS is an independent, international publishing house, incorporated in 1985.

We welcome comments and suggestions regarding any aspect of our publications—please feel free to contact us at the addresses below or at broadview@broadviewpress.com.

NORTH AMERICA   2215 Kenmore Ave.
Post Office Box 1243   Buffalo, New York, USA 14207
Peterborough, Ontario   TEL: (705) 743-8990
Canada K9J 7H5   FAX: (705) 743-8353

customerservice@broadviewpress.com

UK, EUROPE, CENTRAL ASIA, MIDDLE EAST, AFRICA, INDIA, AND SOUTHEAST ASIA
Eurospan Group, 3 Henrietta St., London WC2E 8LU, United Kingdom
TEL: 44 (0) 1767 604972 FAX: 44 (0) 1767 601640
eurospan@turpin-distribution.com

AUSTRALIA AND NEW ZEALAND
NewSouth Books
c/o TL Distribution, 15-23 Helles Ave., Moorebank, NSW, Australia 2170
TEL: (02) 8778 9999 FAX: (02) 8778 9944
orders@tldistribution.com.au

www.broadviewpress.com

Edited by Robert Martin
Cover design and interior by Em Dash Design

This book is printed on paper
containing 100% post-consumer fibre.

 Printed in Canada

Contents

Preface

I am very grateful to Ryan Chynces at Broadview Press for his enthusiasm and encouragement in commissioning this book. Five anonymous referees for Broadview Press gave invaluable advice on an initial plan for the book. I have tried to implement all of their many suggestions on content and structure. Thanks also to Greg Janzen, Ryan's successor at Broadview, for seeing the book through to its printing. Tara Lowes and her production team did wonderful work in preparing the book.

Eve Garrard, David Liggins and Eric Steinhart generously read a draft of the entire manuscript. Their suggestions made tremendous improvements in the material. Rina Arya, Harry Lesser, Carrie Jenkins and Daniel Nolan gave invaluable feedback on several chapters.

Thanks also to Tony Anderson, Eric Barnes, James Robert Brown, Earl Conee, Tim Maudlin, John Norton and Jonathan Vogel for correspondence.

Bob Martin did a wonderful job in copy-editing the manuscript. He also provided a wealth of very helpful philosophical comments.

I have older debts to my former supervisors: Jeremy Butterfield, Peter Lipton, and Hugh Mellor. They have been very influential in many ways. Peter's sudden death in November 2007 remains crushing. He was a wonderful person and his book *Inference to the Best Explanation* has become a classic in its field.

This book is dedicated to Bump and Moula.

Introduction

Philosophers, like scientists, make various claims. But, unlike many scientists, philosophers do not use test tubes, telescopes, cloud chambers, or similar equipment in their work. This raises the question: what kinds of evidence are there for philosophical claims? Philosophical claims are characteristically speculative. Yet, if this means that such claims are unsupported, we might reasonably wonder why anyone should make such claims and why anyone should give them the slightest degree of belief.

Citing the published work of others will not tell us what kinds of support philosophical claims have because it only defers the question. We now need to know what kinds of support there are for those written claims. What reasons did the authors of the claims have for making them? There is a general point about the evidential value of testimony here. Even if testimony can provide us with reason to believe that some **proposition P** is true, the ultimate sources of the testimony — namely, the philosophers who made those claims in the first place — will have to had some other kinds of reason for believing that *P*. We need to know what those kinds of reason are.

Again, it may be an important general lesson in epistemology that it can be reasonable for someone to make certain claims even if that person does not have evidence to support those claims.[1] But presumably not all claims (not even all philosophical claims) have that status. Furthermore, even if it is reasonable for various philosophers to make certain claims without providing supporting evidence, if some of their claims are mutually incompatible we then face the challenge of selecting between those claims. It seems that meeting that challenge will require having reasons for the claims we select.

---

1   For a defence of this view, see van Inwagen (1996).

Suppose we can identify at least some of the kinds of evidence that support philosophical claims. Matters do not end there because we would still need to evaluate the kinds of evidence. We would need to know just how good those kinds of evidence are. At one time people thought that the state of chicken entrails provided evidence about what lay ahead. That was clearly not the best method of predicting the future. But is there any reason why we should suppose that today's philosophers are any less in error? This is not an idle concern. Some philosophers have thought that philosophy's track record of discovering truths, as opposed to promulgating falsehoods, is no better than the track record of examining chicken entrails as a guide to the future.[2] So if one key issue concerns what kinds of evidence support philosophical claims, a second key issue concerns how reliable those claims are — how likely are they to lead to true claims as opposed to false ones.

The fact that philosophers do not have laboratories packed with testing and measuring equipment has perhaps encouraged the belief that they do not need them, and, more generally, that philosophers do not need *any* kind of empirical information in developing and defending their views. The idea is that if philosophers do not rely on empirical data, they must rely on non-empirical data. These data would have to be data of a special kind accessible by intellectual reflection in an armchair. And if philosophers' hypotheses are tested by non-empirical data, then these hypotheses themselves will not be empirical hypotheses. They will not be hypotheses about the empirical world, but hypotheses about how we think about the empirical world. They are hypotheses about our representations of things. Philosophy then becomes an enquiry into the nature of our representations or **concepts** of things. This encapsulates the idea of philosophy as **conceptual analysis**, of philosophical hypotheses as claims about what are concepts are like and how they are necessarily related to one another. This conception of philosophy continues to be influential.

The line of argument in the preceding paragraph, however, can be resisted. Even if philosophers do not have laboratories, and do not run empirical experiments, it does not follow that empirical data are irrelevant to philosophical theories. Such data might even be required by those theories. After all, many theoretical physicists themselves do not have laboratories and do not run empirical experiments. Nevertheless they depend upon the laboratory and field results of experimental physicists to get evidence for their theories.

According to one conception of philosophy — **naturalism** — philosophical hypotheses can receive empirical support (or empirical

---

2   See, for example, Lewis (1991, 58–60) and Taylor (1968, 618–19).

disconfirmation). The support may often be indirect. The support may perhaps be even more indirect than the support that high-level physical theories receive from empirical observations. But the support is there nonetheless. This conception of philosophy may go on to make further claims about this support. In order of increasing strength, it may claim that empirical evidence supplements narrowly philosophical forms of evidence for philosophical claims; that it is the best kind of evidential support that philosophical claims can have; or that it is the only kind of evidential support that philosophical claims can have. We will consider naturalism and its methods particularly in chapter 6.

Something we learn from the discussion so far is that, unlike many other disciplines, not only do philosophers disagree about what claims are warranted, they also disagree about what methods to use and what types of data can support their claims. What methods and data should be used by philosophy is as controversial an issue as any other issue is in philosophy. This book takes a "twin track" approach. It addresses the descriptive issue of identifying some of the methods and types of data that philosophers have used. It also addresses the normative issue of how those methods should be evaluated, and how much support those types of data provide for philosophical claims. To pursue this normative issue, each chapter will contain case studies: actual examples of how certain methods or types of data have been used to support, or undermine, philosophical claims. This brings the descriptive and the normative issues together, as we need to be clear both about what evidence a particular philosopher offered for a certain claim, and also about how reliable that support was. There also seems to be no better way of testing a proposed method or the value of certain data than by examining how well they do in solving a knotty philosophical problem. As Bertrand Russell warned us, "nothing of any value can be said on method except through examples" (Russell 1914, 240). So the use of case studies is itself an indispensable methodological device in philosophy.

This book will be concerned with three broad questions about philosophical methodology:

(Q1) What kinds of data support philosophical hypotheses, and how much support can they provide?

(Q2) Which principles govern the selection of philosophical hypotheses?

(Q3) What kinds of hypotheses are philosophical hypotheses supposed to be?

The data for philosophical hypotheses discussed in the book include the data supplied by **common sense** (chapter 1), **thought experiments** (chapter 3), and science (chapter 6). The principles of selection between philosophical hypotheses to be discussed include principles of **analysis** (chapter 2), simplicity (chapter 4), and explanation (chapter 5).

Issues about the methods and types of data that philosophers should use are entangled with views about the nature of philosophy. Such views belong to what is called "metaphilosophy": the philosophical study of philosophy itself. Conceptual analysis and naturalism are examples of different metaphilosophies. (In fact, "conceptual analysis" and "naturalism" are each umbrella terms that cover a number of metaphilosophical views). Metaphilosophical views are especially hard to argue for. Moreover, many philosophers do not argue for, or even make explicit, whatever metaphilosophical views they hold. Very often whatever metaphilosophical views they may have are background assumptions that are only implicit in their work. This practice is understandable: these philosophers want to get on and tackle "first-order" philosophical problems about the nature of mind, or truth, or the physical world, and so on, not the "second-order" problem of the nature of philosophy. Still, the nature of philosophy is a legitimate area of philosophical inquiry. And since our views about this area, and about the nature of philosophical problems, will bear on how we tackle first-order philosophical problems, it deserves to be investigated as well.

Although philosophical methodology has connections with grand metaphilosophical issues, this should not mislead us. Much philosophical methodology consists in making or evaluating arguments, distinctions and qualifications. These practices are mostly not the special preserve of some particular metaphilosophical faction. For the most part, they form a common venture.

This book's concern with philosophical problems, the principles used to try to resolve them, and the metaphilosophies underlying them reflects a more general concern with disciplined theoretical work in philosophy. Some may worry about how far this neglects the history of philosophy.[3] The issue of the relation of philosophy to the history of philosophy is a controversial one. Although in this book I do not draw upon the history of philosophy, that is not because the book is committed to claiming that the history of philosophy has no important bearing on how philosophy should be studied.[4] The book's scope is intentionally limited in scope in several ways. If the history of philosophy has an important bearing on

---

3   Moore (2009, 116–17) raises just this worry about Williamson (2007).

4   For this issue, see Melnyck (2008b).

how philosophy should be studied, it seems that the relevant historical lessons can complement the non-historical philosophical claims made in this book.

The book's scope is restricted in two further respects. First, it will not explore every potential source of evidence for philosophical theories. For example, the epistemic status of testimony in philosophy will not be explored. Nor will any of the various formal methods that are used in philosophy. These methods have drawn on developments in logic and mathematics to bring increased rigour and precision to philosophy (Anderson 1998, §1). Some of these methods are, however, discussed in (Steinhart 2009), a related text to this book.

The second respect in which the book is deliberately restricted is that, even regarding the topics that it does discuss, not every aspect of those topics will be discussed. But while this book does not aim to be comprehensive, hopefully it provides a useful resource.

ONE Common Sense

1. Introduction

Philosophers have often put forward striking claims. Examples include the claims that time does not exist, that the world consists of only atoms and the void, that the world consists of an infinity of mental substances, that a single cent makes the difference between being rich and not being rich, that no physical object has a colour, that no one knows anything, and that no one has ever believed anything. For each of these claims, one issue is to understand exactly what the claim means. Another issue is to evaluate the claim. What reasons are there for accepting it? What reasons are there for doubting it? Which reasons are the stronger?

G.E. Moore was struck by what seemed to him to be the bizarre consequences of some of the claims that philosophers have made. For example, some idealists denied that time exists. But if their denial were correct, Moore argues, it would not be true that he had breakfast before he had lunch today, or that he put his socks on before he put his shoes on. Yet this conflicts with common sense. Again, some idealists denied that space exists. But their denial entails that nothing is in a spatial relation to anything else. It follows that it is false that Moore's clock is on the mantelpiece, even though common sense says that it is true. In these conflicts between common sense and highfaluting philosophy, Moore wholeheartedly backs common sense. In general, according to Moore, "[the] Common Sense view of the world is, in certain fundamental features, wholly true" (Moore 1925, 44), and any philosophical claim incompatible with common sense claims is false.

Moore's approach draws upon Aristotle's championing of common opinion in *Metaphysics* book B and the common sense philosophy advocated by Thomas Reid in the eighteenth century (Reid 1764). The approach taken by these philosophers raises three questions:

(Q1) What is a common sense claim?
(Q2) What justifies common sense claims?
(Q3) What role (if any) should common sense claims have in philosophy?

Some of our claims belong to common sense, others do not. (Q1) asks on what basis this classification is made. It asks: what does it take for a given claim to be a common sense claim? Having made such a classification, (Q2) asks what significance the classification has. Perhaps a given claim is more credible than some other claim because only the first is a common sense claim. Or perhaps a claim's being a common sense claim does not confer any credibility on it. Given an answer to (Q2), we can address (Q3). (Q3) concerns what the proper role of common sense is in philosophical inquiry.

2. Moore's Defence of Common Sense

Moore begins his paper "A Defence of Common Sense" with a list of claims about his body and its relation to various other physical objects. For example, he claims that he has a body, that this body has existed for some time, that it has grown over that time, that it has not been far from the surface of the Earth during all that time, and that it has been at various distances from various other objects. Moore then makes a list of claims about his mind. He claims, for example, that he is now conscious and that he is now seeing something. Moore also claims to "*know*, with **certainty**" all of the claims in his lists (Moore 1959, 32). He further claims that he knows both that there are many other people and that they know similar lists of truisms about their own bodies and minds.

Moore follows a three-part strategy when a philosopher's argument conflicts with common sense. The first part of Moore's strategy amounts to standing the philosopher's argument on its head. Let's represent the proposition that time does not exist by p. Next, let's represent the proposition that I did not put my shoes on before I put my socks on by q. The idealist offers an argument of the following form:

p,
if p then q,
so q.

Moore offers a counter-argument of the form:

not-q,
if p then q,
so not-p.

Moore argues that because the idealist's conclusion, *q*, is false, so too is the idealist's premise, *p*. This leaves open, however, which of these rival arguments — the idealist's or Moore's — we should accept. The second part of Moore's strategy explains why we should accept his argument:

> The only way ... of deciding between my opponent's argument and mine, as to which is the better, is by deciding which premise is known to be true.... And moreover the degree of certainty of the conclusion, in either case, supposing neither is quite certain, will be in proportion to the degree of certainty of the premises. (Moore 1953, 121–22)

Moore further claims that he is more certain of his claim to knowledge than his opponent is of his own premise. When faced with a philosophical challenge to his claim to know a given common sense statement, Moore responds by saying

> And I think we may safely challenge any philosopher to bring forward any argument in favour of either of the proposition that we do not know [the common sense statement to be true], or of the proposition that it is not true, which does not rest upon some premise which is, beyond comparison, less certain than is the proposition which it is designed to attack. (Moore 1959, 227–28)

Moore's response here appeals to what we might call *differential certainty*. He is more certain that at least one premise of his opponent's argument is false than he is that the common sense statement is false.[1]

The third and final part of Moore's argumentative strategy is that Moore thinks that he can refute his opponent's argument without showing how he knows common sense statements to be true. Again he appeals to considerations of certainty: he is more certain that we know common sense statements than he is of any philosophical theory that would explain how we have that knowledge. Whether or not such an explanation is forthcoming, and whatever form it takes, such an explanation is inessential to our knowing common sense statements to be true.

To sum up, where a philosopher makes a claim that seems bizarre, Moore's strategy is to draw a consequence from that claim that is incompatible with common sense. Doing so shows why the claim is bizarre — it

---

1 Moore's response is endorsed by, amongst others, Chisholm (1982, 68–69), Pryor (2000, 518), Hirsch (2002, 68), Soames (2003, 22–23, 69–70, and 345), Lemos (2004, 11), Armstrong (2006, 160), Lycan (2007, 93–95), and Schaffer (2009, 357).

conflicts with common sense — and it also shows that the claim is false and that any argument in support of the claim is unsound. Any such argument either contains a false premise or a bad inferential step. It remains a further philosophical task to locate this flaw. Moore's strategy is supposed to establish that there is such a flaw, and so that we are reasonable in rejecting the philosopher's claim and any argument that he may have for it.

3. Defining Common Sense

Keith Campbell points out that Moore did not take common sense claims to serve as a foundation for a correct system of philosophy:

> Rather they served as touchstones for propositions arrived at by other routes. Since all propositions must be compatible with them, common-sense beliefs, together with what they entail, serve as a *decisive, negative* yardstick for propositions of all kinds. (Campbell 1988, 163)

Although Moore gives an extensive list of examples of common sense claims, he does not say what makes a claim one of common sense. But unless the argument from differential certainty is to protect *all* popular beliefs from criticism and revision, and not just common sense beliefs, criteria for distinguishing common sense beliefs from merely popular beliefs need to be given (Coady 2007, 101). William Lycan offers a number of ways of characterizing common sense claims. Lycan's characterizations are deliberately conservative. Although all the claims that they count as belonging to common sense are also claims that Moore counts as belonging to common sense, they exclude some of the claims that Moore counts as belonging to common sense. In outline, Lycan's characterization says that a claim belongs to common sense if and only if:

(1) it is "about something noted by someone at a particular time and place,"

(2) that the claim is an instance of a more general claim that most people would accept if it were put to them,

(3) that neither the claim nor the generalization use any specialized or technical terms,

(4) that it is difficult to give up accepting the generalization,

(5) that it would sound strange to assert the generalization because it is so obvious, and

(6) that it would be peculiar to deny the generalization.
      (Lycan 2001, 49–50)

Take, for example, Moore's claim that the Earth existed many years before his body was born. That is a claim that a particular person made at a particular place and time. It is an instance of a generalization (namely, that the Earth existed for many years before many people's bodies were born) that most people would agree to if it were put to them. Both the claim and its generalization are relatively easy to understand: neither of them involves specialized terms or some non-literal form of meaning. It is psychologically difficult for anyone to abandon belief in the generalization. Since the generalization is too obvious to mention, it would be odd to drop it into conversation unless suitable stage-setting had been made. And it would also be peculiar to deny the generalization in the course of a conversation unless, again, suitable stage-setting had been made.

The word "accept" is often used in a quasi-technical manner in philosophy. Presumably Lycan is taking "to accept" to mean *to believe*. But a weaker reading takes it to mean *to behave as if you believe*. When playing chess against a computer you may behave as if you believe that you are playing against an ambitious and imaginative player without your believing that the computer has any mental states. Perhaps our acceptance of the claims of common sense requires that we behave as if we believe them, but does not require that we believe them:

> A common-sense view is a conception on which most of those who belong to that culture at that time habitually rely in their everyday thinking. It is not required that they should actually hold it to be correct — they, or some of them, may know, or think, otherwise: what matters is that their ordinary thinking proceeds *as if* it were correct. (Dummett 1979, 18)

At least for the sake of argument, however, let's grant Lycan's intended characterization of what counts as a common sense claim. We might wonder, though, whether a claim's meeting the conditions set out in his characterization has epistemic significance (Conee 2001, 58). The conditions specify, broadly speaking, various psychological and sociological features: some claims are relatively easy to master and hard to abandon, others are not. But why should a claim's having those features make it more plausible than one that lacks them? A claim's plausibility is either (a) its reasonableness given initial evidence, or (b) its likelihood on all evidence. If (a), then a claim C may be more plausible than another claim C^*, but less justified than C^*, since the degree of justification of a claim depends on more than its reasonableness on initial evidence (Conee 2001, 57). If (b), then the above question becomes pressing: what, if anything, is the connection between being a common sense claim and being a plausible claim?

4. Common Sense and Conservatism

It might be thought that the connection is provided by considerations of theoretical conservatism (hereafter "conservatism" for short). David Lewis writes that:

> It's just that theoretical conservatism is the only sensible policy for theorists of limited powers, who are duly modest about what they could accomplish after a fresh start. Part of this conservatism is reluctance to accept theories that fly in the face of common sense. (Lewis 1986, 134)

According to the principle of conservatism, a person is to some degree justified in retaining a given belief just because that person has that belief. People then have some reason for continuing to believe that p if they already believe that p. We come to philosophy with various prior beliefs, including our common sense beliefs. Given a conflict between a common sense belief and a newly encountered philosophical claim, conservatism says that we are to some degree justified in maintaining the common sense claim just because we already maintain that claim. Conservatism will provide no such support to the newly made philosophical claim.

Two contrasting responses can be made to this appeal to conservatism. One response is concessive because it accepts conservatism; the other response is hard-line because it rejects conservatism. Although the concessive response accepts conservatism, it takes the principle to be *defeasible*. That is, the response allows that the evidence the principle provides can be defeated by counter-evidence. (Lewis [1986, 134–35] agrees.) Conservatism may provide evidence that p, but other factors might together form stronger evidence against p. This view is independently plausible. For example, Copernican theory and observation together provided sufficient reason to revise the long-held belief that the Sun orbits the Earth. Moreover, taking conservatism to be defeasible is not to take it to be peculiar. Many kinds of evidence (including perception, memory, and testimony) are also defeasible. So conservatism is in good company. The concessive response can then assess, in a case-by-case fashion, whether the conservative case for various common sense claims is stronger than any philosophical argument against them.

The hard line response rejects conservatism. This response has two elements. First, it claims that conservatism itself lacks epistemic justification, even defeasible epistemic justification (Christensen 1994, and Vahid 2004). Second, there is reason to reject conservatism. Consider the following example of the opinionated coin flipper (Christensen 1994, 74). This individual flips what he knows to be a fair coin and, without looking, forms the belief that it has landed tails. The fact that he has formed this belief provides no reason for him to maintain his belief that the coin landed tails. The believer is merely dogmatic. Yet conservatism says that the coin flipper is justified in maintaining his belief. The hard-line view concludes that conservatism is false and that it provides no connection between a claim's being common sense and its being justified.

5. Common Sense and Theory

Lycan himself comments that "Moore makes no argument from any proposition's *being common sensical* to that proposition's having any positive epistemic status" (Lycan 2001, 47–48). On the vexed issue of the nature of plausibility, Lycan writes that:

> I maintain that although the psychological basis and normative authority of "plausibility" judgments are thorny and important philosophical issues, they are just that — philosophical issues. (Lycan 2001, 51, endnote 9)

By saying that a plausibility judgement has "normative authority," Lycan means that such a judgment is entitled to tell us what we should believe. The authority of a plausibility judgment partly depends, however, on what it is a judgment about and who is making it. (The epistemology of this issue is very similar to that of the epistemology of testimony.) Lycan invites a comparison in plausibility between Moore's claim that he has hands and the philosophical assumption that every object has proper parts that are themselves substances. That philosophical assumption is not one that most non-philosophers would even understand: What is a proper part? What is a substance? By default they would find the familiar Moorean claim more plausible.

This, however, does not settle matters in Moore's favour. By the same reckoning, most non-scientists would find Moore's common sense claim more plausible than the claims that DNA molecules contain alleles or that photons lack mass. It is hard to see that this observation amounts to a telling criticism of either science or of philosophy.

Lycan appeals to claims which common sense finds plausible. But why restrict ourselves to what is plausible according to common sense? There are other reliable sources of information. For example, there is what is plausible according to modern science (Smart 1966). Now what is plausible according to one such source need not be plausible according to another of the same sort. Moreover, in some cases, what is plausible according to one source is implausible according to another of a different sort. There have been conflicts between scientific and common sense claims, and, at least in some cases, the common sense claims have reasonably been revised.[2] If conflicts between science and common sense can reasonably be settled in favour of science, a reason needs to be given for thinking that conflicts between philosophy and common sense cannot reasonably be settled in favour of philosophy.

This also raises a question about the force of Moore's argument from certainty. If that argument shows that philosophy is not licensed to change our pre-philosophical opinions, then it seems that the same line of reasoning is available to show that science is not licensed to change our pre-scientific opinions. After all, many people have been more confident that whales are fish, that glass is not a liquid, or that the coldness of an ice cube is transmitted to the drink it floats in, than any scientific theory that says otherwise. Moore's argument threatens to prove too much.[3]

Richard Feldman's response to the above point is to allow that empirical results may show that we lack knowledge in certain cases, and then to restrict the argument from certainty as an argument against only "highly abstract philosophical arguments for skepticism" (Feldman 2001, §3). Unfortunately, he provides no reason for maintaining this restricted version of the argument from certainty. It is not clear why empirical results supporting scepticism about our knowledge in some area should have an evidential force that no philosophical argument for scepticism can match. In the absence of a reason for this asymmetrical attitude to empirical results and philosophical argument, Feldman's restriction seems *ad hoc*.

The Moorean may concede that science has corrected some commonly held claims, but deny that those claims were common sense ones. For example, science's discovery that the Sun does not orbit the Earth revised common opinions. David Armstrong, however, queries the extent of the revision:

---

2   McCloskey (1983), and Wolpert (2000, 2–4) each offer examples of errors in common sense thinking about motion.

3   Noah Lemos (2004) presents a book-length defence of common sense. Yet the book's discussion of the critical bearing of science on common sense beliefs is relatively impoverished, as Barber (2007, 179) notes.

What we see really happens. We do see that the sun and the portion of the earth on which we live, are changing their relations to each other. That is certainly knowledge. But we are quite naturally led by this correct perception to acquire a bad theory about which partner in the relation is moving ... Moorean truisms may sometimes come encumbered with false theories that later discovery may reveal to be false. But even so there is always a core of knowledge present. (Armstrong 2006, 161)

This reply may meet the challenge of scientific discovery but it comes at a cost. It threatens to undermine Moore's common sense case against **idealism** and scepticism. The idealist claims that only minds and ideas exist. That claim apparently conflicts with the claims that Moore has hands and that hands are neither minds nor ideas. But now the idealist can take a leaf from Armstrong's book, and make the following speech:

What we see really exists. We see a succession of various sensory ideas in our minds. And we see hands. That is certainly perceptual knowledge. But we are quite naturally led by this correct perception to acquire a bad theory about what we are seeing. The bad theory says that hands are external objects that cause our sensory ideas, and that we perceive hands by having ideas. The Moorean truism that we see hands has been encumbered with a false theory that later philosophical discovery (courtesy of idealism!) has revealed to be false. There is a core of knowledge present, but that knowledge is of those collections of ideas that constitute hands.

The general point is that once a distinction is drawn between Moorean truisms and a (possibly false) theory that interprets those truisms, it becomes a matter of philosophical argument where the line between them should be drawn in any given debate. The Moorean will seek to include more in the content of the truisms in order to generate a conflict between common sense and philosophical theory. The Moorean's opponent will seek to include less in the content of the truisms in order to remove the conflict between common sense and philosophical theory. According to the Moorean's opponent, the conflict is located between rival philosophical theories — his and the Moorean — and the Moorean is guilty of reading claims that properly belong only to his own theory into common sense truisms.

This raises the issue of the analysis of common sense and other claims. Moore himself confessed that he was unsure about the correct analysis of statements about external objects:

> I am not at all sceptical as to the truth of ... propositions which assert the existence of material things.... But I am very sceptical as to what, in certain respects, the correct *analysis* of such propositions is. (Moore 1925, 53)

> It is the analysis of propositions [such as the proposition that *this* is a human hand] which seems to me to present such great difficulties, while nevertheless the whole question as to the *nature* of material things obviously depends upon their analysis. (Moore 1925, 53)

Until it is settled, the issue of the analysis of common sense claims remains a major loophole in the Moorean argumentative strategy. (We will return to this issue in §8 of this chapter.)

On the narrower issue of where to draw the line between Moorean truisms and what (possibly bad) theories say about those truisms, it may be that empirical science can contribute to this (Fodor 1984, Campbell 1988, 166–70, and Bishop 1992). One particular theory in cognitive science takes the mind to consist in a number of modules. According to this theory, each of these mental modules has a fairly specific function (such as memory, language-processing, and so on), and it pursues its function with a great deal of autonomy from the workings of the other modules. Among the modules are the perceptual modules: hard-wired input systems that take information from the body's receptor cells and transducers, and convert it into representations of the body's environment. Their workings are done automatically, unconsciously, and without interference from the mind's other operations. If this theory of the modularity of the mind is on the right lines, then there are empirical grounds for distinguishing between what observation contributes to our claims and what theory contributes to them. As Campbell puts it

> To Observation will belong those propositions which express representations as delivered to central processing by the input systems. To Theory will belong the integration of observational propositions into systematic explanatory systems.... (Campbell 1988, 168)

Fodor also thinks that there are certain linguistic categories ("Basic Categories," as he calls them), such as *dog*, *chair*, and *tree*, that are applied on observational grounds. That is, normal unassisted perception in humans provides sufficient grounds for judging what these concepts should be applied to.[4]

These lines of thought hold out the promise of reinstating the distinction between what perception reveals and what various theories say about what perception reveals. This is not exactly the distinction between what is common sense and what is not. Some of Moore's common sense claims, such as the claim that the Earth existed for many years before his body, do not count as perceptual claims on the above lines of thought. Nevertheless, the latter might reasonably be taken to isolate the content of certain common sense claims (the "Basic Observational Fragment" [Campbell 1988, 170]), and so help to vindicate Armstrong's separation of what common sense perceptions say from what (good or bad) theory says about those perceptions. Whether any of these lines of thought are correct is an empirical matter. Depending on how you regard the role of science in philosophy, you might take this to be a potentially valuable contribution of science to philosophical inquiry, or you might see it as giving hostages to fortune — making philosophical claims hang on the vicissitudes of empirical research. We address this issue further in chapter 6.

So far we have considered the general question of the proper role of common sense in philosophical inquiry. It is worth considering an application of Moore's method to a specific case. Moore himself applied his method to the issue of the existence of the external world. In the next section we will assess this example as a case study of Moore's method. (His method has been applied to other cases besides. For example, Lycan [2003] applies it to the question of whether we have free will.)

6. Case Study: Moore's Proof of the External World

We believe that there is an external world: a world of objects that exist outside of our minds, such as human bodies, rabbits and trees. The problem of the external world is a problem about how such beliefs can be justified. What is the evidence that there is an external world? We have various experiences. But, as Descartes pointed out, those experiences might not be caused by an external world. Descartes offered an alternative possible explanation of our experiences. According to his Evil Demon hypothesis, although there is no external world, a very powerful demon gives us experiences that are just as if they are experiences of an

---

4   For a reply to Fodor, see Churchland (1988).

external world (Descartes 1641, first meditation). One way of formulating the problem of the external world is as the problem of what justifies us in believing the External World hypothesis rather than the Evil Demon hypothesis.

In his paper "Proof of an External World" Moore offered the following argument as a proof that the external world exists (Moore 1939, 146–47). First, he stated that hands exist. (When presenting his proof to an audience, at this point Moore helpfully held up one hand and then another.) If hands exist, they are external objects. It follows that external objects exist.

Moore says that there are three conditions that are individually necessary and jointly sufficient for an argument being a proof (Moore 1939, 41). First, the premise should differ from the conclusion. Second, the premises should be known to be true. Third, the premises should entail the conclusion. Moore takes each of these conditions to be met. Sosa (2007, 50) shows that, even if Moore's conditions for a proof are individually necessary, they are not jointly sufficient.[5] By the first condition Moore seems to have in mind the requirement that an argument should not beg the question: there should be reason to accept the premises that does not assume the truth of the argument's conclusion. We will consider below whether this condition is met. Moore also asserts that his argument is deductively valid, and that he knows the premises: he knows that hands exist, and he knows that hands are external objects. Moore does not prove that he knows these propositions, but he denies that it is a requirement of his argument being a proof that he proves its premises.

Moore might justify this denial in the following way. If it were a requirement that the premises of a proof are proved, then a regress of proofs would ensue. Assume that an argument is a proof only if all its premises are proved. Any putative proof P has premises. To prove P's premises, a new proof, P+1, must be given. But since P+1 is a proof, its premises need to be proven in turn. This requires a further proof, P+2, whose premises also need to be proven. An infinite regress of proofs ensues. Since we cannot provide such an infinite series of proofs, P fails to be a proof. It follows that we cannot prove anything. This invites the Moorean response that we are more certain that there are proofs (at least in mathematics) than that the premises of a proof need to be proved. The Moorean response continues by rejecting our original assumption that an argument is a proof only if all of its premises are proved.[6]

---

5   See also Dretske (2003, 114–15).

6   See also Soames (2003, 20–21).

Moore's proof then runs as follows:

(1)	Here is one hand, and here is another hand.	[Known datum]
(2)	Hands exist.	[By (1)]
(3)	If hands exist, hands are external objects.	[Assumption]
(4)	∴ External objects exist.	[(2),(3)]

Given that the argument is valid, and that Moore knows its premises, it follows that he has proved the conclusion — that external objects exist. (Presumably it is a short step, but one that Moore leaves unremarked, to argue from the claim that external objects exist to the claim that the external world exists.)

Moore offers the following analogy. Suppose you have typed a paper and want to know whether there are any misprints in it. You ask a friend to proofread the paper for you. She tells you that there are some misprints in your paper. You are surprised to hear her tell you that, and so you ask her to prove it. She then proves it as follows:

(1*) A word is incorrectly printed here (she says, pointing to a word on one page), and another word is printed incorrectly here (she says, pointing to a word on another page).

(2*) There are incorrectly printed words in the paper.

(3*) Incorrectly printed words are misprints.

(4*) ∴ There are misprints in the paper.

Your friend has given a good argument for her claim that there are misprints in the paper. Moreover, if your friend knows the premises of her argument, her argument enables her to know its conclusion as well. You can get to know the conclusion too by the same route. The point of the analogy is that if the proofreader's argument for the existence of misprints is a good one, then it seems that so too is Moore's argument for the existence of external objects.

Who is Moore's proof directed at? Suppose that it is directed at the sceptic about the external world. Then it seems that Moore's proof begs the question. Anyone who is a sceptic about the external world will doubt whether there are hands. So premise (2) gives that sceptic no reason to accept (4), Moore's conclusion.

It has been denied, however, that Moore's argument is directed against the sceptic (Baldwin 1990, chapter 9, §5, and Sosa 2007, 53). Baldwin and Sosa argue that Moore was not trying to refute scepticism — the view that we have no knowledge of the external world — but idealism — the view that the external world does not exist. But it is not clear whether Moore's intentions enable him to avoid the charge of question-begging. The idealist will help himself to any line of reply that the sceptic would take to Moore's argument (Hetherington 2001, 170–71). So the idealist may reply that premise (2) of Moore's argument begs the question against him.

Baldwin also suggests that Moore is not trying to prove that he has knowledge of the external world (Baldwin 1990, 291–92). According to Baldwin, Moore is instead trying to put on show, to "exhibit," some of this knowledge in premise (1) and (2) of his proof.[7] But whether anyone has such knowledge to exhibit is precisely what the idealist will dispute.

Baldwin draws a contrast between proving the existence of the external world and showing that one has knowledge of the external world:

> where a proof of knowledge would require refutation of sceptical arguments, an exhibition of knowledge can proceed by means of an appeal to the audience's beliefs concerning what is known. (Baldwin 1990, 291)

Yet Moore is addressing a divided audience. Any realist in the audience will already share Moore's beliefs about what is known — including the premises and conclusion of Moore's proof. A proof can be useful if it shows that there is an entailment between certain propositions, even if we already know those propositions. But the entailment involved in Moore's proof will seem unexceptionable to any realist. So far as the realist is concerned, then, Moore's proof is unnecessary. (Soames [2003, 23] thinks that Moore's purpose in presenting his proof was to show that "there is no need for such a proof in the first place." Sosa [2007, 53], however, disputes this interpretation.) By contrast, no idealists in Moore's audience will share Moore's beliefs about what is known. For instance, they believe that, if hands are external objects, then Moore does not know that he has hands, and so he does not have such knowledge to exhibit. Lastly, it seems that anyone in Moore's audience who is neither already a realist nor an idealist — any "agnostic" — should remain neutral. On the face of it, if Moore's argument shows that an agnostic should form the belief that Moore knows that there are external objects, then the argument would carry equal force against the idealist. The argument would show that the idealist should abandon his belief that no one knows that there are external objects, and he should form the belief that Moore knows there are external objects. But since Moore's argument lacks force against the idealist, it also lacks force against the agnostic. At any rate, it is hard to see how the argument could have force against only one of these parties.

---

7   See also Neta (2007, 79).

The idealist will press the following argument. What is the basis for Moore's asserting premise (1), the premise that he has hands? Presumably Moore takes perceptual experience to give him knowledge of the external world. That assumes, however, that there is an external world and that Moore has knowledge of it. Any reason that Moore has for claiming (2) will assume (4), and so it would be circular to argue for (4) on the basis of (2) and (3). Therefore, it is not the case that Moore can take (2) and (3) as a joint reason to conclude that (4). Wright (1985, 57–60) considers whether Moore's epistemic warrant for his premises (2) and (3) "transmits across" the entailment to (4). In outline, Wright argues that sensory experiences provide epistemic warrant for premise (2) only if there is reason for (4); that the only reason there can be for (4) would be provided by (2); and so there can be no reason for (4).[8]

Note that the idealist's argument does not make any assumptions about the nature of perceptual experience. In particular, it does not assume that perceptual experience consists of a flow of impressions and ideas from which the existence of external objects is inferred (*pace* Hetherington 2001, 171). The idealist's argument assumes only that Moore's having experiences, even his having experiences that are apparently of physical objects, does not entail that there exist external objects, and so does not entail that Moore knows that there exist external objects. The Moorean may stipulate that an experience is a perceptual experience only if there exists some external object *o* such that the experience is an experience of *o*. But that stipulation generates the problem of how you would know whether any of your experiences are perceptual experiences so understood.[9]

Furthermore, the idealist's argument does not assume that "knowledge that there are external things in general is *epistemically prior* to knowledge of some particular external thing" (Hetherington 2001, 172). Propositions in set S are epistemically prior to propositions in set S^* if and only if

> it is possible to know all the propositions in set S without knowing any propositions in set S^*, but not conversely.

The idealist does not assume that you would already have to know that there are external objects in order to be in a position to know that you have hands. Consider, as an analogy, scepticism about knowledge of

---

8   See also Wright (2002). For pro-Moorean replies, see Pryor (2000, 2004) and Davies (2000, 2003). Wright (2007) and Neta (2007) assess these pro-Moorean replies.

9   Wright (2002, §§VIII–X) argues that appealing to direct realist theories of perception does not resuscitate Moore's proof.

angels. A sceptic of this sort will thereby be a sceptic about knowledge of such alleged species of angels as seraphim. But this sceptic is not committed to an **epistemic priority** thesis whereby knowledge that there are angels in general is epistemically prior to knowledge that there are seraphim. Instead of being committed to an epistemic priority thesis, a sceptic about knowledge of Xs is committed to the following epistemic **equivalence** thesis: knowledge that there are Xs in general is exactly as difficult to get as knowledge of any species of X. A sceptic about knowledge of angels will take it to be exactly as difficult to get knowledge that there are angels in general as it is difficult to get knowledge that there are seraphim. Similarly, the sceptic about knowledge of the external world will take it to be exactly as difficult to get knowledge that there are external objects in general as it is difficult to get knowledge that there are hands — a species of external object.

Hetherington argues that Moore can be in a position to know that he has hands without being in a position to know that there are external objects. Hetherington argues that you could know that you have hands without having the concept of an external object, and so without entertaining the proposition that there are external objects. This is so because "unlike the concept of a hand, the concept of an external object is at least partly a philosophical concept (the **explication** of which occupied much of Moore's paper)" (Hetherington 2001, 173). Since it is possible for you to know that you have hands without knowing that there are external objects, Moore does not beg the question in arguing in his proof from (2) and (3) to (4).

It is doubtful that the charge of question-begging can be countered in this way. Suppose that you are wondering whether a certain politician, Richie Nix, is a liar. Nix's press officer then offers the following argument:

Richie Nix believes everything that he says.
∴ Richie Nix is not a liar.

It is possible to have all the concepts used in the premise — the concepts of belief, proposition, speech, universal quantification, and of Richie Nix — without having the concept of a liar. You might have all of those concepts although it never occurs to you that anyone might deliberately tell what they believe to be false. In that case, you would be in the position of knowing the premise without knowing the conclusion. Even so, it remains the case that the press officer's argument is question-begging. More generally, whether an argument is question-begging does not depend on whether it is possible to understand (or know) its premises without understanding (or knowing) its conclusion. An argument directed at a particular audience is question-begging if and only if it contains at least one premise that would not be accepted by the argument's intended audience unless they already accept the conclusion of the argument (Walton 1989, 52 and Govier 1992, 85).[10]

One lesson of the shortcomings of Moore's proof of the external world lies in the shortcomings of appeals to *phenomenology*. These are appeals to how things appear to us pre-theoretically. It is open to doubt whether there is such a thing as how things appear to us that does not make any general or theoretical assumptions. At a sub-personal level (i.e., at a level below that of conscious attention) our minds classify information before making it available to conscious access. (Recall the discussion of Fodor's mental modules in §5.) It is for cognitive science to discover empirically what kinds of classification our minds make. Philosophers have no particular insight into what classifications are made, and so they have no insight into what is pre-theoretical data and what is not. Appealing to what cognitive science has discovered is very different from appealing to phenomenology. The appeal would be based on what science, not naïve perception, tells us. (Such an appeal is characteristic of the philosophical view known as naturalism and its advocacy of scientific methodology and scientific results. See chapter 6.) Furthermore, even if there is a domain of how things pre-theoretically appear to us, it is unclear how we could identify these things. Consider a debate between J.L. Austin and David Hume about what we perceive. Austin believes that we perceive physical objects, "medium-sized dry goods," and that talk of sense impressions is a philosopher's fantasy (Austin 1962). Hume believes that we perceive sense impressions, and that talk of physical objects is a projection of the mind (Hume 1739–40, book I, part IV, section II). They disagree about the phenomenology of perception. If we wired them up to a lie detector, no doubt the machine would record their honest but conflicting accounts of what we perceive. Perhaps one of the parties is self-deceived: he believes all along what the other party does and he is reporting only what he believes he believes we perceive. Well perhaps, but phenomenology will not tell us which (if any) of the parties is self-deceived. Some independent means would be needed to achieve that. Once again the appeal to phenomenology goes by the board.

---

10 For other statements of the charge that Moore's proof is question-begging, see Jackson (1987, 113–14), and Beebee (2001, 359). For defences against this charge, see Lemos (2004, 85–91) and Coady (2007, 108–09).

7. Moore's Argument from Certainty

Lycan also defends Moore against the charge of **begging the question**. He admits that Moore's proof of an external world "comes close" to begging the question (Lycan 2007, 90). But he reminds us of the second stage of Moore's strategy in his defence of common sense. This was Moore's appeal to certainty.

We have degrees of belief or degrees of certainty. We are more confident, or more certain, about some things than others. We are more certain about what our own names are than whether there is life on other planets; we are more certain that the Empire State Building is very tall than that it is 443 meters tall. We differentiate between the relative certainty of different propositions.

Moore made just such a differentiation. He differentiated between common sense claims and the premises and conclusions of sceptical philosophical arguments. Lycan sees Moore as arguing as follows. Moore has hands, and since hands are external objects, there exist external objects. Moore knows those facts too. Now the **premise set** of any argument that concludes that Moore does not know that external objects exist is less plausible than the claim that Moore knows that he has hands. So it is less plausible that any argument for scepticism about knowledge of the external world is sound than that Moore does not know that there is an external world (Lycan 2001, 39).

Lycan claims that "no particular *criterion* of plausibility, credibility or comparative certainty is or need be invoked" (Lycan 2001, 40). But even if no particular criterion of plausibility is being invoked, certain claims about what is more plausible than what are being made, and there is an issue about the basis on which they are made. The Moorean appeal to certainty faces a dilemma (Baldwin 1990, 270–71). If it is intended simply as a psychological claim ("I, the Moorean, am more certain that p is true than that it is false"), then it is unclear whether the Moorean claim has any force in an argument. It seems to be merely an autobiographical remark. Alternatively, if it is intended a normative claim ("I, the Moorean, have reason to be more certain that p is true than that it is false"), then why should we accept the claim? If any reason can be given, it must not beg the question against Moore's opponents, and it cannot rest on a claim about plausibility since that is the kind of claim that the reason is supposed to support. The appeal to certainty leaves this dilemma unresolved.[11]

---

11 For another criticism of the appeal to differential certainty, see Wright (1985, 57).

The dilemma is not avoided by claiming that each of us is more certain that we have hands than any philosophical theory that says that we are not justified in believing that we lack hands. If the claim is a sociological one — a description of what something commonly believed — it is unclear what argumentative force it has. If the claim is intended as a normative one — that we should have that degree of certainty — then an argument is needed to take us from the sociological fact that we share a high degree of belief to the normative claim that we are entitled to have that high degree of belief. Now some philosophers think that psychological or sociological claims ground normative claims (e.g., Hanna 2006). Perhaps the Moorean is tempted by this view. But the view in question needs to be made precise and it also needs defending since it is far from obvious. So taking this view would require the Moorean to formulate and defend an elusive and controversial philosophical view. Yet that was something that Moore's argument from certainty had originally promised to avoid. The premise set of that argument was advertised as containing only obvious and truistic premises.

Here is a second attempt that the Moorean might make. Lycan rejects the above dilemma. According to Lycan, Moore is concerned about "rationality, the normative notion," and

> [f]or it to be normatively rational to prefer the knowledge
> claim to one of the skeptic's purely philosophical assumptions,
> we need not drag in any further material that "establishes" the
> knowledge claim…. (Lycan 2007, 93, footnote 23)

Despite avowedly rejecting the dilemma, Lycan appears to be addressing the second limb of the dilemma. This said that if the Moorean claims to have reason to be more certain that he has hands than that he lacks them, then the Moorean needs to justify that claim. Lycan agrees that the Moorean has more reason to be certain that he has hands than that he lacks them, but Lycan denies that the Moorean needs to justify that claim. Consider the debate leading up to this point. The idealist claims that external objects do not exist. Moore replies that external objects exist and that he knows that they do. Moore argues for his claim on the ground that it is more rational to believe that there are external objects than it is to believe the premises of any argument that the idealist offers for *his* claim. Why accept that defence? Lycan thinks that we do not need to justify it. But if that is so, is it not clear why we even need to justify Moore's earlier claim that there are external objects and that he knows that there are. There seems no need to appeal to the argument from certainty. In short, if Lycan's response is a good one, it can be used at an earlier stage of the debate — the stage at which Moore declares that there are external objects and that he knows that there are — thereby making the argument from certainty redundant.

It might be replied that the argument from certainty is not redundant because it provides justification for the claim that there is an external world (and also for Moore's claim to know that). But unless the normative claim that the argument from certainty makes is itself justified, that argument fails to provide justification for Moore's claim to know that there is an external world. We are no further forward.

Lycan's defence of Moore's appeal to certainty also involves a pointed contrast between philosophy and common sense:

> Just as there is no such thing as an idealist argument that does not appeal to some abstract metaphysical or epistemological principle that is simply assumed without defence, there is no such thing as a skeptical argument that does not do the same thing. Which is to say that *there is no good reason to accept the argument*; the unargued principle is only philosophical stuff.... [There] is no rational ground for pledging allegiance to the [principle] *in preference to* a plain truth of common sense. (Lycan 2001, 41)

> I for one do not think that any philosophical claim is known to be true. Indeed, Moore himself had a low regard for philosophical claims in general, and I believe he was right in that. (Lycan 2007, 86 [footnote omitted])

By defending in this way the greater plausibility of common sense claims over purely philosophical ones, Lycan may have overplayed his hand. In arguing against the idealist thesis that there are no external objects, Moore relies not only on the premise that hands exist, but also on the premise that hands are external objects. (And, like the other premises of his proof, Moore assumes that he knows it.) But the premise that hands are external objects is a philosophical principle that is drawn from a piece of philosophical analysis. So the various aspersions that Lycan casts against purely philosophical claims should be levelled against it. It too is an "unargued principle" and "only philosophical stuff."

The point applies more generally to Moore's defence of common sense claims against any other philosophical claim. To generate an incompatibility between a philosophical claim *p* and a common sense claim *not-q*, Moore needs a principle of the form *if p then q* so that he can argue: *not-q*, *if p then q*, so *not-p*. Lycan's aspersions against philosophical principles cut equally against a premise of the arguments of Moore's opponents but also against a premise of Moore's counter-arguments. The result is that Lycan's intended defence of common sense undermines Moore's counter-arguments.

What Lycan needs to offer is a still more qualified defence of common sense claims. The defence should show why common sense claims are more plausible than the premises of any philosophical arguments against such claims. Yet the defence should not be committed to saying that purely philosophical claims provide "no good reason" to accept arguments, or that they are "only philosophical stuff."

8. Moore and Philosophical Analysis

Moore's proof was intended as a refutation of idealism. But statements about the external world are open to analysis. One such analysis is **phenomenalism**. Phenomenalism seeks to analyse every statement about an external object as a conjunction of statements about actual and possible experiences. So, for example, the statement that there is a tree in the garden is analysed in terms of a conjunction of statements about certain tree-like experiences that people have, or would have, when having certain garden-like experiences. The phenomenalist can then accept Moore's proof but deny that external objects exist independently of minds. Consequently, Moore's proof has no force against phenomenalism. (For this reason, Baldwin [1990, 295] regards Moore's proof as a "total failure." Curiously, Moore was fully aware that phenomenalism consistently claims both that there are no external objects, as understood according to a realist analysis of "external objects," and that there are human hands [Moore 1942, 669–70].)

So premise (3) of Moore's proof ("hands are external objects") is too weak since a phenomenalist analysis of what it is to be an external object is available. It seems that what Moore needs is an analysis of what it is for something to be a hand (or, more generally, of what it is for something to be an external object) that is not available to his opponents. The question is then how this is to be established. The premise could be strengthened by building in a realist analysis along the lines of (3'):

(3')   Hands are external objects in the sense of being mind-independent objects.

The problem here is that Moore's opponents will question whether (3') is true. The original premise that hands are external objects was introduced as a definition. Definitions of terms are either stipulations or they report the meaning of a term already in use. If Moore were simply to stipulate that "external object" means *mind-independent object*, the substantive issue would then be whether hands (or anything else) are external objects in that sense. That is not a matter that can be settled by stipulation. It calls for philosophical argument. On the other hand, if Moore were to claim that, as the phrase is used in everyday life, "external object" means *mind-independent object*, the substantive issue would then be whether Moore's claim correctly reports the meaning of "external object." The phenomenalist would dispute its correctness. On either count, what goes by the board is Moore's swift, clear-cut attempt to prove the existence of the external world.

We will consider another argument for the existence of the external world in chapter 5, §7. It is the argument that positing the external world provides the best explanation of our sensory experiences.

9. Conclusion

There is no agreement on whether, and to what extent, common sense claims should have a role in evaluating philosophical claims (Byrne and Hall 2004). Even those philosophers who think that common sense claims have an important role here disagree about where this leaves philosophy. They disagree about whether philosophy should set an ambitious agenda or a more modest one. On the ambitious agenda, philosophy can make substantive metaphysical claims that are consistent with common sense, but that also go beyond it.[12] On the more modest agenda, philosophy's role is to reconcile the claims of science with the claims of common sense.[13]

Alex Byrne and Ned Hall think that the lesson to be drawn from Moore's work on common sense is that we should prefer modest philosophy to ambitious philosophy. They argue as follows: Ambitious philosophy is very hard. Arguments for substantive metaphysical claims about what exists, or what is more fundamental than what, often contain some hidden defect. Our increased recognition of this has shown how high the bar is for reaching novel and substantive metaphysical conclusions.

Moore, however, endorsed the ambitious agenda. He thought that philosophy should give

> a general description of the whole of the universe, mentioning
> all the most important kinds of things which we do not abso-

---

12   See e.g., Sider (2001, xiv–xvi).
13   See e.g., Jackson (1998, 42–44).

lutely know to be in it, and also considering the most important ways in which these various kinds of things are related to
one another. (Moore 1953, 2)

One of Moore's own contributions to this description was to claim that
there are truths about moral goodness, that those truths are not analysable in terms of truths about the natural world, and that knowing those
truths requires having a special faculty of moral **intuition**. (We will consider his influential argument for this non-naturalistic view about morality in chapter 2, §5. It is known as Moore's **"open question" argument**.)

Still, even if Moore himself did not draw the lesson that Hall and
Byrne draw from his work on common sense, perhaps they have drawn
the correct lesson from it, one that Moore sadly missed. Their argument
for that lesson is based on the claim that ambitious philosophy is difficult to do. While that claim is correct, it does not settle the matter. Their
argument has to assume that modest philosophy is less difficult to do
than ambitious philosophy. Such an assumption, however, is debatable.
Arguments for so-called modest metaphysical claims about what things
can co-exist with what other things, and about what common sense
claims are consistent with what scientific claims, often contain some
hidden defect too.[14] The bar for reaching well-founded conclusions on
the modest agenda seems as high as the bar for reaching well-founded
conclusions on the ambitious agenda.

Looking ahead to chapter 6, the approach known as philosophical
naturalism also subscribes to the ambitious agenda. This approach
deliberately draws upon the methods and claims of natural science. In
particular, it draws upon natural science's readiness to revise its claims in
the interests of achieving the most informative but economical account of
observations. Quinean naturalism shares this revisionary attitude to our
philosophical claims, and the observation-driven nature of any revisions.
As we will see, however, beyond having these attitudes of deference to
science and a willingness to revise our current beliefs, it is unclear what
else Quinean naturalism involves. Naturalism is modest in one respect:
it refrains from making claims that go beyond those made by science.
But even the significance of this is unclear until it is established just what
claims science makes and what the philosophical consequences of those
claims are.

---

14 By way of illustration, see the responses to Jackson (1998) made by Stalnaker (2000), and
Laurence and Margolis (2003).

Questions for Discussion

1. Moore does not offer criteria for what counts as belonging to common sense. Does his failure to do so undermine his project? Why should providing such criteria be important? Can you provide criteria on Moore's behalf? (In fact, what kinds of thing can you provide criteria for? Try dogs, chairs, or games. After you've tried that, has your opinion about the viability of Moore's project changed?)

2. Reid thought that one of the "marks" of common sense claims is that they are widely believed because it is part of human nature to believe them:

> I think that the constitution of our nature leads us to believe certain principles that we are compelled to take for granted in the common concerns of life, without being able to give a reason for them. If I am right about this, then those are what we call "the principles of common sense," and we dismiss as obviously "absurd" anything that obviously conflicts with them. (Reid 1764, ch. 2, §6)

Does Reid's view have any advantages over Moore's? Does it have any disadvantages?

3. Are common sense claims revisable? What was Moore's view on this issue? See Moore (1953, 6–8), but then compare Lycan (2001, 40) with Coady (2007, 114–15). What would be Reid's view?

4. The examples of common sense claims that have been given in this chapter seem humdrum. But are there common sense claims that are not humdrum, claims that would strike many non-philosophers as controversial? For example, could it be a common sense claim that God does not exist? Georges Rey argues that it is part of common sense at least in the Western world that God does not exist, and that adult Westerners who take themselves to believe that there is a God are deceiving themselves (Rey 2006, 2007). Is Rey right, or is he reading into (modern Western) common sense something that is not part of it? Can we answer that question without settling beforehand criteria for what counts as part of common sense?

5. Some philosophers think that many common sense claims such as "I have a hand" are known, or are reasonably believed, non-inferentially.

That is, that these common sense claims are known, or reasonably believed, although not on the basis of their being inferred from some epistemically superior basis. Our knowledge, or reasonable belief, in these common sense claims is said to be "**properly basic.**" This raises the question of which claims we are entitled to count as basic. Have you any suggestions? Alvin Plantinga thinks that, because that question is difficult to answer, there is no objection to counting claims such as "I am aware of the divine presence" as properly basic (Plantinga 1981). Is Plantinga's view a reasonable one? Is his argument persuasive?

Core Reading for Chapter 1

Armstrong, D.M. (2006) "The Scope and Limits of Human Knowledge."
Baldwin, Thomas (1990) *G.E. Moore* ch. IX.
Campbell, Keith (1988) "Philosophy and Common Sense."
Coady, C.A.J. (2007) "Moore's Common Sense."
Kelly, Thomas (2008) "Common Sense as Evidence: Against Revisionary Ontology and Skepticism."
Lemos, Noah (2004) *Common Sense: A Contemporary Defense.*
Lycan, William G. (2001) "Moore Against the New Skeptics."
Moore, G.E. (1925) "A Defence of Common Sense."
Moore, G.E. (1939) "Proof of an External World."
Moore, G.E. (1953) *Some Main Problems of Philosophy* ch. 1.
Soames, Scott (2003) *Philosophical Analysis in the Twentieth Century, volume 1 The Dawn of Analysis* ch. 1.

two Analysis

1. Introduction

Analysis is often taken to be a characteristic activity of philosophy, and especially of philosophy belonging to the tradition inaugurated by Gottlob Frege, Bertrand Russell, Bernard Bolzano and G.E. Moore. The tradition in question is even called "analytic philosophy."

First, we want to know what distinguishes this kind of analysis from (say) Freudian analysis or functional analysis. Being told that it is a characteristic activity of a tradition ("analytic philosophy") inaugurated by certain named philosophers amounts to this: this kind of analysis is philosophical analysis, not psychoanalysis or functional analysis. While true, that is not very illuminating.

Second, philosophers in the Frege-Russell-Bolzano-Moore tradition pursue analysis in order to deepen their understanding and to remove confusion and error. Yet philosophers of many traditions have been trying to do that. It needs to be said *how* philosophical analysis furthers understanding and removes error.

In chapter 1 we saw that Moore thought that philosophical views should be consistent with widely held pre-philosophical intuitions. Especially during the 1950s, many philosophers in the analytic tradition thought that philosophical analyses need to be consistent with what people commonly believe, or are inclined to believe, before reflection. In particular, these philosophers thought that what people commonly believe, or are inclined to believe, about particular actual or possible concrete cases before reflecting on them should constrain philosophical analyses.[1] (These pre-philosophical beliefs or inclinations to belief are called "philosophical intuitions.") The primary data for assessing

---

1   E.g., Chisholm (1966, ch. 2).

philosophical analyses was taken to consist in these philosophical intuitions. It was further thought that an analysis was acceptable only if it was consistent with our intuitions, and so that a conflict between an analysis and a strongly held intuition was a good reason to reject the analysis. In more recent years, philosophers have been much more critical about this methodology. They have wanted to know what the nature of philosophical intuitions is, what their source is, and why they should be taken to have such epistemic authority.

The above considerations set the agenda for this chapter. There are three general questions that need answering:

(Q1) What is a philosophical analysis supposed to be?
(Q2) Can there be philosophical analyses in that sense?
(Q3) How can a philosophical analysis be tested?

2. What Is Philosophical Analysis?

A purely descriptive answer to (Q1) would try to describe what philosophers in the analytic tradition are doing when they are doing analysis. A normative answer to (Q1) would say what the best account of philosophical analysis is; it would be an account of what philosophers should be doing when they do analysis. We want an answer that has both descriptive and normative aspects. It is not enough to describe philosophical practice; we may need to improve it.[2]

There are several kinds of philosophical analysis even within the analytic tradition. It is not a straightforward matter how best to classify them. Instead of offering a classification of kinds of analysis, we will consider three influential philosophers in the analytic tradition and contrast their views about the nature of philosophical analysis. These are the views of Moore, Russell, and Quine. Each of their views marks important subtraditions within the broader analytic tradition.[3]

MOORE

Moore held the following views about philosophical analysis. *Philosophical analysis is meaning analysis*: philosophical analysis gives the meaning of a term. *Meaning analysis is decompositional*: meaning analysis consists in giving the complex meaning of a term by stating its simpler component meanings. The meaning of a term is often called a concept. Hence Moore talks of analysing complex concepts into simpler

---

2   These questions are adroitly addressed in the account of analysis offered by Petersen (2008).
3   For Frege's views on philosophical analysis, see Frege (1879, preface), Dummett (1991, ch. 2), Blanchette (2007), and Horty (2008).

ones. Such an analysis is a kind of explicit definition. The concept being analysed is called "the *analysandum*," and the concepts providing the analysis are collectively called "the *analysans*." Such an analysis has various formal features (Došen 1994, §3). One of particular importance is that the analysis is not circular. The analysandum is "eliminated": it does not occur in the analysans. By avoiding circularity, the analysis can be informative.

There is an issue about what the objects of analysis are — whether they are terms or the meanings that those terms express (concepts). We will not pursue this issue. It is arguable that talk of analysing a term is elliptical for talk of analysing sentences containing that term, and that talk of analysing a concept is elliptical for talk of analysing propositions containing that concept. The issue then is whether the objects of analysis are sentences or propositions.

Moore's views on analysis have been highly influential, and especially in his application of those ideas to metaethics. We will consider this application in §5.

RUSSELL

Russell developed the following pioneering views about analysis. *Grammatical form versus logical form*: the grammatical structure of a sentence may diverge from its underlying logical form. For Russell, the logical form of a sentence is a structure that the sentence has that determines the sentence's logical role and its logical properties. In particular, a sentence's logical form specifies what valid inferences it figures in: which sentences it can be validly inferred from and which sentences can be validly inferred from it. *Uniqueness of logical form*: each sentence has exactly one logical form (Russell 1914, 33–53). Russell illustrated these claims with his theory of descriptions. That theory was concerned with sentences of the grammatical form "the F is a G." According to Russell's theory, although a sentence such as "the garden is overgrown" has the grammatical form of a subject-predicate sentence, its logical form is quite different. According to Russell, its logical form is that of a quantified proposition, a proposition that says that there exists something that uniquely is both a garden and is overgrown (Russell 1905, and 1919, ch. XVI). More generally, Russell's analysis of sentences of the form "the *F* is *G*" has the following form:

The *F* is *G* if and only if there exists exactly one *F* and it is *G*.

This kind of analysis does not give an explicit definition of terms of the form "the *F*." Instead, the analysis offers an implicit definition of "the

F" by analysing any sentence containing that term. For any sentence containing "the *F*," the analysis provides as its analysans a sentence that is **logically equivalent** but which does not contain "the *F*."

QUINE

Quine represents a view of analysis that is closer to Russell than to Moore (Quine 1960, §§53–54). It is a view of analysis that Quine shares with Tarski and Carnap.[4] Quine rejects Moore's above views on analysis, not least because of his rejection of the assumption that there are truths about what terms mean (Quine 1960, ch. 2).

Quine holds that *philosophical analysis is regimentation*. It is the replacement of a philosophically problem-ridden language with a language that is not philosophically problem-ridden. Quine takes from Russell the idea that to analyse a philosophically troublesome sentence from a natural language, we should **paraphrase** that sentence into a philosophically more perspicuous language, such as the language of predicate logic. Quine calls such a translation a "regimentation" of natural language. Regimenting a fragment of language will avoid any confusion that arises from our being misled by the grammatical form of the original sentence. But whereas Russell takes each sentence to have a unique logical form, Quine drops this assumption (Quine 1960, 260). There is no unique way of translating a sentence of a natural language into a sentence of an artificial language. And since Quine eschews propositions, he is not committed to saying that the logical form that a given regimentation attributes to a given sentence is a matter of saying what type of proposition that sentence expresses. What logical form a sentence is assigned depends upon how the sentence is best regimented. In different contexts — where we are interested in different linguistic functions that the sentence serves — what counts as the best regimentations may differ.

These three views on analysis — Moore's, Russell's and Quine's — indicate something of the range of views available on this topic. Of these three philosophers, Moore places the strongest requirements on an analysis. In the next section, §3, we will consider a working model of philosophical analysis that draws on Moore's views. In §4 we will assess whether there can be successful philosophical analyses given the model.

3. A Working Model of Philosophical Analysis

In the previous sections we got some indication of the range of views that have been advanced on the topic. It is helpful to fix on a particular

---

4   See especially Carnap (1950, ch. 1).

model of analysis. The model in question is relatively simple. It draws upon Moore's views on analysis. Moore's views on analysis — or what have been taken to be his views — have been highly influential in analytic philosophy. Many philosophers have endorsed the model of analysis in question. Many others though have rejected it in part or as a whole. By setting out the model, we can locate various philosophical views on analysis depending upon which parts of the model they accept, which parts they reject, and what they replace them with.

The model will be set out as a model of the analysis of terms. An equivalent way of setting out the model would be as a model of the analysis of concepts.

The model makes the following five claims:

(1) *An analysis has the logical form of a universally quantified biconditional*:

$$(\forall x)\,(Fx \leftrightarrow Gx)$$

The above formula says that, for any thing x, x is F if and only if x is G. As a matter of convention, the analysandum is taken to be the formula on the left-hand side of the biconditional, and the analysans is taken to be the formula on its right-hand side. An analysis gives necessary and sufficient conditions for something to be F.

(2) *An analysis is necessarily true.* The analysis does not apply only to every actual thing that is F. It applies to everything that could be an F. An analysis of, for example, the term "cause" does not apply only to every actual cause. The analysis applies to everything that could be a cause, to every possible cause. So an analysis is to be read as saying that, for every possible thing, that thing is F if and only if it is G. So, if the analysis is true, it will be necessarily true. Furthermore, if the analysis is true, it is true because of the meanings of the terms in it. Hence if the analysis is true, it is analytically true — true in virtue of the meaning of the terms involved. Let's spell this out a little.

Suppose that F and G are concepts or word-meanings, and that it is a **conceptual truth** that Fs are Gs. A conceptual truth is supposed to be a proposition that is true solely in virtue of its constituent concepts and the relations between those concepts. For example, defenders of the view that there are conceptual truths often claim that the proposition that all vixens are foxes is true solely in virtue of the concepts VIXEN, FOX, and UNIVERSAL QUANTIFICATION, and entailments between those concepts. These philosophers also often contrast this example with the proposition that some vixens are hungry, which they claim is not true solely in

virtue of the concepts VIXEN, HUNGRY, and EXISTENTIAL QUANTIFICA-
TION and entailments between those concepts. Now suppose the English
word "vixen" expresses the concept *F*, and that the English word "foxes"
expresses the concept *G*. Then the English sentence (S)

(S) Vixens are foxes.

expresses the conceptual truth that *F*s are *G*s. Sentence (S) is true in virtue of expressing a conceptual truth. Another way of saying this is that
(S) is an **analytic truth** (as opposed to a **synthetic truth**). A conceptual
truth is a conceptually **necessary truth**. So (S) expresses a conceptually
necessary truth. Another way of saying this is that (S) is an analytically
necessary truth.

(3) *An analysis is informative.* The analysis of the term *"F"* in terms of
"G" provides novel information about the meaning of *"F."* One way in
which this requirement has been met is by further requiring that the
analysis is non-circular. This means that if *"F"* is analysed by *"G,"* *"G"* is
not analysed by *"F."* This non-circularity requirement also establishes *the
direction of analysis*: it establishes which term is the analysandum and
which the analysans.

A good illustration of this requirement is the Euthyphro dilemma.
Plato's dialogue *Euthyphro* contains a discussion between Socrates and
Euthyphro about what it is to be pious. Socrates asks the following question: "Is what is pious loved by the gods because it is pious, or is it pious
because it is loved by the gods?" (Plato *Euthyphro* 10a). Socrates' question
can be seen as posing a dilemma. Socrates is asking what the relation is
between being pious and being loved by the gods. Which one is to be
analysed in terms of the other? There are two options: either things are
pious because they are loved by the gods, or the gods love pious things
because they are pious.

Consider the first option. This says that the analysis of why things
are pious is that they are loved by the gods. But unless some reason is
given as to why the gods love those things and not other things instead,
it seems arbitrary and gratuitous that the gods should love the things
that they do. The gods might have loved other things instead. So if we are
going to analyse what it is for a thing to be pious by saying that the gods
love it, we need to say why the gods love that thing.

Furthermore, what is so special about the gods? Mortals love various things too. Why is a thing's being pious to be analysed in terms of
the gods loving it rather than in terms of the mortals loving it? Unless
some reason is given as to why there is an analytic connection between

the gods loving a thing and that thing being pious, it seems arbitrary to analyse piety in terms of what the gods love rather than in terms of (say) what mortals love. So we need to show that there is an analytic connection between *the gods* loving certain things and those things being pious.

If we were to say that the gods love those things because those things are pious, we would have shifted to the second option. Notice that the two options are mutually exclusive. It cannot be the case both that things are pious because the gods love them *and* that the gods love those things because they are pious. That would be a vicious circle. It says that things are pious because (following the circle around) they are pious. So the analysis of why things are pious cannot be because things are pious.

The second option analyses why the gods love certain things in terms of those things being pious. To avoid circularity, what it is for things to be pious cannot then be analysed in terms of its being loved by the gods. It will have to be analysed in some other way.

The dilemma that Socrates poses then comes to this. The claim that a thing is pious because it is loved by the gods seems to make an arbitrary connection. Why the gods? And why do the gods love those things? On the other hand, if the claim is that the gods love certain things because those things are pious, what it is for a thing to be pious has to be analysed in some independent way — some way that is independent of the claim that the gods love those things.

The Euthyphro dilemma has immediate relevance for the divine command theory of morality. This theory analyses what it is to be morally wrong as what God forbids and what it is to be morally right as what God commands. The dilemma this theory faces is that either things are morally wrong because God forbids them, or God forbids certain things because they are morally wrong. The first limb of the dilemma raises the issue of arbitrariness. Why should God forbid certain things and not others? If God has no reason for forbidding those things, then his ruling seems arbitrary. The second limb of the dilemma analyses why God forbids certain things in terms of those things being morally wrong. To avoid a vicious circle, what it is for something to be morally wrong cannot be analysed in terms of God's forbidding it. To sum up, the dilemma is that either the divine command theory arbitrarily takes what is morally wrong to be what God forbids, or things are not morally wrong because God forbids them.[5]

The general point behind the Euthyphro dilemma is the claim that the relation of analysis is irreflexive: the analysis of a concept F cannot involve the same concept. Consequently, it is not possible to analyse F in

---

5   The Euthyphro dilemma remains controversial. See Joyce (2002) for criticism of it.

terms of the concept G and analyse G in terms of F. This is the basis for the charge of vicious circularity made above. Another consequence is that analysis is also an asymmetric relation: if F is analysed in terms of G, then G cannot be analysed in terms of F.

Let's now continue with the remaining claims of our working model of philosophical analysis.

(4) *An analysis is knowable a priori.* The biconditional stating the analysis

$$(\forall x)\,(Fx \leftrightarrow Gx)$$

can be known *a priori*. Furthermore, it can be known *a priori* that the biconditional is necessarily true, that it is analytic, and that it provides the analysis of "*F*."

Given certain assumptions about the connection between what is analytic and what is knowable *a priori*, all of these claims can be derived from requirement (2) above. Assuming that an analysis states an analytic truth, and that every analytic truth is knowable *a priori*, it follows that the biconditional stating the analysis can be known *a priori*. An analytic truth is a sentence that is true solely in virtue of its meaning. Given that we can know *a priori* what a sentence means, we can know *a priori* that it is true in virtue of its meaning. If the biconditional is an analytic truth, it is knowable *a priori* that the biconditional is an analytic truth. Lastly, if it is an analytic truth that the biconditional states the analysis of "*F*," then, again given the assumption that every analytic truth is knowable *a priori*, it is knowable *a priori* that the biconditional provides the analysis of "*F*."

(5) *An analysis is testable by the method of hypothetical cases.* This method concerns how philosophical analyses are tested. By considering whether you would be inclined to apply a certain term in various hypothetical situations, you can, without further reflection, discover *a priori* various analytic truths about the necessary or sufficient conditions for the correct application of a term. This is the method of hypothetical cases — of appealing to philosophical intuitions — mentioned in §1.

For example, a theory in the philosophy of mind called "analytical behaviourism" analyses claims about mental states as claims about how people behave and are disposed to behave. On this theory, the claim that Ned believes that it is sunny is to be analysed as the claim that Ned does, or is disposed to do, such things as loosening his collar, putting on sun cream, turning up the air conditioning, and so on. How plausible is that analysis? Suppose that Ned turns out to be a robot controlled by radio by computer scientists. All of his behaviour and his dispositions to behave are produced by the scientists at their controls. Would you be inclined to say that the thing we have been calling "Ned" believes that it is sunny? Would you be inclined to apply the phrase "believes that it is sunny" to Ned? What you are inclined to say, what your intuitions are, can be enough to give you *a priori* **knowledge** of what is required for the phrase "believes that it is sunny" to apply to anything.

Intuitions are used to test an analysis in the following way. The analysis says that, necessarily, anything is an *F* if and only if it is a *G*. We imagine a hypothetical case in which something is an *F*. We then see whether we have the intuition to describe that thing as a *G*. If we do, the intuition is some evidence for the analysis being true. If we have the intuition that the thing is not *G*, that intuition is some evidence that the analysis is false. If we have no intuitions, we consider another hypothetical case and proceed as before.

It might be that some intuitions provide evidence for an analysis whereas others provide evidence against the same analysis. Depending on the balance of evidence, various intuitions may need to be revised or discarded. Some intuitions may provide evidence against a given analysis but, because the analysis is especially simple or fruitful or illuminating, the balance of evidence may be against those intuitions. Our earlier hypothetical example of Ned might produce an intuition against analytical behaviourism. But here is another hypothetical example that might produce an intuition *for* it. Suppose that you were to discover that none of your best friends' heads contain brains but instead cogs and motors that regulate their behaviour towards you. Do you have the intuition that this would be a situation in which you discovered that what you took to be your friends never had any mental life at all, or (as analytical behaviourism would claim) that you discovered something about the inner goings on of friends who thought and cared about you all along? Reaching a philosophical analysis will then be a matter of weighing up proposed analyses against intuitions and reaching a reasoned balance between them. This method is known as *reflective equilibrium*.[6]

The above five claims, (1)–(5), characterize a widely held model of philosophical analysis. Claims (1)–(4) describe the nature of philosophical analysis. Claim (5) describes how philosophical analyses are tested. The remainder of this chapter will be concerned with the nature of philosophical analysis, and the next chapter will be concerned with the method of hypothetical cases.

---

6   Goodman (1955, 61–66), Rawls (1971, 19–20), DePaul (1998), and Henderson and Horgan (2000, 72–73). But see also Cummins (1998).

Here, in summary form, are the five claims that constitute our working model of philosophical analysis:

(1) An analysis has the logical form of a universally quantified biconditional: $(\forall x)\ (Fx \leftrightarrow Gx)$
(2) An analysis is necessarily true.
(3) An analysis is informative.
(4) An analysis is knowable *a priori*.
(5) An analysis is testable by the method of hypothetical cases.

It is helpful to have an example or two of how this model is supposed to apply. A simple example in which the model appears to apply is the following analysis of "x is an even number":

$(\forall x)$ (x is an even number $\leftrightarrow$ x is divisible without remainder by 2)

Another example: Suppose that we want to analyse sentences of the form "x is the same person as y." An analysis in terms of our working model would be:

$(\forall x)\ (\forall y)$ (x is the same person as y $\leftrightarrow$ (x is a person and y is a person and x = y))

The analysis says that, for any x and y, x is the same person as y if and only if x and y are persons and x is identical to y. This analysis has the form of a universally quantified biconditional. It states necessary and sufficient conditions for a pair of things being the same person. It also is necessarily true: it applies to any possible pair of things. It is at least moderately informative. And we can know it to be true *a priori* by understanding the terms involved, and by considering what we would say about hypothetical cases of things that are the same person or hypothetical cases of things that are people and are identical. This example leaves open how sentences of the form "x is a person" should themselves be analysed. That task faces difficulties of its own.

The tripartite analysis of knowledge also seeks to meet the requirements of our working model. This analysis runs:

$(\forall x)\ (\forall p)$ (x knows that p $\leftrightarrow$ x has a justified true belief that p)

Whether this analysis is correct was notably challenged by Gettier (1963).

4. Is Analysis Possible?

Having set up our model of philosophical analysis, we will spend the next five sections trying to knock it down. Moore's own views on analysis raise an issue about the limits of analysis — about whether some concepts cannot be analysed and, if so, which ones these are. In the next section, §5, we will assess Moore's "open question" argument that the concept INTRINSIC GOODNESS cannot be analysed. (It is helpful to follow the convention of writing names of concepts in capital letters. It helps avoid conflating the concept *F* with the property of an *F* or with the meaning of the word "F." There are substantive issues about how these things are related and we should not beg any questions about them.) If Moore's argument that the concept INTRINSIC GOODNESS cannot be analysed is successful, we might wonder whether the argument can be generalized. If so, perhaps it can then be argued that *no* concepts are analysable. That would be a surprising result because it would render our working model of analysis idle. There would be no analysable concepts for it to apply to. This line of thought is taken up in §6 in terms of what is known as "the **paradox of analysis**."

A further issue is that not only do some concepts seem to be analysable, it seems that they can be analysed in more than one way. The availability of multiple analyses for the same concept is a further problem for our model of philosophical analysis. This problem will be presented in §7.

Another problem is that people can have concepts without being able to specify necessary and sufficient conditions for their correct application. This subject matter has been emphasized by the later Wittgenstein and also by some recent psychological theorizing. Its bearing on our model of philosophical analysis will be taken up in §8.

Lastly, are there any successful philosophical analyses? The track record of philosophical analysis is open to question. This issue will be reviewed in §9.

5. Case Study: Moore's Open Question Argument

Moore argues that certain concepts are simple and unanalysable. In particular, he argues that the concept INTRINSIC GOODNESS cannot be analysed in terms of any of the concepts that the sciences use (including psychology and the social sciences) (Moore 1903, ch. 1). His argument is known as "the open question argument." The argument is interesting in its own right because it has a very ambitious conclusion, but it is also of interest because of the issues it raises for the view that philosophical analysis is meaning analysis. On such a view, how are proposed analyses to be tested? Are any concepts unanalysable? If so, how can we tell which ones are and which ones are not?

Moore is concerned with what it is for something to be intrinsically good. He distinguishes between instrumental goods and intrinsic goods. Some things are instrumentally good: they are good because they are a means to something else. A roof over your head is instrumentally good: it keeps out the rain. Socks on your feet are instrumentally good: they keep you warm. Something's keeping out the rain or its keeping in the warmth is itself instrumentally good: it is good for keeping you alive. What about your being alive? Is that also an instrumental good? Perhaps it is — if you are alive you can experience life's pleasures — or perhaps it is good in itself. At any rate, it seems to Moore that some goods are instrumental whereas others are intrinsic. Instrumental goods are things that are good for getting certain other things. Intrinsic goods are things that are good not because they get you other things, but because they are good in themselves.

This line of thought prompts two questions. First, which things are good? It is widely agreed that if anything is an intrinsic good, then pleasure is an intrinsic good. It is controversial, however, whether anything else is an intrinsic good. The second question asks what intrinsic goodness is. Moore takes it that another way of asking this second is to ask what the meaning of the phrase "intrinsic goodness" is. Moore further thinks that there are exactly three possible answers to this last question:

> The meaning of "intrinsic goodness" is simple and unanalysable.
> The meaning of "intrinsic goodness" is complex and analysable.
> The phrase "intrinsic goodness" is meaningless.

Moore thinks that the third answer is implausible. Anyone who debates about which things are intrinsically good, or simply agrees that some things are instrumentally good, understands talk of things being intrinsically good. If someone understands such talk, that person understands what that talk means. It follows that such talk has meaning (and that that person has understood what that meaning is). Moore also rejects the second answer. His reason is provided by his open question argument. By elimination, Moore concludes that intrinsic goodness is simple and unanalysable.

Before we consider the open question argument, it is worth assessing Moore's preceding strategy. His assumption that there are only three possible answers to his question is debatable. In particular, Moore seems to have overlooked some complexities in what it is for talk to be meaningful. For instance, some philosophers distinguish between descriptive and expressive meaning. The sentence "Ottawa is a capital city" describes a certain city; the sentence has descriptive meaning. By contrast, the sentence "Well done Ottawa!" does not describe Ottawa. The sentence lacks descriptive meaning. Someone who sincerely utters that sentence typically expresses a positive attitude towards Ottawa — an attitude of appreciation or affection. According to a view in metaethics called expressivism, a sentence such as "Pleasant things are intrinsically good" lacks descriptive meaning and has only expressive meaning. On this view, someone who sincerely utters that sentence typically expresses a positive attitude towards pleasant things, an attitude of approval (Ayer 1936, ch. 6). Now the first and second possible answers that Moore canvasses assume that "intrinsic goodness" has a descriptive meaning, that the phrase is used to describe things in a certain way. Expressivism rejects that assumption. The third possible answer says that "intrinsic goodness" is meaningless. Presumably it is saying that the phrase lacks descriptive meaning. Expressivism offers a further answer. It says that "intrinsic goodness" lacks descriptive meaning but has expressive meaning. Interestingly, many expressivists have accepted Moore's open question argument as an argument against the second answer (Ayer 1936, 138–39). So even if Moore's strategy is flawed, his open question argument may remain useful. Let's turn to Moore's argument.

The argument is directed against the claim that the (descriptive) meaning of "intrinsic goodness" is complex and analysable. That claim is made, for instance, by ethical naturalism. Ethical naturalism seeks to analyse the meaning of "intrinsic goodness" and all other ethical terms with the use of natural terms. When discussing ethical naturalism, Moore appears to take natural terms to be terms used by the natural sciences broadly construed so as include the science of psychology (Moore 1903, 40).[7] Ethical naturalism claims that the meaning of "intrinsic goodness" can be analysed using so-called natural terms such as "pleasure," "happiness," or "desire." Beyond agreeing that there is such an analysis, ethical naturalists disagree among themselves about which natural terms provide the analysis. One such analysis says that "intrinsic goodness" means what we desire to desire. (This analysis was proposed by Russell [1897] and revived by Lewis [1989].)

Moore argues against ethical naturalism by taking this particular analysis of "intrinsic goodness" as a good illustration of the view and then by trying to show why the analysis fails. He writes that:

> To take, for instance, one of the most plausible, because one
> of the more complicated, of such proposed definitions, it may

---

7   See also Lewy (1964, 295).

> easily be thought that, at first sight, that to be good may mean to be that which we desire to desire. Thus if we apply this definition to a particular instance and say "When we think that A is good we are thinking that A is one of the things which we desire to desire," our proposition may seem quite plausible. But if we carry the investigation further and ask ourselves "Is it good to desire to desire A?" it is apparent on a little reflection, that this question is itself as intelligible as the original question "Is A good?" ... But it is also apparent that the meaning of this second question cannot be analyzed into "Is the desire to desire A one of the things that we desire to desire?": we have not before our minds anything as complicated as the question "Do we desire to desire to desire to desire A?" (Moore 1903, §13)

There is much debate about exactly what Moore's argument is. Without pursuing Moore scholarship, let's take it that Moore is running two lines of argument (Fumerton 2007, 231). We will also take these arguments to be concerned with questions understood as sentence-types. For example, when an argument concerns the question whether what we desire to desire is good, we will take the argument to be concerned with sentence-type "Is what we desire to desire good?"

The first line of argument runs as follows:

(1) Suppose that "A is good" means the same as "A is what we desire to desire."

(2) Then "Is what we desire to desire good?" is the same question as "Is what we desire to desire what we desire to desire?"

(3) But the first question is significant — there would be a point in asking it — whereas the second question is trivial — there would be no point in asking it.

(4) So the two questions are not the same.

(5) So "A is good" does not mean "A is something we desire to desire."

Premise (1) states (roughly) the ethical naturalist view that Moore is going to argue against. Premise (2) states what Moore takes to be a consequence of premise (1). Suppose "A is good" means the same as "A is something we desire to desire." Then we can take a sentence containing the term "is good" and substitute this term with the complex term "is what we desire to desire," and the result would be the same sentence. As a special case, we can take a question that uses the term "is good" and substitute this term with "is what we desire to desire," and the result is the same question. For instance, the term "good" occurs in the question "Is what we desire to desire good?" If we substitute that term with "what we desire to desire," the result is the question "Is what we desire to desire what we desire to desire?" If premise (1) is true, those should be the same question. Premise (3), however, points out a difference between the two questions. The answer to the question "Is what we desire to desire good?" is significant. There would be a point to asking the question because its answer is not obvious. There is what we desire to desire, and the question is asking whether it is good. We may have to reflect and argue about what the answer to the question is — about whether it is good or not. In that sense, the question is "open." This case contrasts with the other question. The answer to the question "Is what we desire to desire what we desire to desire?" is trivial. There would be no point in asking that question because its answer is obvious. There is what we desire to desire, and the question is asking whether it is what we desire to desire. Obviously the answer is "Yes." We don't need to reflect and argue about what the answer to the question is. In that sense, the question is "closed." If one question is significant and the other question is trivial, then the questions are not the same. Premise (4) draws the consequence from premise (3) that the questions are not the same. It follows that premise (2) is false. But premise (2) follows from premise (1). Premise (5) concludes that "A is good" does not mean "A is something we desire to desire." The ethical naturalist analysis is refuted.

The second line of argument in Moore runs as follows:

(1) Suppose that "A is good" means the same as "A is what we desire to desire."

(2) Then "Is what we desire to desire good?" means the same as "Is what we desire to desire what we desire to desire?"

(3) But the first question is significant — there would be a point in asking the question — whereas the second question is trivial — there would be no point in asking the question.

(4) So the two questions do not mean the same.

(5) So "A is good" does not mean "A is something we desire to desire."

This line of argument closely resembles the first, but they importantly differ. The first concerns identifying questions in terms of which sentence-type they belong to. The second concerns identifying questions in terms of their meaning.

In the case of the second line of argument, as before premise (1) states the ethical naturalist view that "A is good" means the same as "A is what we desire to desire." Premise (2) states what Moore takes to be a consequence of premise (1). Here the claim is that the two questions mean the same. Premise (3) is the same as before. It claims that one of the questions is significant (is "open") whereas the other is not (is "closed"). Given this difference, premise (4) infers that the questions differ in meaning. It follows that premise (2) is false. But premise (2) follows from premise (1). Premise (5) concludes that "A is good" does not mean "A is something we desire to desire."

Let's now examine each of these lines of argument. In the case of the first line of argument, the inference from (1) to (2) is open to criticism. We need to distinguish two questions having the same meaning from their being the same sentence-type. Perhaps the best way to see this distinction is by considering a non-philosophical example. Consider the sentences "Where is the cat?" and "Ou est la chat?" Those sentences have the same meaning. But they are not the same sentence-type. Inscribing them involves different types of patterns of ink when inscribed, and uttering them involves different types of patterns of sound (Fumerton 2007, 231). If we individuate questions in terms of the sentence-types that express them, "Where is the cat?" and "Ou est la chat?" do not ask the same question. Returning to the first line of argument, premise (1) does not entail premise (2). Suppose that "A is good" means the same as "A is what we desire to desire." It does not entail that "Is what we desire to desire good?" is the same question as "Is what we desire to desire what we desire to desire?" Those questions are expressed by different sentence-types. Since premise (1) does not entail premise (2), the argument is invalid.

If Moore is running two lines of argument, talk of *the* open question argument is strictly a misnomer. When philosophers talk of the open question argument, typically they have the second line of argument in mind. In the case of this argument, premise (1) entails premise (2). If "A is good" means the same as "A is what we desire to desire," then "Is what we desire to desire good?" means the same as "Is what we desire to desire what we desire to desire?" But the inference from premise (3) to premise (4) is questionable. Premise (3) notes a difference between the two questions. What is doubtful is whether the difference is a difference in meaning between the two questions. If it is not a difference in meaning, the inference from (3) to (4) does not go through.

Premise (3) says that the question "Is what we desire to desire good?" is significant — there would be a point in asking the question because its answer is not obvious. It goes on to say that the question "Is what we desire to desire what we desire to desire?" is trivial — there would be no point in asking the question because its answer is obviously "Yes." The ethical naturalist, however, can reply that what this shows is that although (at least according to ethical naturalism) the two questions have the same meaning, it is not *obvious* that they have the same meaning. Consequently, substituting one of these terms for the other in a sentence that some people bear a certain psychological attitude to may result in a sentence that the same people do not bear the same attitude to, despite the fact that these people fully understand both sentences. For example, the sentence:

A is intrinsically good if and only if A is intrinsically good

will strike anyone who understands it as obviously true. Substituting "what we desire to desire" for the first occurrence of "intrinsically good" in that sentence results in the sentence:

A is what we desire to desire if and only if A is intrinsically good

and people may understand that sentence without it striking them that it is obviously true. But this is not damaging to ethical naturalism because it is not part of the view that its analysis of "intrinsically good" should be obviously true. Indeed, its analysis will be interesting only if it is not obviously true. A similar point holds for the questions that Moore uses in his second line of argument. The question:

Is what we desire to desire what we desire to desire?

will strike anyone who understands it as having an obvious answer. Substituting "good" for the second occurrence of "what we desire to desire" in that question yields:

Is what we desire to desire good?

People can understand that sentence without it striking them as having an obvious answer. They can find the first question "closed" and the second question "open" even though they understand both sentences. But again this result is not damaging to ethical naturalism, and the reason is the same as before. Since ethical naturalism does not require that its analysis of "intrinsically good" is obviously true, asking whether the analysis is true need not have an obvious answer. Yet that is precisely what the second question, the "open" question, is asking. So it is on these grounds that the ethical naturalist can question the inference from premises (3) to (4) in Moore's second line of argument.[8]

Moore appeals to what is "before our minds" when we consider his questions. He says that what is before our minds when we consider the second question is more "complicated" than what is before it when we consider the first question. Assuming that what is before our minds are the meanings of the questions, he concludes that the meanings of the questions differ.

This appeal to introspection raises a number of issues. First, we have seen that Moore apparently runs together two lines of argument. One concerns certain linguistic entities, i.e., certain questions individuated in terms of sentence-types. The other concerns the meaning of those questions. Moore is supposedly holding the meanings of the questions before his mind, but in this passage he slips into discussing the questions themselves:

> But it is also apparent that the meaning of this second question ["Is it good to desire to desire A?"] cannot be analyzed into "Is the desire to desire A one of the things that we desire to desire?": we have not before our minds anything so complicated as the question "Do we desire to desire to desire to desire A?"

The ethical naturalist can agree that "Do we desire to desire to desire to desire A?" is a more complicated sentence than "Is it good to desire to desire A?" When we hold each of these questions "before our minds" (i.e., when we compare them), we can tell that the first question has more words in it than the second, and so that it is more complicated. But the issue is not whether the questions—those sentence-types—differ in complexity. The issue is whether the meanings of those questions differ. It begs the question against the ethical naturalist simply to claim that they do.[9]

Second, Moore assumes that our introspective access to the meanings of our terms is straightforward. He apparently thinks that, for any pair of terms that we understand, if we bring the meaning of one term "before our minds" and then the meaning of the other term, we will immediately conclude on that basis whether or not those meanings are the same. According to the Moorean:

---

8   For further criticism of this inference, see Kalderon (2004).
9   This charge of question-begging was originally made by Frankena (1939). The charge remains controversial: see Pigden (2007, 246) and Nuccetelli and Seay (2007, 277–78).

> ... where a definition is legitimate, anyone who understands
> both the term to be defined and its definition should, on
> reflection, be able to recognize the definition as a way of elu-
> cidating the considerations which guide the application of the
> term.... However much we reflect on our understanding of
> the terms "good" and ["what we desire to desire,"] the ques-
> tion of whether something which [we desire to desire] is good
> remains significant. (Baldwin 2003, 321)

There are several reasons to reject the above requirement on legitimate
definitions. First, take a pair of terms with the same meaning, such as
"wager" and "bet." People can understand those terms and yet doubt (and
so not know) whether they have the same meaning. People could learn
each of these terms normally but separately. They could also even believe
that, for any act, that act is a wager if and only if it is a bet. Nevertheless,
these people could coherently doubt, and so not know, that "wager" and
"bet" have the same meaning. Perhaps they have had a track record of
taking pairs of terms to have the same meaning, only later to find out
that the terms differ in meaning. Their awareness of this bad track record
makes them doubt whether "wager" and "bet" have the same meaning. It
even causes them to believe that the two terms differ in meaning. Despite
this eccentric belief, their use of "wager" and "bet" is otherwise as competent as anyone else's (Rieber 1992).[10]

Here is another reason for rejecting Moore's requirement that you can
tell by introspection whether any pair of terms that you understand have
the same meaning. Consider some actual examples. Does "point" as used
in Euclidean geometry mean the same as "point" in any non-Euclidean
geometry? When atomic physicists describe a table as "solid," do they
mean what Shakespeare and his contemporaries meant by that word? Do
physicists today mean the same by "atom" as physicists in the nineteenth
century? When physicists describe glass windowpanes as liquids, do they
mean by "liquids" what you mean by that word? Introspection does not
seem to answer any of these questions:

> ... introspection does not provide a general ground for the
> truth or falsity of synonymy claims even where the terms in the
> relevant class are well understood by us. (Lance and O'Leary-
> Hawthorne 1997, 26)[11]

---

10   See also Salmon (1989, 265–66) and Soames (2003, 46–47).
11   See also Baldwin (1990, 63–64, 88).

Some defenders of Moore think that although the open question argument does not entail that "good" and "what we desire to desire" differ in meaning, the argument provides some degree of evidence that the two terms differ in meaning.

> Moore is suggesting that the mere fact, as he puts it, that we ordinarily find at least "questionable" or doubtable a proposition equating a pair of terms ["good" and "what we desire to desire"] is relevant to determining whether such a theory is correct.... The main strategy is to use openness as a test for synonymy. (Ball 1988, 207)[12]

> ... [T]he presence of doubt merely suggests that the analysis is incorrect. (Strandberg 2004, 182)

> Moore's argument ... suffices to create a burden of proof on the ethical naturalist.... [The latter has] the argumentative burden of showing how two apparently different things — [goodness] and [what we desire to desire], for instance — are really one and the same thing. (Shafer-Landau 2003, 57–58)

The above passages claim that if someone doubts whether "intrinsic goodness is what we desire to desire" is true without doubting whether "intrinsic goodness is intrinsic goodness" is true, then that is evidence against "intrinsic goodness" having the same meaning as "what we desire to desire." But the point made in the "wager"/"bet" example equally applies here. According to the above passages, if someone doubts whether "a wager is a bet" is true without doubting whether "a wager is a wager" is true, then that is evidence against "wager" having the same meaning as "bet." And since this was an arbitrarily chosen pair of synonymous terms, the point applies quite generally to any pair of terms with the same meaning. This generates a dilemma. Either the fact that someone can doubt whether "intrinsic goodness" and "what we desire to desire" have the same meaning provides no evidence against the ethical naturalist analysis. Or, if it does provide evidence against it, it provides very weak evidence, because exactly the same kind of evidence is available against any pair of synonymous terms having the same meaning.

Under what circumstances does a body of information e provide evidence against a hypothesis h? One suggestion is that e provides evidence against h if the best explanation of why e occurs is that h is false (Harman

---

12 See also Ball (1991, 8–17) and Pigden (2007, 258).

1965, esp. 90–91). But, to apply this suggestion to the present case, Mooreans would need to show why the best explanation of why someone doubts that "intrinsic goodness is what we desire to desire" is true is that the ethical naturalist analysis is false. They would have to show why that was a better explanation than the hypothesis that the person does not know the meaning of "good," something that the ethical naturalist analysis specifies. And they would also have to show why their tactic does not over-generalize so that, for example, they are committed to saying that the best explanation of why someone doubts that "a wager is a bet" is true is that "wager" and "bet" differ in meaning. (The idea of **inference to the best explanation** will be discussed at more length in chapter 5, §5.)

Tom Baldwin identifies a further argument in Moore, an argument to be distinguished from Moore's open question argument. Baldwin calls it Moore's "distinct question" argument (Baldwin 1990, 88–89 citing Moore 1903, 13). In the following passage Baldwin states how the argument would run against the ethical naturalist analysis that "good" means the same as "pleasant":

> ... however much we may try to persuade ourselves that "good" ... just means "pleasant," the fact that we continue to regard the question whether all pleasures are good as significant shows that "good" and "pleasant" are not synonymous. What is important here is the persistence of the sense that such questions are significant, that their answer is always an "open question." ... [It] is reasonable to demand of an analysis of meaning that it should illuminate the concepts with which it deals in such a way that, because it enhances our understanding, we come to find it natural for us to guide our judgments according to it. It is in the light of this requirement that the persisting sense of the significance of Moore's questions is problematic for the ethical reductionist. It is evidence that his reductive analysis is simply not persuasive, and therefore not correct. (Baldwin 1990, 89. Baldwin himself queries the foregoing argument though not its conclusion)

The argument that Baldwin reconstructs includes the premise that it is an open question whether "good" means *pleasant*. It also introduces a premise that if "good" is analysed as meaning *pleasant*, that analysis should enhance our understanding of "good," and we should find it natural to use the analysis in making judgments. The puzzle is how those two premises are supposed to entail that "good" and "pleasant" differ in meaning. There seems to be an assumption that so long as the question whether "good" means *pleasant* persists as an open question, we would not find it natural to make judgments according to the claim that "good" means *pleasant*. But what does "natural" mean here?

One suggestion might be that a question is an open one if and only if its answer is not obvious. If an answer to a given question is not obvious, it is not obvious that we make judgments in accordance with that answer. So if "what we find natural" means "what we find obvious," then the assumption is correct. So long as it is an open question whether "good" means *pleasant*, it is not obvious that we make judgments in accordance with the claim that "good" means *pleasant*. It is unclear, however, that the conclusion that "good" does not mean *pleasant* follows from this. Since ethical naturalists need not (and should not) regard their analyses as obvious, they need not think that it is obvious that we make judgments about which things are good on the basis of their analyses.

In another sense, "what we find natural to do" means *what we do spontaneously or readily*. On this reading, the assumption says that so long as the question whether "good" means *pleasant* persists as an open question, we would not spontaneously or readily make judgments according to the claim that "good" means *pleasant*. The assumption, however, is debatable. An analysis of "good" might not be obviously true. Nevertheless, people who believe the analysis might become so conversant with it that they spontaneously use it in judging which things are good. The general point here has nothing specifically to do with meaning analysis. What seems obvious and what seems natural to someone in this sense are psychological issues, and even if a claim is not obvious to someone, other psychological factors can make reliance on that claim natural to them. For example, it is not obvious — it is not beyond doubt — that there is a correlation between temperature and the height of a certain liquid in a glass tube. But a doctor who believes that there is such a correlation might spontaneously use a mercury thermometer to take a patient's temperature.

Lastly, suppose we grant this second reading of the assumption. That is, suppose that so long as the question whether "good" means *pleasant* persists as an open question, we would not spontaneously make judgments according to the claim that "good" means *pleasant*. Even so, it is still unclear how it follows that "good" and "pleasant" differ in meaning. In sum, Moore's "distinct questions" argument seems as unsuccessful as his "open question" argument.

6. The Paradox of Analysis

An important issue that Moore's open question argument raises is a general one about philosophical analysis. A philosophical analysis of a term's meaning needs to be both true and interesting. If the analysis is uninteresting, then it does not deepen our understanding of the term's meaning. For instance, an analysis that said that "intrinsically good" has the same meaning as "intrinsically good" would be true but uninteresting. But for an analysis to be interesting, it needs to be not obviously true. Ethical naturalism offered an analysis of "intrinsic goodness" that attempts to meet these twin requirements of being true and being interesting. Moore, by contrast, seems to require that an analysis of "intrinsically good" should be both true and obvious. Taken together his requirements rule out the possibility that there is any true and interesting analysis of the meaning of "intrinsically good." But notice that his requirements rule out the possibility that there is any true and interesting analysis of the meaning of any term whatsoever. Suppose, for instance, that we tried to analyse the meaning of "knowledge" by saying that it has the same meaning as "justified true belief." That would be an interesting analysis. But Moore could point out that whereas "knowledge is knowledge" is obvious to anyone who understands it, "knowledge is justified true belief" is not obvious to anyone who understands it. Moore would be committed to rejecting this analysis of the meaning of "knowledge" for just the same reason as he rejected the ethical naturalist's analysis of the meaning of "intrinsically good." More generally, if Moore's open question argument were valid, it would show that the meanings of no terms are analysable (Lewy 1964, 302 and Baldwin 1990, 88). It would follow that philosophical analysis, understood as meaning analysis, is impossible. It then seems that Moore's argument proves too much. A likely diagnosis of where the argument goes wrong is that it erroneously assumes that any analysis, and more generally any conceptual truth, will be recognized as obviously true by anyone who understands it. That assumption seems mistaken. Here is another counterexample. Someone may have the concept GREAT-GRANDPARENT and the concept SECOND COUSIN (i.e., the concept CHILD OF SOMEONE WHO IS A CHILD OF SIBLINGS). Nevertheless, it may not be obvious to them — it may be an open question to them — whether second cousins share two great-grandparents. It may take a little time and reasoning for them to realize that it is a conceptual truth.[13]

Moore's open question argument apparently trades on what has been called the paradox of analysis, a paradox that precisely says that philosophical analysis, understood as meaning analysis, is impossible (Wisdom 1934, 79 and Langford 1942). Langford writes:

---

13   See also Baldwin (1990, 210–11), and Darwell, Gibbard and Railton (1992, 115).

Let us call what is to be analyzed the analysandum, and let us call that which does the analyzing the analysans. The analysis then states an appropriate relation of equivalence between the analysandum and the analysans. And the paradox of analysis is to the effect that, if the verbal expression representing the analysandum has the same meaning as the verbal expression representing the analysans, the analysis states a bare identity and is trivial; but if the two verbal expressions do not have the same meaning, the analysis is incorrect. (Langford 1942, 323)

The paradox can be set out a little more fully as follows:

(1)   A philosophical analysis of a concept, F, should say what that concept is identical to.

(2)   Suppose that a given philosophical analysis of the concept F says that it is identical to the concept G.

(3)   So if the concepts F and G are not identical, the analysis is false. (By (1) and (2)).

(4)   Alternatively, if the concepts F and G are identical, then what the analysis says (that the concept F is identical to the concept G) has the same content as the claim that the concept F is identical to the concept F.

(5)   But it is uninteresting ("trivial," as Langford calls it) that the concept F is identical to the concept F.

(6)   So if the concepts F and G are identical, what the analysis says is uninteresting. (By (4) and (5)).

(7)   So either the analysis is false or it is uninteresting. (By (3) and (6)).

Premise (4) can be supported in two ways. Here is the first way. An analysis of the concept F says what that concept is identical to, namely the concept G. So the analysis says that concept F is identical to itself. The claim that concept F is identical to concept F also says that concept F is identical to itself. So that claim says the same as the analysis. Here is the second way. There is a principle of semantics known as the principle of compositionality. This principle says that the meaning of a sentence is determined by the meaning of each of its components (the concepts that they express) and by how they are arranged. Suppose that the analysis is correct and so that concept F is identical to concept G. Then the claim that concept F is identical to concept G, and the claim that concept F is identical to concept F, consist of the same terms arranged in the same way. By the principle of compositionality those claims have the same meaning — they say the same thing.

The argument (1)–(7) poses a dilemma for any philosophical analysis, where philosophical analysis is understood as a meaning analysis. Either the analysis captures the content of the concept in question, or it does not. If it does not, then the analysis is not informative and so is not interesting. If it does, then the analysis is false. The paradox arises because intuitively it seems possible for philosophical analysis to produce true and interesting analyses of concepts. In fact, the paradox of analysis is doubly paradoxical because the paradox seems to be an interesting result of an analysis of the concept of a philosophical analysis.

A simple attempt at a solution would be metalinguistic (Ackerman 1981, 1990). Consider the following analysis:

(A) (∀x) (x is procrastinates ↔ x defers action)

A metalinguistic solution would construe (A) as being about not just the concepts of procrastinating and deferring action, but also about the terms "procrastinates" and "defers action." (A) would be construed as (B):

(B) (∀x) (the concept expressed by "procrastinates" applies to x ↔ the concept expressed by "defers action" applies to x)

A problem with this attempt is that the same analysis can be expressed in different words. For example, assuming that "procrastinate" is synonymous with "postpones things he or she should be doing," (A) can be expressed as:

(C) (∀x) (x is procrastinates ↔ x postpones things he or she should be doing)

(C) does not say anything about the term "defers action." So (C) does not mean the same as (B). But (A) means the same as (C). So (A) does not mean the same as (B) (Rieber 1994, 107–09).

A more promising line of solution would be that in an analysis the term for the analysandum and the term for the analysans should differ syntactically and should have different semantic structures. What is a semantic structure? Let T be a term and each of $T_1, \ldots, T_k$ be its components. The semantic structure of T is the property of *being a term each of whose components have the respective meanings of $T_1, \ldots, T_k$*. For example, the semantic structure of "female fox" is the property of *being a term with* *two components whose respective meanings are the property of being female and the property of being a fox.*

> [Two] expressions have the *same semantic structure* if and only if they are synonymous and for each meaningful component of one there is a corresponding component of the other which means the same. (Rieber 1994, 110)

It follows that "female fox" and "vixen" have different semantic structures. For each semantic structure there is a corresponding concept. There may be more than one semantic structure corresponding to the same concept. For example, the semantic structures of "female fox" and "vixen" both correspond to the concept FEMALE FOX (i.e., the concept VIXEN). Consequently, semantic structures are more finely individuated than concepts. Different terms can have the same semantic structure. So terms are more finely individuated than semantic structures. Let's introduce the notation "« »" to indicate that a term refers to its own semantic structure. Recall (A):

> (A) ($\forall$x) (x is procrastinates $\leftrightarrow$ x defers action)

What (A) says is given by (D):

> (D) ($\forall$x) (the concept corresponding to «procrastinates» applies to x $\leftrightarrow$ the concept corresponding to «defers action» applies to x)

The terms "procrastinates" and "defers action" in (D), and so in (A), refer to their semantic structures. What (A) says can be said using other expressions provided that they refer to the same semantic structures.

How does this apparatus solve the paradox of analysis? A statement of an analysis refers to the semantic structures of the terms flanking the biconditional. Recall premise (4) of the paradox:

> (4) If the concepts F and G are identical, then what the analysis says (that the concept F is identical to the concept G) has the same content as the claim that the concept F is identical to the concept F.

That premise assumes that the analysis is simply about the concept F. That assumption is rejected by the current suggestion. It takes the analysis to say that concept F, the concept corresponding to one semantic structure, is identical to concept G, the concept corresponding to another semantic structure.

The argument from compositionality says that the meaning of a sentence is determined by the meanings of its components, and how those components are combined. But compositionality does not apply to expressions that refer to their own semantic structures. "[The] contribution made by an *expression which refers to its own semantic structure* to the meaning of a sentence depends not on its own meaning — or at least not solely on its own meaning — but rather on its semantic structure" (Rieber 1994, 112).

To sum up, the paradox of analysis is a powerful challenge to the model of philosophical analysis that we are working with. Nevertheless, that model can be supplemented with an account of the semantics of sentences stating analyses that offers a promising solution to the paradox.[14]

7. The Problem of Multiple Analyses

Here again are the five claims that characterized our working model of philosophical analysis:

(1) An analysis has the logical form of a universally quantified biconditional:
$(\forall x)\,(Fx \leftrightarrow Gx)$
(2) An analysis is necessarily true, indeed analytically true.
(3) An analysis is informative.
(4) An analysis is knowable *a priori*.
(5) An analysis is testable by the method of hypothetical cases.

This model requires that the analysandum and the analysans express the same concept — that "F" and "G" have the same meaning. This entails that the analysandum has a unique analysis. If "G" provides the analysis of "F," then, for any term "H," "H" provides the analysis of "F" if and only if "H" has the same meaning as "G."

The **problem of multiple analyses** faces this model of philosophical analysis because it seems false that every analysandum has a unique analysis, and consequently it seems false that an analysis gives the meaning of the term for the analysandum. If correct analyses are to be found anywhere, they are to be found in mathematics. Let's consider some mathematical analyses. Euclid said that:

---

14 For other recent solutions to the paradox, see Richard (2001) and King (2007, ch. 7).

> a circle is a plane figure contained by one line, which is called the circumference, and is such that all straight lines drawn from a certain point within the figure to the circumference are equal to one another. (Euclid *The Thirteen Books of the Elements* Volume 1, Book I, Definition 15)

Leibniz said that a circle is:

> a figure described by the motion of a straight line around a fixed end. (Leibniz 1679, 230)

Lastly, differential geometry says that a circle is a closed plane curve of constant curvature. These three analyses are equivalent, but they are not synonymous. Leibniz's analysis, for example, uses the concept MOTION, and so it also uses the concept TIME. Yet neither of the other analyses uses these concepts. Since the three analysans concepts are distinct, they are not all identical with the concept CIRCLE. It would be arbitrary to select one of these analysans concepts. Our working model of philosophical analysis is committed to claiming that none of the three analyses is correct. This runs counter to mathematical practice as it treats each of them as *bona fide* and correct analyses (Anderson 1987, 127–28, 139–41; 1990, 69–71; and 1993, 215–18). Furthermore, the same considerations arise in philosophy. For example, as a first attempt Nozick analyses "s knows that *p*" as:

(i)   *p* is true,
(ii) *S* believes that *p*,
(iii) If it were not the case that *p*, it would not be the case that *S* believes that *p*. (Nozick 1981, 172–78)

A logically equivalent, but distinct, analysis would drop (i) but retain (ii) and (iii) (Anderson 1987, 161–62, n. 25). To take another example, Russell's theory of descriptions provides several analyses of sentences of the form "S believes that the *F* is *G*" that are not synonymous.[15] One might take a hard line and think that these results show that the examples are not philosophical analyses. But it is not clear why philosophy should require that its analyses state synonymies although mathematics does not make that requirement. It is not clear what benefit such a requirement would bring, a benefit that mathematical analyses lack.

---

15 For supporting argument, see Anderson 1990, 169–71.

8. Family Resemblance

In our working model of philosophical analysis in §3, it was claimed that an analysis has the logical form of a universally quantified biconditional:

$$(\forall x)\,(Fx \leftrightarrow Gx)$$

An analysis then gives necessary and sufficient conditions for something to be *F*. It was also claimed that it is knowable *a priori* what these conditions are.

The later Wittgenstein has often been taken to challenge these claims (1953, §§65–67). The challenge is simple and direct. Take a particular example of a concept, such as the concept GAME. What conditions are necessary and sufficient for something to be a game? A plethora of activities are called games. Not all games involve competition (e.g., patience) or fun for the participants (e.g., gladiatorial games). So those are not necessary conditions. And it is not only games that are governed by rules or that have objectives, since political debates and initiation ceremonies share those features. So those are not sufficient conditions. Pairs of games resemble each other in certain respects, but what respects these are, differ between different pairs of games. Wittgenstein draws an analogy with how the faces of pairs of people from the same family may resemble each other in certain respects — perhaps you have your father's eyes and chin, and your sister has your mother's nose — although what these respects are differ from pair to pair.

Some philosophers have interpreted Wittgenstein to be making two claims. First, because we have been unable to give *a priori* knowable necessary and sufficient conditions for the application of various terms (such as "game"), those terms lack such conditions. Second, we call different things by the same term only because these things bear certain **family resemblances** to each other. It is then a mistake to suppose that there are certain necessary and sufficient conditions for something to be correctly called a "game." Although this interpretation once enjoyed near-orthodoxy among Wittgensteinians, it has come under question by some of them in more recent years (Bangu 2005, 57–58). As Wittgenstein recognized, the fact that to date we have failed to formulate such conditions provides little support for the claim that there are no such conditions (Bangu 2005, 58 cites Wittgenstein 1964, 18, 35).

An alternative interpretation offers the weaker thesis that a competent user of a term "F" need not know necessary and sufficient conditions for the application of "F" (Baker and Hacker 1992, 131, Bangu 2005, 60–61).[16] This interpretation is consistent with the term's having such conditions. It claims only that, even if there are such conditions, someone can be ignorant of them despite being a competent user of "F." But, on this interpretation, Wittgenstein's claim is consistent with our working model of philosophical analysis. According to that model, it is for philosophers to find out what conditions are necessary and sufficient conditions for the correct application of terms. If ordinary users of terms already knew what those conditions were, philosophical analysis would have little to do.[17]

A psychological theory known as prototype theory has claimed that people do not access concepts by knowing individually necessary and jointly sufficient conditions (Smith and Medin 1981, Rosch and Mervis 1975, and Rosch 1987). It further claims that people access concepts by having certain typical examples of the concept in mind (prototypes) and judging that other cases are also examples of these concepts if they are sufficiently similar to the prototypes. Since prototype theory is a scientific theory, the issues that it raises are ones that arise via the naturalistic method in philosophy (see chapter 6).

Certain data taken as supporting evidence for this theory consist in typicality effects or prototypical effects. People classify some instances of a concept as better examples of the concept than others are. For example, people classify robins as better examples of birds than ostriches. People's reaction times for classifying things as birds are also faster in the case of robins than ostriches. If these findings are correct, some psychologists and philosophers think that would support the theory that people's concepts lack necessary and sufficient conditions for correct application (Stich 1992, 249 and Ramsey 1992).

No doubt most people frequently use "quick and dirty" methods, such as the use of prototypes and other rules of thumb, in classifying things. But these same people often also know the shortcomings of those methods. They know that there can be "imposters": things that fit the prototype of a bird although they are not birds (such as bats). They also know that there can be atypical cases: things that do not fit the stereotype of a bird although they are birds (such as ostriches and penguins) (Rey 1983, 1985; Keil 1989, and Fodor and Lepore 1994). Moreover, people often use prototypes even in the case of concepts that have necessary and sufficient conditions of application, and where these people know these conditions. For example, most people who have the concept PRIME NUMBER take numbers such as 3, 5, 7 and 11 to be stereotypical prime numbers. When

---

16 See also Geach's criticism of what he calls the Socratic fallacy in Geach (1972, 33–34).

17 For another response to the family resemblance challenge, see Chalmers (1996, 53–55).

invited to think of prime numbers, these are the ones that readily come to mind and which people most rapidly verify are prime. These people are less quick off the mark in classifying numbers such as 823, 1097, and 3469 as prime. Yet all these numbers are prime because they each satisfy a necessary and sufficient condition for being prime (being divisible without remainder only by itself or by 1), and people with the concept PRIME NUMBER invariably know that condition. (Armstrong, Gleitman and Gleitman (1983) present very similar results with respect to people's possession of the concept EVEN NUMBER.)

The first lesson of these considerations is that people's concepts should not be conflated with the prototypes they use as heuristic devices. The second lesson is that the inference from "People do not access necessary and sufficient conditions in order to apply concepts" to "Those concepts lack necessary and sufficient conditions of correct application" is a dubious one.

Another response to the prototype data is that, far from prototype theory denying that concepts have necessary and sufficient conditions of application, the theory offers a distinctive take on what those necessary and sufficient conditions are. For example, it takes a necessary and sufficient condition for being a bird something's being sufficiently similar to prototypical birds (Jackson 1998, 61). The claim here is that prototype theory itself offers analyses of the form:

(Proto) $(\forall x)$ (x is $F \leftrightarrow$ x is sufficiently similar to prototypical Fs)

An apparent difficulty with analyses of this form is that they are circular. Understanding what a prototypical F is requires understanding what an F is, and that returns us to the left-hand side of the biconditional. Or so it might seem.

There are two ways of responding to this. One response is to supplement (Proto) by listing or pointing to some prototypical Fs. We can thereby learn, of certain things, that they are prototypical Fs. By that means, and (Proto), we can then come to understand what an F is. Something is an F if and only if it is sufficiently similar to the things that have already been picked out as prototypical Fs. (Lewis (1997, especially §§V and VII) develops this idea in the case of the analysis of colour terms.)

Another response is to query the significance of the non-circularity requirement. In §3 the requirement that analyses are informative was enforced by the requirement that analyses should be non-circular. Prototype theory cannot then be taken as offering analyses of concepts in terms of necessary and sufficient conditions. Some philosophers have thought that analyses can be informative whilst also being circular.[18] The idea here is that an analysis of a term "F" may be informative by describing some of the analytic connections between "F" and other terms, even if a full understanding of any of these other terms would itself require understanding "F." Strawson puts the view in terms of concepts:

> A concept may be complex, in the sense that its philosophical elucidation requires the establishing of its connections with other concepts, and yet at the same time irreducible, in the sense that it cannot be defined away, without circularity, in terms of those other concepts to which it is necessarily related. (Strawson 1992, 22–23)

To start with some non-philosophical examples, there are conceptual connections between the economic terms "producer," "consumer," "supply," and "demand," but such concepts are not non-circularly analysable. By definition, a producer supplies a good to a consumer to meet some demand. And also by definition a consumer has a demand for some good that a producer supplies. These definitions use the same members of a small family of terms. There are also such connections between the concepts of the days of the week — it is a conceptual truth that Tuesdays immediately succeed Mondays and immediately precede Wednesdays — although such concepts cannot be non-circularly analysed. Philosophical examples are more controversial. Carroll takes the concepts CAUSATION, CHANCE, COUNTERFACTUAL CONDITIONAL and LAW OF NATURE to stand in conceptual connections to each other, but he further holds that they are not non-circularly analysable (Carroll 1994, 5–7). Gupta and Belnap claim that concepts as diverse as those of TRUTH, PREDICATION, NECESSITY and PHYSICAL OBJECT cannot be non-circularly analysed (Gupta and Belnap 1993, ch. 6 and 7). Technical work has been done on saying which kinds of circular analysis are admissible (Gupta and Belnap 1993, ch. 4; Humberstone 1997). It remains unclear, though, whether a formal demarcation of admissible circular analyses from non-admissible ones can be given (Keefe 2002). Yet even if such a demarcation cannot be given, that does not discredit the suggestion that there can be informative but circular analyses.

---

18 Shoemaker (1984, 222); Strawson (1992, ch. 2); Anderson (1993, 213–14); and Carroll (1994, 3–16).

9. The Track Record of Philosophical Analysis

Philosophical analysis seems to have a poor track record. There are relatively few philosophical analyses that are widely agreed to be correct. In one way or another, almost every philosophical analysis that has been proposed faces objections. Such objections may say that there are actual or possible counter-examples to the analysis, or that the analysis is circular, or that the analysans is more obscure than the analysandum. Perhaps these objections can be overcome, but there is no agreement about that either. In short, philosophical analysis has a history of little success and widespread failure (Fodor 1998, 69–70).

Even if the track record of philosophical analysis is as bad as is being claimed, this history of failure might in fact count as evidence in support of the project of philosophical analysis. Georges Rey compares the track record to the combination of success and failure that science has had in positing unobservable entities (Rey 2004, 243–44). The measure of success indicates that science is "onto something." The measure of failure indicates that what science does is not all wishful thinking. For if it were all wishful thinking, science would not undergo any setbacks. It would be able to spin out its fiction without check. In the case of philosophical analysis, all parties agree that we find reasons to reject many analyses. Our rejecting these analyses is a measure of our failure in discovering philosophical analyses. But the fact that we have reasons for rejecting them is a measure of success in our tracking things that supplies those reasons. Rey takes it that what we are tracking are concepts, and the tracking itself consists in our conceptual competence — our understanding of the concepts in question. At any rate, these patterns call out for explanation.

Quine sought to explain in other ways the patterns of linguistic behaviour that other philosophers took to be exhibiting grasp of analytic truths. In his view, they reflected claims that were central to our belief system, and so they reflected claims that are tenaciously held. Quine's centrality hypothesis, however, is of dubious value here. For example, Moorean common sense claims ("here is a hand," "I have been alive for a number of years") are central to our belief system, and they are strongly held. Yet they seem unlike conceptual truths. Furthermore, Quine takes claims central to our belief system to be explanatorily important. But not every conceptual truth is explanatorily important (e.g., that vixens are female foxes) unlike scientific laws.[19]

---

19   For some further differences, see Rey (2004, 244–45).

Returning to the issue of the track record of philosophical analysis, the search for analyses has been valuable even if there is no agreement about which analyses are correct. Consider the attempt to analyse the concept KNOWLEDGE. This has shed light on such issues as "the defeat of evidence, causal and counterfactual conditions on knowledge and justification, and the epistemic role of external factors like social context and the reliability of belief-forming mechanisms" (Conee 1996, 265, n. 9). Similar observations hold for other concepts of philosophical interest, such as those of CAUSATION, PERCEPTION, and RATIONALITY. In this respect, the track record of philosophical analysis looks much more satisfactory.

The previous section canvassed the idea that there can be informative but circular analyses. If this idea is tenable, then the track record of philosophical analysis can be re-assessed. If we consider only non-circular analyses, then it might be conceded that philosophical analysis has a poor track record. If, however, we consider informative circular analyses, then things may look a bit better. As we have seen, the analysis of "producer" in terms of "consumer" is circular because "consumer" is itself analysed in terms of "producer." Notwithstanding circularity, the application of one concept may be an important necessary condition for the application of another; or it may be an important sufficient condition for the application of another concept. This kind of mapping of "conceptual geography" can be philosophically valuable (Carroll 1994, 15–16).

Lastly, there is some reason why we should expect philosophical analysis, even circular analysis, to be difficult and its results controversial. A correct analysis of a concept would express a rule governing the application of that concept. But a possessor of that concept need not be consciously aware of that rule, let alone know how to formulate it. Such a rule is "sub-doxastic": it is below the level of conscious belief. If people need not know the semantic rules that guide the application of their concepts, their only route to knowing what the contents of their concepts are, what these semantic rules specify, is by theorizing on the basis of what they introspect and observe about linguistic behaviour. Since such behaviour is the outcome of a number of influences besides the semantic rules governing concepts, it is unsurprising that it should be difficult to reach consensus on what those semantic rules specify. This observation is also relevant to the family resemblance issue of the previous section. If the rules governing the content of concepts are sub-doxastic, and so people do not have conscious access to them, the information that they do have conscious access to may have a quite different character, such as a family resemblance character.

10. Taking Stock

Let's take stock of the discussion so far. We began with a certain model of philosophical analysis (§3). We then considered various problems facing this model. Not all of those problems seem insuperable. Moore argued that the concept INTRINSIC GOODNESS cannot be analysed, but his open question argument appeared flawed (§5). The paradox of analysis (§6) is the problem of how there can be informative analyses if the analysandum and the analysans express the same concept. One promising avenue for a solution took the informativeness of an analysis to result from syntactically different terms with different semantic structures expressing the same concept. A more serious problem is the problem of multiple analyses (§7). The problem here is that there can be equally good analyses of the same analysandum that differ in meaning. Another problem concerns family resemblance cases (§8). People do not know necessary and sufficient conditions for the application of many concepts although they can apply those concepts successfully across a wealth of cases. All too often people know only of a series of loose resemblances between the things that fall under a given concept. We saw, however, that it is questionable to infer from this that concepts lack necessary and sufficient conditions of application. Lastly, there is a problem about the apparent dearth of successful philosophical analyses (§9). The key replies were that philosophical analysis's degrees of success and of failure are in accordance with what we should expect if it is engaging with a genuine subject-matter, and that its degree of success is higher if we include whatever informative circular analyses have been given.

In the remainder of this chapter we will consider three accounts of analysis that are alternatives to the model presented in §3. These accounts are particularly motivated by the concern to "naturalize" philosophical analysis — to show how philosophical analysis is compatible with scientific enquiry and its empirical methods. (This discussion looks ahead to the extended treatment of naturalism in chapter 6.) The accounts are ones offered by David Lewis and Frank Jackson (§11), Georges Rey (§12) and W.V. Quine (§13) respectively. The discussion of Quine's account will explore his view of philosophical analysis as explication. This will lead on to a discussion of the use of paraphrase in philosophy (§14).

11. Naturalizing Analysis: Lewis and Jackson's Account

A recent important version of conceptual analysis is known as the *Canberra Plan* (Lewis 1994, esp. 298–303; Jackson 1998, esp. ch. 1–3; Nolan 2005, ch. 9; and Braddon-Mitchell and Nola 2009, ch. 1). (The name is a label for how philosophy is meant to be done in the School of Philosophy in the Research School of Social Sciences at the Australian National University, Canberra.) Suppose we want to know what a certain philosophically interesting subject matter is. Suppose, for instance, we want to know what temporal change or personal identity or colour is. The Canberra Plan offers the following three-step programme for finding out the nature of the subject matter.

First: assemble folk platitudes about the subject matter. The first task is to draw up intuitions about the subject matter. What are wanted are intuitions that are widely, if not unanimously, shared. They are intuitions that all the folk have. To be widely shared, the content of these intuitions needs to be obvious and uncontroversial. (Recall Moore's list of common sense claims in chapter 1, §2.) Hence the intuitions to be assembled are folk platitudes about the subject matter. Insofar as discovering what intuitions we have can be done *a priori*, this part of the programme is an *a priori* exercise. For example, the list of folk platitudes about colour provides a description of the concept COLOUR. The list includes such platitudes as that colours appear to be visible properties of objects, that they can persist through changes in lighting conditions, that they cause sensory experiences of colour, that there is something visible that all things of the same colour have in common, and so on. By describing the concept COLOUR, the list of folk platitudes is thereby describing a certain role, "the colour role," as we might call it.

Second: discover what occupies the role. Having used the folk platitudes to delineate a certain role, there is then a question as to what occupies that role. Folk platitudes about colour say that colour is, amongst other things, a visible property of the surfaces of things and the cause of our sensory experiences of colour. But what kind of thing is it that occupies this role? If folk platitudes delineate a role, it is another task to discovery what occupies that role.

At least in the case of some roles, it is a contingent fact what occupies those roles. Perhaps at one possible world a thing undergoes change over time by remaining identical through time and differing in its properties at different times. Perhaps at another possible world a thing undergoes change over time by its having different temporal parts. We cannot tell *a priori* which of these ways is involved for a thing to change over time at the actual world (Jackson (1994)). So we need to use *a posteriori* means to discover what occupies the role of change over time.

Furthermore, even in the case of roles where we can tell *a priori* that exactly one kind of thing *could* occupy that role, it is a further question whether anything actually occupies that role. For example, perhaps our folk intuitions about freedom of action include the libertarian intuition that a free action cannot be determined by events in the distant past.

Assuming that in the actual world our actions are determined, it follows that nothing perfectly realizes the freedom of action role. But it may be that there is something about our mental life that meets many of the other folk intuitions about freedom, especially many of the more import-ant ones (Jackson 1998, 44–45). In that case, although there is no per-fect occupier of the freedom of action role, there may be an "imperfect occupier" of it and an "imperfect deserver" of the expression "freedom of action." As Lewis puts it, "[when] it comes to occupying a role, and thereby deserving a name, near enough is good enough" (Lewis 1996, 58).[20] We would have freedom of action, although what we have does not exactly match the list of folk intuitions about freedom. Once again, it requires *a posteriori* investigation to tell what occupies, or is the best candidate for occupying, the role marked out by a list of folk intuitions.

Third: identify the subject matter with what occupies the role. The first stage of the Canberra Plan programme said that the folk platitudes about a subject matter determine a certain role, and that whatever occupies that role is identical to that subject matter. The second stage instructs us to discover what occupies that role. It follows that whatever it is that occupies that role is identical to the subject matter. In slogan form: to be *F* is to occupy the *F*-role.

Jackson officially assigns conceptual analysis the modest task of iden-tifying the *F*-role by assembling folk platitudes about *F*s, and of establish-ing whether the folk platitudes are consistent with what science claims about the world (Jackson 1998, 42–44). Yet he also puts conceptual analy-sis to the much more ambitious task of specifying conceptual entailments between different descriptions of the world. Take any true description of anything in the world. This might be people's psychology or the col-ours of objects, to take two of Jackson's examples. The ambitious task is this: given physicalism — the claim that everything is physical — every true description of anything in the world is *a priori* deducible from a description of the world in terms of fundamental physics. To defend the view that there are colours or minds in our world, we need to show how things as told in the vocabulary of fundamental physics make true things told in the vocabulary of colour or of psychology. This requires us to define the subjects, and to do this we must do conceptual analysis. This is Jackson's "entry by entailment" thesis applied to the case of physical-ism (Jackson 1998, 6–8). Notice that this ambitious entry-by-entailment role for philosophical analysis goes beyond any role of assembling and systematizing folk intuitions. It is doubtful that there are even any folk

---

20   See also Lewis (1989, 92–94) and Nolan (2005, 223–27).

platitudes about how microphysical descriptions relate to psychological or colour descriptions.[21]

12. Naturalizing Analysis: Rey's Account

Rey has sought to show how philosophical analysis can be made "naturalistically acceptable" (Rey 2004, 2005a, b). This involves showing how philosophical analysis can cohere with empirical investigations by cognitive science into the structure of concepts, and broader scientific investigations into the properties of substances and processes. This section will outline and assess Rey's attempts at reconciliation between conceptual analysis and empirical science.[22]

A concept is a means of representation. It is something like a map. The concept TIGER represents tigers: it provides information about tigers (if there are any). Likewise, the concept GHOST represents ghosts: it provides information about ghosts (if there are any). And so on. As these examples show, some concepts represent actual things (such as tigers) whereas other concepts fail to represent actual things (such as ghosts). The concept GHOST represents ghosts in the same way as a map of Atlantis represents Atlantis. In a useful piece of terminology, concepts such as TIGER are "full" whereas ones such as GHOST are "empty."

In either case, one source of information about a concept is provided by information encoded in the concept itself. For example, the concept WIDOW encodes such information as that a widow is someone whose husband has died. It also encodes inferential information. For example, it encodes the information that any inference of the form "x is a widow, so x is female" is valid. The entire inferential information encoded by a concept fixes what is called the concept's "inferential role." To have the concept WIDOW is to have a mental representation that encodes the relevant information, both propositional and inferential. This kind of information is available on reflection ("in the armchair") to anyone who possesses the concept. For that reason, such information is traditionally regarded as *a priori* knowable by possessors of the relevant concept, and the information encoded in the concept as consisting in conceptual truths.

In the case of full concepts, an additional source of information is available. This is information provided by the actual things represented by the concept. The concept TIGER represents actual things, tigers; information about tigers constitutes additional content to that concept.

---

21 Similar worries are expressed by Beaney (2001, 523–25). For other criticisms of the Canberra Plan, see Block and Stalnaker (1999), Laurence and Margolis (2003), Miščević (2001), Schroeter (2006), Melnyck (2008a), Williamson (2007, 121–29), Polger (2008), and Balaguer (2009).
22 See also Miščević (2005).

Furthermore, if tigers have essential properties — properties that are essential for something's being a tiger — and we can know only *a posteriori* what these essential properties are, then scientific investigation is needed to provide this information about tigers, and thereby about the concept TIGER. Suppose, for example, that it is essential to tigers that they have a certain DNA sequence. Creatures that lack that DNA sequence are not tigers even if they look and behave strikingly like typical actual tigers. They are fake tigers. And creatures that have that DNA sequence are tigers even if they look and behave strikingly unlike typical actual tigers. They are atypical tigers. Then the concept TIGER represents only things that have that DNA sequence. The concept does not represent the fake tigers but it does represent the atypical tigers. Moreover, the information that it is essential to tigers that they have a certain DNA sequence is knowable only *a posteriori*. It follows that it is knowable only *a posteriori* that the concept TIGER represents things that look and behave strikingly unlike typical actual tigers but have the same DNA sequence as typical tigers. Likewise, it follows that it is knowable only *a posteriori* that this concept does not represent things that superficially resemble typical tigers but that lack the DNA of typical tigers. It will require scientific inquiry and theorising to uncover that information.

In sum, there are two sources of information about a full concept. There is what the concept says about the actual things it represents — the information that the concept encodes — and there are the actual things the concept represents. There seems nothing untoward about using both sources where we can to find out about a given concept. Getting substantive and reliable information about anything, including the contents of concepts, is difficult. We need all the help we can get.

Let's consider the first source of information further. Three questions are worth asking:

(Q1) How do we tell what information is encoded in a concept?
(Q2) Does the information encoded in a concept have to be true?
(Q3) If not, how can we tell when the information is true?

How do we tell what information is encoded in a concept? That information is standardly taken to consist in conceptual truths. So the question can equivalently be put: how do we tell what information expresses conceptual truths? Take an example. Almost every person has many beliefs about tigers. Which of those beliefs express conceptual truths about tigers — information encoded in the concept of TIGER — and which do not? Perhaps we can get evidence for a given proposition's being a conceptual truth by polling people on which sentences they find intelligible, which they find unintelligible, which they find obviously true, and so on. But, first, the category of conceptual truth cross-classifies some of these categories: an obvious truth (such as that money doesn't grow on trees) need not be a conceptual truth, and a conceptual truth (such as that second cousins share two great-grandparents) need not be obvious. Furthermore, people's judgements about intelligibility and obviousness are sensitive to their beliefs about the world and also to how dull, or over-excited, their imaginations are (Rey 1994, 88). The issue here is sometimes put in the following way by Quineans: How do you tell the difference between a dictionary and an encyclopaedia? The idea behind the question is that if a dictionary lists truths of meaning whereas an encyclopaedia lists other matters of fact, how can you tell which information should go in which book? It may be that conceptual truths about tigers are available to you in your armchair, but lots of extraneous information about them is also available to you in your armchair. As Gilbert Harman puts it, there is no distinction between our mental dictionary and our mental encyclopaedia. Each of us has beliefs about tigers, but there is no sharp line between those beliefs about tigers that are true (supposedly) in virtue of meaning and those that are true because of the facts (Harman 1973, 97).

It is tempting to try to filter out this extraneous information by saying that conceptual truths about tigers consist in information about tigers that you had to acquire when you learnt the meaning of the word "tiger," or that is derivable from what you learnt. One difficulty here is that if conceptual truths about tigers are learnt in this way, then there has to be a distinction between the information needed to learn the meaning of "tiger" and all other information about tigers. But how do you tell what falls on which side of this distinction? We are back where we started.

Here is one suggestion about how to tackle the issue. It draws upon what are called "locking theories" of mental content and concept possession (see Stampe 1977 or Dretske 1988). These theories get their name from their claim that words and concepts get their content by picking out, or "locking onto," features of the world. What people mean by a word — that is, the concept they associate with the word — determines what they would apply the word to, under ideal epistemic circumstances. If someone has the concept RAVEN, they will apply that concept to some things and not to others. They do so partly because of the content of that concept — the concept's saying that ravens are thus-and-so — and partly because of what information they have about what things are thus-and-so. Typically, a person's information about the world is incomplete or flawed, and they do not process what information they have in a fully rational way (e.g., they do not iron out any contradictions in their information). Consequently, the person would not apply the concept to all and only ravens. Although they would apply the concept to some ravens, they would also misapply the concept because they would not apply it to some other ravens or they would apply it to some non-ravens.

To meet this difficulty, consider a person in idealized epistemic circumstances. Suppose that the person is fully rational and is fully informed about which things are thus-and-so. Given that their concept says that ravens are thus-and-so, they would apply the concept to all and only ravens. In general, a person has the concept F if and only if that person would apply that concept to all and only Fs, under ideal epistemic circumstances. Those circumstances are ones in which the person is fully rational and is informed about everything except about which things were F and which were not.

This account of concept-possession offers an answer to the Quinean challenge of how to distinguish between matters of meaning and matters of fact. Perhaps you and I disagree about what to apply the word "raven" to. Do we mean different things by what we mean by "raven" or do we mean the same thing but have different beliefs about ravens? According to the suggested account, you and I mean the same by "raven" if and only if: given that we were completely rational and otherwise fully informed, we would agree about which things were ravens. If, however, we were in such epistemically ideal circumstances, and yet we were to disagree about what things to apply "raven" to, then each of us would be using that word with a different meaning (Rey 1983, 255–56; and 1994, 92–95).

A correct analysis of a concept would express a rule governing the application of that concept. But a possessor of that concept need not be consciously aware of that rule, let alone know how to formulate it. Such a rule is "sub-doxastic." It is below the level of conscious belief and inaccessible by introspection. There is nothing untoward in this. The grammatical rules that linguists seek to formulate are also sub-doxastic.[23] If people need not know the semantic rules that guide their application of concepts, they will have to theorize about them on the basis of whatever semantic information that introspection and behaviour provides. People's linguistic behaviour, however, is not determined solely by the semantic rules that govern their concepts. In particular, their beliefs and preferences influence their behaviour. Differences in the beliefs and preferences of people can lead to differences in what they would apply a given concept to, despite the fact that the same semantic rule governs that concept. For example, a semantic rule governing the concept FISH might be that the concept applies to any cold-blooded aquatic creature with fins

---

23 For more on sub-doxastic rules, see Stich (1978) and Rey (2004, 84).

and scales. A person might have this concept, but, because they have the erroneous belief that whales are cold-blooded aquatic creatures with fins and scales, they misapply the concept by applying it to whales. Again, a person might have this concept, but, because they misperceive freshwater fish as lacking scales, they misapply the concept by not applying it to freshwater fish. Despite how their behaviour differs from typical possessors of the concept FISH, provided that these people have a concept involving the same sub-doxastic rules, they too have the concept FISH.

Up to this point we have taken the Quinean challenge to be broadly metaphysical: "What is the difference between a matter of meaning or a matter of fact, between a change of meaning and a change of belief?" The challenge might instead be made as an epistemic challenge: "How can we tell whether something is a matter of meaning and a matter of fact, between a change of meaning and a change of belief?" We can look to the above locking theory to help address this challenge. Suppose we take someone to have the concept RAVEN despite their tendency to misapply it in some cases (at least by our lights). Then we should expect them to correct some of those misapplications when they acquire more information or when they reflect on their classificatory practices. If these predictions are confirmed, that is evidence for the hypothesis that the subject has the concept RAVEN. If the predictions are disconfirmed, that provides evidence against the hypothesis and for the hypothesis that the subject has some other concept whose extension overlaps with the concept RAVEN.

At any rate, locking theories of concept-possession hold out some promise of providing a principled distinction between semantic issues and epistemological issues. Note, however, that the epistemological methods that locking theories appeal to in explaining how we can tell which concepts someone has are empirical methods. Yet the traditional project of philosophical analysis requires that we have *a priori* access to the contents of our concepts, and that we can know *a priori* which information belongs to the contents of concepts and which does not. That requirement would then be unmet. In fact, it has been argued that "all available accounts of what it is to possess a concept with a given content either entail that [the requirement] is false or fail to provide an adequate explanation of how it could be true" (Melnyck 2008a, 269).

Does the information encoded in a concept have to be true? Many philosophers talk of conceptual truths, and their thinking seems to be that the fact that a concept contains a certain piece of information guarantees that that information is true. Hartry Field has trenchantly challenged that line of thought:

Why should the fact, if it is one, that certain beliefs or inferences are integral to the meaning of a concept show that these principles are correct? Why should the fact, if it is one, that abandoning those beliefs or inferences would require a change of meaning show that we shouldn't abandon those beliefs or inferences? Maybe the meaning we've attached to these terms is a bad one that is irremediably bound up with error, and truth can only be achieved by abandoning those meanings in favour of different ones (that resemble them in key respects but avoid the irremediable error). (Field 2005, 85)

Suppose that a concept C encodes some piece of information, a certain proposition p. Talk of p's being a conceptual truth is open to two readings. One reading goes: if a concept C encodes p, then p is true. This is the reading that Field is challenging. A concept is a way of representing the world. The fact that p is represented as being true does not obviously entail that p is true. For example, the fact that a guru, or a prized book, represents the proposition that the world will end tomorrow as being true, does not obviously entail that the world will end tomorrow. Gurus' pronouncements, books, and concepts are all forms of representation. Similarly, then, the fact that a concept represents a certain proposition p as being true does not entail that p is true.

There is another way to read the claim that proposition p is a conceptual truth. This reading goes: according to concept C, p is true. According to this reading, C represents p as being true. It does not follow from this that p is true. Consider a parallel: it might be that, according to a certain novel, Ottawa won the match. It does not follow that Ottawa won the match. The novel might have made things up. It is one thing for something (a concept, a novel, a guru) to represent p as being true. It is another thing for p to be true. On this reading, to say that p is a conceptual truth is not to say that p is true. It is only to say that, according to some concept, p is true.

If the information encoded in a concept does not have to be true, how can we tell when it is true? One way is by comparing the information encoded in the concept with information about the actual things the concept applies to. If the two pools of information yield mutually incompatible claims, and the latter pool of information is thought to be more reliable, then there is reason to reject the information encoded in the concept.

Rey suggests that:

> ... we'll find that, in the case of many [full concepts], our defer-
> ence to the world undercuts the amount of *a priori* knowledge
> we can expect to have with regard to them. (Rey 2005b, 478)

In his work on this topic, Rey seems to work with a dichotomy: either information about a concept is about information encoded in the concept, and so is knowable *a priori*, or information about a concept is information about instances of the concept, and so is knowable only *a posteriori*. This dichotomy could be resisted.

First, the dichotomy overlooks the possibility of *a priori* knowable information about a concept that is not information encoded in the concept. Some philosophers argue as follows. Mathematical truths are not conceptual truths — true in virtue of their constituent concepts. Those truths are also knowable *a priori* because they are knowable but not testable by observation. *A priori* knowledge of a mathematical truth provides *a priori* knowledge of its constituent concepts — *a priori* knowledge that we could not otherwise have. For example, *a priori* knowledge that $7 + 5 = 12$ provides *a priori* knowledge about the concepts 7, 5 and 12. This is the *a priori* knowledge that what these concepts apply to (namely, certain numbers) stand in a certain relation. It has been argued that what goes for mathematical truths also goes for certain philosophical principles, such as the principle that, for every property, there exists an **abstract object** that has (in a special primitive sense) that property (Linsky and Zalta 1995.) On this view this enables us to have *a priori* knowledge about some philosophically interesting concepts, such as the concepts ABSTRACT OBJECT and PROPERTY, that is not information encoded in those concepts.

Second, the dichotomy states that information about the actual instances of a concept is information that is knowable only *a posteriori*. That claim is true only if the actual instances of every concept are empirical, concrete things. But that assumption is open to question. If the concepts PROPOSITION, NUMBER and SET have instances, their instances are abstract objects — objects that are not empirical, concrete things. Some philosophers who believe that there are such abstract objects think both that we can have *a priori* knowledge of them, and that we cannot have *a posteriori* **knowledge** of them.[24]

Even if the instances of a given concept are concrete instances, some philosophers doubt whether empirical research could provide philosophically significant information about the concept. Consider the concept KNOWLEDGE. Its instances are certain psychological

---

24 See again Linsky and Zalta (1995).

states, states of knowing. But can knowledge be empirically examined as (say) aluminium can? Richard Feldman is doubtful. He considers a comparison that Hilary Kornblith makes between metallurgy and epistemology. Metallurgy does not use *a priori* methods to study the concept ALUMINIUM, but uses empirical methods to study aluminium. Kornblith thinks that epistemology should follow suit. It should not use *a priori* methods to study the concept KNOWLEDGE, but should use empirical methods to study knowledge (Kornblith 1995, 243–44). Feldman comments that:

> It's difficult to see, however, exactly why we should think that knowledge is relevantly like aluminium. For one thing, what we seek in the case of aluminium is an understanding of its physical constitution. We want to know what it is made of, how it interacts with other materials and why, and what we can use it for. Our analysis of knowledge does not call for an account of its physical constitution. It's doubtful that there's any such thing. We might also seek scientific analyses of processes, such as cell division. But knowledge isn't a substance like aluminium or a process like cell division. So, analogies such as these don't provide reasons to seek naturalistic analyses of knowledge. (Feldman 1998, 26)[25]

What Feldman says here about Kornblith's suggestion has obvious application to Rey's account of conceptual analysis. Feldman would presumably think that both approaches are misconceived. On his view, science cannot tell us what knowledge is, and, for the same reasons, it cannot tell us about the concept KNOWLEDGE. This rejoinder raises important issues about the role of science in philosophy. We will take up this matter at length in chapter 6.

Resistance to the second limb of the dichotomy comes from another quarter as well. According to minimalism about semantics, semantic concepts, such as the concepts TRUTH and REFERENCE, refer to properties, but those properties have only a logical role. In particular:

> Unlike most other properties, being true is unsusceptible to conceptual or scientific analysis. (Horwich 1998, 5)

> ... different kinds of property correspond to different roles that predicates play in our language, and ... unless these differences

---

25   See also Feldman (2002, 179).

> are appreciated, we will be tempted to raise questions regard-
> ing one sort that can legitimately arise only in connection
> with another sort ... According to minimalism, we should ...
> beware of assimilating being true to such properties as being
> turquoise, being a tree, or being made of tin. Otherwise we will
> find ourselves looking for its constitutive structure, its causal
> behaviour, and its typical manifestations.... We will be puzzled
> when these expectations are inevitably frustrated.... (Horwich
> 1998, 37–38)

Whether or not minimalism about semantics is correct, it represents an important position that seems overlooked by the dichotomy.

Near the beginning of this section we asked three questions, (Q1–3). It is time to summarize our answers. The three questions were:

(Q1) How do we tell what information is encoded in a
       concept?
(Q2) Does the information encoded in a concept have to be
       true?
(Q3) If not, how can we tell when the information is true?

In answer to (Q1), locking theories of content offer an account both of what information is encoded in a concept and of how we can tell what that information is. These theories, however, offer an account on which we can know only *a posteriori* what information is encoded in a concept. Next, we saw Field's answer to (Q2) that the information encoded in a concept need not be true. The fact that a concept represents a certain proposition *p* as being true does not entail that *p* is true. Lastly, our means for telling whether the information encoded in a given concept is true will be the same means we use for telling whether any piece of information is true.

Our investigation of Rey's attempt to naturalize analysis has a mixed message. Locking theories of content provide a promising account of the distinction between information encoded in a concept and information not encoded in it. A further issue is whether the information encoded in a concept is correct. Here Rey claimed that, in the case of concepts that have instances, "our deference to the world undercuts the amount of *a priori* knowledge we can expect to have with regard to them." Rey's claim, however, made some questionable assumptions. Those not already com-mitted to naturalism would not accept all of those assumptions.

In the above quotation, Rey qualified what he said by saying that it applied to *many* full concepts, not all. Perhaps the qualification is to indicate that his account applies to only concepts such as DOLPHIN and MESON whose instances can be investigated by empirical science. But such a restriction in the scope of his account would lessen its interest. The account would not apply to concepts of perennial philosophical interest such as the concepts SET and PROPOSITION, and it would remain open to debate whether it applied to other ones such as KNOWLEDGE, TRUTH or REFERENCE.

13. Naturalizing Analysis: Quine's Account

According to Quine, philosophy explores how theories are best systematized, simplified, and clarified. There are a number of aspects to this process.

(1) *Regimentation*: systemization is achieved by stating a theory in a clear and rigorous language (the "canonical notation," as Quine calls it). This involves selecting a certain language as the canonical language (for Quine, it is the language of first order logic), and then stating the theory in that language.

(2) This process of translation requires *explication*: replacing imprecise terms with more precise ones.

(3) *Ontological reduction*: certain fragments of language apparently carry commitment to certain kinds of entities, but those patterns can be paraphrased away in terms of other fragments, and the apparent **ontological commitment** is thereby avoided.

(4) *Ontological commitment*: having stated the theory in the canonical language, we then determine what needs to exist (the "**domain of quantification**") in order for the theory to be true. What entities the theory says exist, what it is ontologically committed to, consists in all and only those entities that are quantified over when the theory is set out in its canonical notation.

What is the relation between the unregimented and the regimented versions of the theory? It is not synonymy (Quine 1960, 159). Instead, the regimented version should perform whatever functions of the unregimented version that we find important. "We fix on the particular functions of the unclear expression that make it worth troubling about, and then devise a substitute, clear and couched in terms to our liking, that fills these functions" (Quine 1960, 258–59). Where a fragment s of a language is regimented as s', Quine says that:

> there is no call to think of s' as synonymous with s. Its relation to s is just that the particular business that the speaker was on that occasion trying to get on with, with help of s among other things, can be managed well enough to suit him by using s' instead of s. We can even let him modify his purposes under the shift, if he pleases. (Quine 1960, 160)

Since the acceptability of a paraphrase depends on the "scientific and philosophical purposes" served by certain fragments of a language, for Quine a proposed paraphrase is assessed in terms of what functions need to be served, and how those functions would be better served by the paraphrase. What makes a paraphrase a good one is that it makes our theory simpler and clearer (Harman 1967, 352–56 and Suppes 1968).

Quine takes the idea of explication from Carnap. Explication is "the transformation of an inexact, prescientific concept, the *explicandum*, into a new exact concept, the *explicatum*" (Carnap 1950, 3). There is a number of requirements on an explication. The explicans should be more exact than the explicandum. It should also be similar in some way to the explicandum, although "close similarity is not required and considerable differences are permitted" (Carnap 1950, 7). The explication should also be simple and fruitful (i.e., it should generate theoretically interesting hypotheses). Carnap's central example of an explication is the explication of the vague term "warm" by the more precise term "temperature." The latter term has a role in the theory of thermodynamics, and the simplicity and inventiveness of that theory contribute to the simplicity and fruitfulness of the explication of "heat" by "temperature."[26]

Quine summarizes his view in the following paragraph:

> [In an analysis, we] do not claim synonymy. We do not claim to make clear and explicit what the users of the unclear expressions had in mind all along. We do not expose hidden meanings…. We fix on the particular functions of the unclear expressions that make it worth troubling about, and then devise a substitute, clear and couched in terms to our liking, that fills these functions. Beyond those conditions of partial agreement, dictated by our interests and purposes, any traits

---

26 For more on explication, see Goodman (1951, ch. 1), Goodman (1963), Hanna (1968), and Gustafsson (2006).

of the explicans come under the head of "don't cares." (Quine 1960, 258–59)

It is useful to consider how far Quine departs from the working model of philosophical analysis outlined in §3. That model said:

(1) An analysis has the logical form of a universally quantified biconditional.
(2) An analysis is necessarily true. Indeed, it is analytically true.
(3) An analysis is informative.
(4) An analysis is knowable *a priori*.
(5) An analysis is testable by the method of hypothetical cases.

In an explication, the explicans needs to capture only the important functions of the explicandum. So an explication need not claim that regimented sentences are materially equivalent to their pre-regimented twins. So Quine is not committed to (1). The explicans and the explicandum are not synonymous — a notion that Quine finds obscure. Consequently, Quine avoids the paradox of analysis since the paradox requires that the relata of an analysis are synonymous. Quine rejects the view that there is such a thing as *a priori* justification (as we will see in chapter 6, §2). And he is dubious about the philosophical use of hypothetical cases. The overall result is that Quine rejects our working model of philosophical analysis and replaces it with his ideas about regimentation, explication, and paraphrase.

Paraphrase is a ubiquitous device in philosophical analysis. Just as there are different views of what philosophical analysis is, however, so too there are different views of what a paraphrase is and what the point of paraphrase is. It will be useful to consider some widely held views about paraphrase before considering Quine's own view of it. This is the task of the next section.

14. Paraphrase

To paraphrase a sentence is to use another form of words to convey at least part of what the original sentence says more clearly or succinctly. Many philosophers have been ambitious in what they think paraphrases can achieve. For example, Arthur Pap, Frank Jackson and David Armstrong have claimed that sentences such as "Red is a colour" and "Red resembles orange more than it resembles blue" appear to be about certain colour properties (such as the property of *redness*). They argue that those sentences cannot be paraphrased as sentences that are not about colour properties. They conclude that those sentences are about colour properties and that the sentences are true only if those colour properties exist (Pap 1959, Jackson 1977, and Armstrong 1978, ch. 6).

Philosophers with ambitious views about the role of paraphrase follow a five-step programme:

(1) *Apparent ontological commitment*: Suppose that a class of sentences, the K-sentences, apparently refer to Ks or require that Ks exist if those sentences are true. (Where sentences require that Ks exist if those sentences are true, those sentences "quantify over" Ks.) The K-sentences might include such sentences as "That is a K and so is this," "there are at least two Ks," or "there are as many Ks as planets." The first example apparently refers to Ks, and the next two examples apparently quantify over Ks. Assuming that a sentence that refers to something, or that quantifies over something, is true only if that thing exists, the sentences in our examples are true only if Ks exist. These sentences are apparently ontologically committed to Ks. That is, they appear to be committed to the existence of Ks.

(2) *Paraphrase*: Suppose that all K-sentences can be paraphrased by sentences that do not refer to, or quantify over, Ks.

(3) *Sameness of truth conditions*: Given the paraphrase, each paraphrased sentence and the sentence that paraphrases it have the same truth conditions. They are true (false) in the same possible circumstances.

(4) *Sameness of logical form*: A paraphrased sentence and the paraphrasing sentence have the same logical form, but the syntax of the paraphrasing sentence better reflects what that logical form is.

(5) *Genuine ontological commitment*: The syntax of the paraphrased sentences is misleading and those sentences are not ontologically committed to Ks.

Here is an illustration of this programme. Certain sentences apparently refer to, or quantify over, sensory appearances or sense data. When Rachel the alcoholic hallucinates a pink rat, she does not see a pink rat, but still it seems that she sees something. So we might say such things as "Rachel sees a pink rat appearance." That sentence apparently describes a relation between Rachel and something else, a mental picture or sense datum. The sentence seems to be true only if there is a sense datum to which Rachel is related. What we have said, then, is apparently committed to the existence of sense data. Given that we believe what we have said, we are thereby apparently committed to the existence of sense data.

Roderick Chisholm offered a paraphrase of sentences that apparently refer to, or quantify over, sense data. Such sentences are paraphrased by sentences applying one-place predicates to people. For example, the sentence "Rachel sensed a pink rat appearance" would be paraphrased as "Rachel sensed-pinkly-and-ratly." Chisholm called this the "adverbial theory" of perceptual reports (Chisholm 1959, ch. 8 and 1966, 94–96). As he put it:

> For in saying "He is appeared to white," or "He senses whitely," we are not committed to saying that there is a thing — an appearance — of which the word "white," in its sensible use, designates a property. We are saying, rather, that there is a certain state or process — that of being appeared to, or sensing or experiencing — and we are using the adjective "white," or the adverb "whitely," to describe more specifically the way in which that process occurs. (Chisholm 1966, 96)

Having seen an illustration of how the programme of paraphrase is supposed to work, let's assess the programme. Three questions need to be asked:

(Q1) Why paraphrase?
(Q2) Are paraphrases available?
(Q3) What can paraphrases show?

These questions overlap, and we have already seen indications of likely answers. (Q1) asks for the motivations for paraphrasing sentences. What is the point of the programme? (Q2) asks whether paraphrases can be given (as opposed to their being only on a philosophical wish list). (Q3) asks what paraphrases can provide. In particular, can paraphrases establish the claims about logical form and ontological commitment made in (4) and (5)?

Why paraphrase? Paraphrases simplify theories. One way that they can do this is by problem avoidance. Suppose that a certain fragment of language generates certain problems. If those same problems are not generated by the paraphrase, the problems can thereby be avoided. For example, a fragment of language may contain sentences such as "The Equator is 25,000 miles long" and "We crossed the Equator." Those sentences apparently refer to a certain entity, the Equator, which (like a river or a bridge) has a length and can be crossed. But what kind of thing would the Equator be? If it is taken to be a physical object, does it have a mass? Does it rotate around the Earth (like a fan belt) or is it stationary relative to the Earth? How could you tell? If the Equator is taken to be a geometrical object, it is an abstract object. Abstract objects are typically taken to lack spatial location. But if there is such a thing as the Equator, it encircles the Earth and is crossed by ships and jet planes. How could something be both abstract and have a location? Now suppose that sentences involving the apparently referring term "the Equator" can be paraphrased as sentences of the form "__ is nearer the Equator than ...," where this five word phrase is treated as a relative term (Quine 1960, 254). Loose talk of our crossing the Equator can then be paraphrased in terms of our being nearer the Equator than our destination at one time, and, at a later time, our not being nearer the Equator than our destination. The sentences provided by the paraphrase do not raise the same problems as before. The expression "the Equator" does not occur as a singular term in a subject place in the sentences produced by the paraphrase. Consequently, it no longer appears to be an expression that refers to a certain object. In addition, the paraphrasing sentences do not raise any problems of their own (Stern 1989, 35–36). More generally, Quine talks of:

> problems [that] are dissolved in the important sense of being shown to be purely verbal, and purely verbal in the important sense of arising from usages that can be avoided. (Quine 1960, 261)

Being able to paraphrase K-sentences does not by itself show that Ks do not exist. What paraphrase is supposed to show is that K-sentences are not committed to the existence of Ks. Perhaps such a paraphrase plus considerations of **ontological simplicity** together provide reason for claiming that Ks do not exist. (These considerations will be discussed in chapter 4, §2). Ontological simplicity, however, is only one kind of simplicity. Chisholm's adverbial theory requires the introduction of a range of primitive one-place predicates. This increases the ideology of his theory — the number of primitive non-logical terms employed by the theory — and this is a cost for the theory. (For **ideological simplicity**, see again chapter 4, §2). It is then a matter for debate whether the ideological complexity of the adverbial theory is sufficiently compensated for by its ontological economy and problem avoidance.

A final way in which a paraphrase contributes to our theories is by clarifying inferences. Regimentation assigns certain logical forms to various classes of sentences, and it clarifies the logical connections between the sentences of these various classes.

Are paraphrases available? In an earlier example, we saw that paraphrasing sentences containing the expression "the Equator" is supposed to show that such sentences are not committed to the existence of a certain kind of object, the Equator:

> There is a systematic method of translating (reducing) discourse which might seem to presuppose a given sort of object into discourse which serves the same purpose but does not make that presupposition. (Hylton 2007, 246)

But is there such a method, let alone a systematic one? In the Equator example, Quine does not specify the method. He only reassures us that the unregimented sentences can be regimented and that the resulting sentences lack the undesirable features of the originals. Peter Hylton offers "the average family has 1.8 children" as another example of a sentence needing regimentation. Presumably that sentence would be regimented as "the number of children in families divided by the number of families is 1.8." What that does, however, is to pair up the unregimented sentence with its regimented twin. It does not tell us how to go about pairing the two sentences — how to select which sentence provides a suitable paraphrase. Moreover, even if it did that, it is not clear whether it is a method that tells us, for any unregimented sentence containing the expression "the average family," which regimented sentence it should be paired up with. It is still less clear whether it would be an entirely general method that tells us, for any sentence, which regimented sentence it should be paired with (in a given context). In short, it is not clear that the would-be method is systematic.

We might instead offer paraphrases on an *ad hoc* basis, paraphrasing specific sentences in the disputed class when they confront us. The weakness in that approach, however, is that, in the absence of a specified method of paraphrase, it is unclear what confidence we should have in supposing that we could paraphrase any sentence in the disputed class. So we need to have some systematic method of paraphrasing — a "paraphrase algorithm." The most promising way of devising, and justifying, such an algorithm would be to devise and justify something still more ambitious: a compositional semantic theory for the fragment of language in question, and then show how the algorithm fell out as a consequence of that theory (Lewis 1983b, 16–17).

What can paraphrases show? We have seen what the alleged benefits of paraphrase are. This raises the question of what exactly the relation between the paraphrased sentence and the paraphrasing sentence is and how it can confer those benefits. There are two difficulties to overcome here. First, there are the deficiencies of particular suggestions of what the paraphrase relation is. Second, there is a more general difficulty about capturing the asymmetry of the paraphrase relation. Take these difficulties in turn.

If the paraphrased and the paraphrasing sentence are supposed to have the same truth conditions, then, as a first attempt, we might take the relation between the two sentences to be material equivalence. This faces the problem that any two sentences with the same truth value will stand in the paraphrase relation to each other. Two ways of revising this first attempt suggest themselves. One way is to add an epistemic constraint: that it is knowable *a priori* that the two sentences are materially equivalent. Another way is to add a modal constraint: that it is necessarily true that the two sentences are materially equivalent. Both revisions, however, face a common problem. Any two logical truths meet these constraints, but it is not the case that any two logical truths stand in the paraphrase relation. For example, any sentence of the form "p v $\neg p$" and any sentence of the form "$((p \supset q)$ & $(q \supset r)) \supset (p \supset r)$" are logical truths. They are necessarily equivalent, and we can know that *a priori*. Nevertheless, no such sentences stand in the paraphrase relation to each other. They are not even of the same logical form.

A different attempt would be to take paraphrased and paraphrasing sentences to be synonymous. A more guarded variant would be to require that the sentences are "normally used to make the same assertion" (Alston 1958, 10). Quine rejects talk of synonymy, but we have seen how he takes paraphrased and paraphrasing sentences to share important functions. Each of these suggestions avoids the problems faced by the attempts canvassed in the previous paragraph. Like those attempts, however, the present suggestions do not capture the asymmetry of the paraphrase relation. Whether sentences p and q are materially equivalent, or necessarily equivalent, or synonymous, or serve the same important functions, the relations they stand in are symmetric. But if p paraphrases q, the relation between them is asymmetric. Suppose that p is (for example) synonymous with q. Should p be used to paraphrase q, or q be used to paraphrase p? This bears on the issue of ontological commitment. Suppose that p is apparently ontologically committed to Ks, whereas q is not. It is tempting to think that if p is paraphrased by q, then p is shown to be only apparently ontologically committed to Ks, and genuinely not ontologically committed to Ks. But that would be to assume that because q is not apparently ontologically committed to Ks, it is not genuinely ontologically committed to Ks. If p is apparently ontologically committed to *K*s, and appearances are not deceptive, then *p* is genuinely ontologically committed to *K*s. Moreover, since *p* and *q* are synonymous, if *p* is genuinely ontologically committed to *K*s, it follows that *q* is also genuinely ontologically committed to *K*s, and that *q*'s appearance of not being ontologically committed to *K*s is misleading. More generally, the paraphrase tactic requires some means of distinguishing between merely apparent ontological commitment and genuine ontological commitment (and also between merely apparent lack of ontological commitment and genuine lack of ontological commitment) (Alston 1958; Searle 1969, 107–12; and Oliver 1996, esp. 65–66). Whereas paraphrase is an asymmetric relation, the relations canvassed here — material equivalence, *a priori* necessary equivalence, synonymy, sameness of important function — are all symmetric relations, and so they shed no light on what sentence should paraphrase what other sentence. (The same problem will arise in the case of non-symmetric relations too.) What the paraphrase tactic needs, then, is a "symmetry breaker."

A good way to bring out this point is to consider an argument that David Lewis uses for the existence of possible worlds. Lewis argues that sentences of the form "possibly, *p*" can be paraphrased as "at some possible world, *p*." There are some true sentences of the form "possibly, *p*." Therefore, there are some true sentences of the form "at some possible world, *p*." Sentences of the latter kind are ontologically committed to possible worlds. Therefore, so too are sentences of the former kind. Here is what Lewis says:

> It is uncontroversially true that things might have been otherwise than they are.... [T]hings could have been different in countless ways. But what does this mean? Ordinary language permits the paraphrase: there are many ways things could have been besides the way they actually are. On the face of it, this sentence is an existential quantification. It says that there exist many entities of a certain description, to wit "ways things could have been." I believe that things could have been different in countless ways; I believe permissible paraphrases of what I believe; taking the paraphrase at its face value, I therefore believe in the existence of entities that might be called "ways things could have been." I prefer to call them possible worlds. (Lewis 1973, 84)

For our purposes, what is most important about this passage is that Lewis uses paraphrase as a device of ontological inflation. A sentence of the form "there might have been talking donkeys" does not seem to be ontologically committed to a possible world where there are talking donkeys. The sentence can be "permissibly" paraphrased as "at some possible world, there are talking donkeys." At face value, the latter sentence is ontologically committed to a possible world where there are talking donkeys. Therefore, so too is the sentence that it paraphrases. The sentence "there might have been talking donkeys" does not appear to be ontologically committed to at least one possible world where there are talking donkeys, but the paraphrase shows that it is so committed. The challenge facing devotees of paraphrase is to explain why a paraphrase should be given an ontologically deflationary reading — "Talk of possible worlds and what goes on in them amounts to no more than talk of what is possibly or necessarily the case" — rather than an ontologically inflationary reading — "Strange but true, talk of what is possibly or necessarily the case is a disguised way of talking about possible worlds and their inhabitants."[27]

All this reinforces the point that the paraphrase tactic needs a "symmetry breaker." Various candidates have been offered. We have seen that Quine thinks that a paraphrasing sentence does not merely serve the same important functions as the paraphrased sentence. The paraphrasing sentence explicates the paraphrased sentence; the former uses more precise and theoretically fruitful terms. This gives Quine his materials for breaking the symmetry (see also van Inwagen 1991).

Another candidate is unabashedly metaphysical. According to some philosophers, some kinds of thing are metaphysically more fundamental than other kinds. In their terminology, the more fundamental kinds "ground" the less fundamental kinds. The suggestion is then made that sentences describing less fundamental kinds of thing should be paraphrased by sentences describing more fundamental kinds of thing, and not vice versa. For example, if cricket players are more fundamental kinds of thing than cricket teams, than sentences describing the team (such as sentences describing team spirit) should be paraphrased in terms of sentences describing the cricket players, rather than vice versa. The direction of paraphrase follows the direction of grounding (Schaffer 2009, 370).

This last suggestion is intriguing, but it looks more promising in some cases rather than others. Philosophers use the term "paraphrase" in a quasi-technical sense, and we have been taking it that a paraphrase of K-sentences can show that K-sentences are not ontologically committed to Ks. The current suggestion is not working with that understanding. Cricket players ground cricket teams only if both cricket players and cricket teams exist. So the suggestion does not take it that a paraphrase

---

27 For discussion of Lewis's argument, see Stalnaker (1984, 44–58) and Jubien (1988, 300–02).

of *K*-sentences entails that *K*-sentences are not ontologically committed to *K*s. Instead, the suggestion requires that a paraphrase of *K*-sentences entails that *K*-sentences are ontologically committed to *K*s. This may be admissible in the case of sentences about cricket teams; it looks more awkward in the case of sentences about (say) the average family. Sentences about the average family are often taken to be prime examples of sentences requiring a paraphrase, where that paraphrase shows that the truth of those sentences does not require the existence of a certain mysterious entity, namely the existence of the average family. Now it may be that there are two notions of paraphrase at play — the Quinean eliminative one and the non-eliminative grounding one — and we can work with both of them, provided that we do not confuse them. Nevertheless, the grounding suggestion does not then give us a general solution to the symmetry problem. It has nothing to contribute to cases where what is at issue is whether commitment to entities of a certain kind is genuine or merely apparent.

Alternatively, it might be replied that there is only one notion of paraphrase, the non-eliminative grounding one. To take the example of sentences about the average family: the reply says that the average family exists but it is a fictional entity. Fictional entities form a species of abstract object, and abstract objects are themselves grounded by **concrete objects**. (This reply draws on Schaffer [2009, 359].) Positing fictional entities might seem ontologically uneconomical and so at odds with **Ockham's razor**. But, the reply continues, Ockham's razor should be taken to concern only fundamental entities. Properly formulated, the principle says: Do not multiply fundamental entities without necessity (Schaffer 2009, 361).

Now restricting the scope of Ockham's razor in this way avoids the charge of being ontologically uneconomical. Without an independent rationale for the restriction, however, it seems an *ad hoc* manoeuvre. The restriction is made solely to avoid the charge of being ontologically uneconomical. Furthermore, the proposed restriction is not one that is reflected in our inferential practice. The detective uses Ockham's razor to infer from the presence of only one set of fingerprints at the crime scene that there was only one murderer (rather than two or more murderers). The scientist uses Ockham's razor to infer from Beta decay that a single neutrino with spin ½ is emitted (rather than two particles each with spin ¼, or three particles each with spin ⅙, and so on).[28] The detective and the scientist are engaged in good inferential practices, but their practices

---

28   For the neutrino example, see Nolan (1997, 333).

do not require that they take murderers or neutrinos to be fundamental kinds of thing.

15. Conclusion

We began this chapter by seeing something of the range of ways in which philosophical analysis can be classified and the range of ways in which it can be practised. Here is a debunking view. It is little wonder that there is a proliferation of ways of doing philosophical analysis. Talk of doing philosophical analysis is just a fancy way of talk of doing philosophy. The differences between different views of philosophical analysis are just differences in how to philosophize, and there are better or worse ways of doing that. This debunking view advises us to give up on trying to figure out what analysis is, and to think more about what kind of work we want philosophical theories to do and how they should do it. This reorientation of philosophical energies will be taken up in chapter 5 where we consider the topic of explanation in philosophy.

Questions for Discussion

1. Some philosophers claim that epistemology should study knowledge, not the concept KNOWLEDGE.[29] Does their view have to assume that knowledge can be investigated only scientifically?

2. Williamson's view says that epistemology should not be concerned with the concept KNOWLEDGE, but with knowledge itself. It thereby assumes at least that there is such a thing as knowledge. Presumably other branches of philosophy are entitled to make corresponding assumptions. Metaethics should not be concerned with the concept MORAL VALUE, but with moral values, and it would thereby be assuming that there are moral values. Philosophy of religion should not be concerned with the concept GOD, but with God, and it would thereby be assuming that there is a God. And so on.

Does Williamson's view really have these ramifications? If so, are they weaknesses in the view? Do they provide a case for taking epistemology and the other branches to be concerned with concepts, not with what those concepts are allegedly about? (See Rey 2005a.)

3. Feldman says that since knowledge is neither a substance nor a process, it cannot be empirically investigated. Does his premise ("neither a substance nor a process") exhaust every kind of entity that can be studied by science? How would space-time points or radioactive fields fit into his classification? If they do not fit, just how important is it that knowledge does not fit either? Lastly, even if what Feldman says is correct, our *acquiring* knowledge is a process. Can Feldman give any reason for denying that it can be empirically studied by science?

4. If knowledge can be scientifically studied, as Kornblith claims, is there anything of philosophical interest that cannot be scientifically studied? For example, philosophers have wanted to know what it is to exist. Can science discover what it is to exist? What might such a discovery be like? (Or is it unreasonable to ask what such a discovery might be like in advance of the discovery?)

---

29   E.g., Williamson (2007, 206, 211).

Core Reading for Chapter 2

Beaney, Michael (2007) "Analysis" *Stanford Encyclopedia of Philosophy*.

Hylton, Peter (2007) *Quine* chs. 3, 9 and 10.

Jackson, Frank (1998) *From Metaphysics to Ethics* chs. 1–3.

Moore, G.E. (1903) *Principia Ethica* ch. 1, esp. §13.

Nolan, Daniel (2005) *David Lewis* ch. 9.

Rey, Georges (2004) "The Rashness of Traditional Rationalism and Empiricism."

Rieber, S.D. (1994) "The Paradoxes of Analysis and Synonymy."

Williamson, Timothy (2007) *The Philosophy of Philosophy* ch. 4.

THREE Thought Experiment

1. Introduction

A thought experiment is an experiment carried out in our imagination. It is a device used both in science and philosophy. In a thought experiment, we imagine a certain situation, we follow through some of the consequences of that situation, and then we draw a general conclusion — typically, a certain theoretical claim. A thought experiment is in some ways similar to an experiment in a physical laboratory. As a convenient label, call the latter kind of experiment a "concrete experiment." A difference between these two kinds of experiment is that a thought experiment concerns an imagined example whereas a concrete experiment concerns an actual example. But this contrast goes deeper. Concrete experiments are relatively familiar to us. (It is only relatively recently, though, that philosophy of science has recognized some of the complexities involved in experimental design and practice: see Gooding 1990.) But thought experiments seem more puzzling. The following three questions will be the focus of this chapter:

> (Q1) A thought experiment is about an imagined situation. How can thinking about an imagined situation give new knowledge about the actual world?
> (Q2) Are thought experiments special cases of a more familiar kind of phenomena, or are they *sui generis*?
> (Q3) Are there particular difficulties facing philosophical thought experiments?

A thought experiment involves imagining a situation, not perceiving it. (Q1) asks how imagining a situation can tell us about what that situation would be like if it were actual, and what its theoretical consequences would be. Furthermore, what kind of thing is a thought experiment? (Q2) asks whether we can understand thought experiments in terms of some more familiar, or better understood, ways. Lastly, thought experiments are of particular importance in philosophy because of many philosophers' epistemic ambitions. Many philosophers take themselves to have **modal knowledge** — knowledge about what is merely possible or about what is necessary. Some of them take thought experiments to be a fundamental source of modal knowledge. Some thought experiments seek to show that something imaginable is possible. Others seek to show that something that is apparently imaginable is impossible. Other philosophers, however, believe that there are special problems facing thought experiments in philosophy. Their criticisms chiefly concern how far removed the situations imagined in philosophical thought experiments are from actual situations, and the lack of background detail in these thought experiments. (Q3) asks whether any of these criticisms are good ones.

Before we embark on these large issues, it is well to stock up on lots of examples of thought experiments. That is the task of the next section.

2. Examples of Thought Experiments

IS THE UNIVERSE FINITE?
Imagine that the universe is finite and has a boundary. Now imagine throwing a spear at this boundary. Either the spear stops at the boundary or it passes through it. Lucretius argued that if the spear stops at the boundary, there must be something on the other side of the boundary that is stopping the spear, and so the so-called boundary is not a genuine boundary. Lucretius also inferred that if the spear passes through the so-called boundary, then again there is no genuine boundary. Either way space has no boundary. The thought experiment's conclusion is that space is infinite (Lucretius *The Poem on Nature: De Rerum Natura* p. 40).

NEWTON'S BUCKET
Imagine that a bucket filled with water begins to rotate. Initially, the surface of the water remains flat, but, as the water acquires the motion of the bucket, its surface becomes concave. The concave shape shows that the water is rotating. But the water is not rotating relative to the bucket because they have the same rotating motion. Newton infers that the water is rotating relative to absolute space (Newton 1686, book 1, *Scholium*).

DO HEAVIER BODIES FALL FASTER THAN LIGHTER ONES?
Galileo took Aristotelian mechanics to claim that heavier bodies fall faster than lighter ones. (There is some controversy whether this was

Aristotle's view, but we will let this pass for the sake of argument.) Galileo offered the following thought experiment as an objection. Imagine that a body H is heavier than a body L. Imagine further that H is connected to L by a cord. According to Aristotle, heavier objects fall faster than lighter ones. So will the composite body $H+L$ fall faster than H or will it fall slower than H? On the one hand, given Aristotle's claim that heavier bodies fall faster than lighter ones, and since $H+L$ is heavier than H, $H+L$ will fall faster than H. On the other hand, since L is lighter than H, and again given Aristotle's claim that heavier bodies fall faster than lighter ones, L will retard the fall of H when they are joined together, and so $H+L$ will fall slower than H. Conjoining these results, Aristotle's claim that heavier bodies fall faster than lighter bodies involves a contradiction (Galileo 1638, 66–68).

TRAVELLING AT LIGHT SPEED
Imagine what you would see if you travelled at the speed of light. According to Maxwell's theory of electrodynamics, you would observe the light beam as an electromagnetic field at rest. But since there is no such thing, according to Maxwell's theory, the thought experiment disconfirms the theory (Einstein 1949, 53).

THE MISSING SHADE OF BLUE
Imagine that you have not seen a certain shade of blue but that you have seen shades of blue slightly lighter or slightly darker than it. Could you imagine that "missing" shade of blue? Hume thought that you could. He concluded that not every simple idea we have needs to be a "copy" of a corresponding sense experience (Hume 1739-40, bk. I, pt. I, sec. I).

THE BRAIN IN A VAT
Imagine that your brain is placed in a vat wired up to a computer. The computer sends certain electronic signals directly to your brain thereby inducing experiences which are introspectively exactly like the experiences you would have if you were living a normal life and perceiving an external world. This imagined situation prompts the intuition that you cannot tell whether or not you are a brain in a vat. The conclusion is that you do not know whether you perceive an external world.

SWAPPED MEMORIES
Imagine that a cobbler lost all memories of his former life but apparently acquired all the memories that a prince has. John Locke inferred that the cobbler would be the same person as the prince, although they are different men (i.e., different human beings). Locke concludes that there

is a distinction between *being the same human being* and *being the same person*; these need not coincide (Locke 1694, bk. II, ch. 27, sec. 15).

THE CHINESE ROOM

Imagine that you are in a room with an input slot and an output slot. Through the input slot come messages in (say) Chinese. You have a manual that tells you what message in Chinese to post in reply through the output slot. The manual does not tell you what any of the Chinese messages mean in English; using the manual requires only that you match up the shapes of input Chinese characters with what's in the manual, and copy out characters just on the basis of their shape. John Searle has the intuition that you do not understand Chinese, even though you (unwittingly) give appropriate answers in Chinese to questions in Chinese. He concludes that understanding a language is not a matter of appropriate symbol manipulation, and, more generally, that the mind is not merely a symbol manipulating device analogous to a computer (Searle 1980).

MARY THE COLOUR SCIENTIST

Imagine that Mary is a colour scientist who has spent her whole life in a room in which everything is black and white and shades of grey. The physical sciences of her day are so advanced that their textbooks state all the physical facts involved when someone sees a red object. By reading these textbooks Mary learns all the physical facts involved when someone sees a red object. So Mary comes to know all the physical facts about what happens in people's nervous systems when they see red objects. According to physicalism, all the facts about what happens when someone sees a red object are physical facts. There are no non-physical facts involved. But when Mary leaves her room and sees a ripe tomato for the first time she will learn something that she did not know before. She will learn what a red object looks like. So Mary will learn a new fact about what is involved when someone sees a red object. But previously Mary knew all the physical facts involved when someone sees a red object. Therefore, this new fact that she learns is not a physical fact. It is a non-physical fact. So physicalism is false (Jackson 1982).

Lastly, here are briefer versions of some other philosophical thought experiments.

INVERTED SPECTRA

Imagine that I see as red everything that you see as green, and vice versa. Our behaviour and behavioural dispositions would be the same. So seeing things as red (or as green) cannot simply be a matter of behaving or being disposed to behave in certain ways. This thought experiment for "inverted spectra" is in Locke (1694, bk. II, ch. xxxii, sec. 15), although the anti-behaviourist conclusion was drawn only after the rise of behaviourism in the 1930s.

ZOMBIES

Imagine an atom-for-atom replica of you that lacked any conscious experiences. This would be a physical replica of you that physically resembled you through and through and that behaved like you (a *Doppelgänger*), although it had no mental life. Such a physical replica would be a "zombie." Physicalism, however, says that you are nothing but a physical object. Since you differ psychologically from your zombie twin, the thought experiment concludes that physicalism is false (Chalmers 1996).

COULD THERE BE MORE THAN ONE SPATIAL WORLD?

You can travel from Toronto to Berlin. NASA can send a rocket from Earth to Neptune. More generally, it seems that there is a spatial route linking any two spatial regions. But is this a necessary truth? Imagine that every time that you fell asleep in your humdrum urban life, you then seem to wake in a sunny paradise with a different body from the one you have in your humdrum life. The people and sights around you are also quite unlike the ones in your humdrum life. And, whenever you seem to fall asleep at the end of a glorious day in this paradise, you awake again in your humdrum life. You set out on expeditions in your humdrum world but you never find the paradise, and vice versa. Anthony Quinton suggested that in this situation you would be experiencing life in two spatially unrelated worlds. He concluded that it is not a necessary truth that any two spatial regions are spatially connected (Quinton 1962).

MOLYNEUX'S CUBE

Imagine that someone blind from birth felt cubes and globes of about the same size. Imagine that that person later had his or her sight restored. Could that person tell just by looking which objects are cubes and which are globes? Molyneux, who devised the thought experiment, and Locke both thought that the person could not tell which was which. Locke concluded that our perceptions are altered by unconscious automatic inferences and that these inferences are due to our past experiences: "the ideas we receive by sensation are often in grown people altered by the judgment, without our taking notice of it" (Locke 1694, bk. II, ch. ix, sec. 8).

TWIN EARTH

Imagine a sample of liquid that had all manifest qualities of water, but which was not H_2O. (It might help to imagine this liquid to be found on another planet, Twin Earth.) Would that liquid be water? Putnam intuited that it would not. Consequently, since the word "water" would not apply to that liquid, the meaning of "water" is not determined by its manifest qualities alone. The microstructure of water, its being H_2O, determines what the word "water" correctly applies to. Since people may be ignorant of what the microstructure of water is, Putnam concluded that "'meanings' just ain't in the head" (Putnam 1975, 227).

THE VIOLINIST

Imagine that you found yourself wired up to a complete stranger whose life depended on the huge inconvenience of your remaining wired up to them for nine months. Would you have the right to sever the wiring? The situation you imagine yourself in is relevantly similar to a woman who finds herself pregnant. Judith Jarvis Thomson concluded that if you have a right to sever the wiring, by parity of argument the woman has a right to an abortion (Thomson 1971).

COULD EVERYTHING DOUBLE IN SIZE OVERNIGHT?

Imagine everything in the universe doubling in size at midnight. If you cannot imagine this, some philosophers think that this is evidence to show that objects are not located in absolute space like raisins in a pudding. Objects are simply in spatial relations to each other: there is no absolute space. (This is a variant of Leibniz's thought experiment for the relational nature of space: Leibniz 1715–16, 26.)

DUPLICATE PEOPLE

Imagine that two exact physical and psychological duplicates of Captain Kirk stepped out of the transporter room. Would those two people each be Captain Kirk? Parfit argued that they cannot each be Kirk since there is only one Captain Kirk, and it would be arbitrary to identify one of the duplicates with him. Parfit concluded that personal identity is a less important issue than has often been thought, and that what is more important is psychological continuity with past selves (Parfit 1984, 119–20, 282–87).

The variety of the above examples suggests to some people that thought experiments do not have a single role (Jackson 2009, 100–01). Some thought experiments clarify a theory. Other thought experiments clarify a consequence of a theory. Still others reveal otherwise unobvious connections. And yet others provide test cases for philosophical analyses or scientific theories. Given that thought experiments may have any of these roles, the task of devising a theory of thought experiments becomes that much harder. The next section will review some attempts.

3. Theories of Thought Experiments

What kind of thing is a thought experiment? How does it work? In particular, how can we get new knowledge about the actual world just by imagining a situation? In this section we will outline five theories of thought experiments that seek to answer these questions.

(1) *Thought experiments as triggers* (Kuhn 1964). Anomalies, or results that conflict with prediction, turn up during scientific research. Often scientists ignore them by writing them off as experimental error or by hoping to tackle them at a later stage. The function of a thought experiment is to trigger scientists' memories of anomalies and thereby to retrieve knowledge of them. Imagining the situation presented by a thought experiment prompts scientists to remember the situation and what its consequences were. By drawing on their memories of the actual situation, scientists can reliably say what would happen if the imagined situation were actual. Kuhn claims that a thought experiment can precipitate a crisis in a scientific theory and so initiate a change of theory. By retrieving knowledge of an anomaly, scientists can spot some of the weaknesses of their current theory and then seek to change it.

Kuhn admits that his theory does not apply to all scientific thought experiments. Thought experiments describing physically impossible situations are exceptions (e.g., Einstein's moving at light speed). More generally, thought experiments describing unobserved types of situation do not fit Kuhn's theory. For example, Poincaré devised a thought experiment (his "Flat Land" thought experiment) which involved two-dimensional people living in a two-dimensional environment (Poincaré 1952, 37–38). Gendler (1998, 2000, 2004) develops Kuhn's idea that thought experiments can make us think about our theories in new ways, but she does so without relying on Kuhn's remembering account of thought experiments.

(2) *Thought experiments as a priori knowledge of a Platonic realm* (Brown 1991a, b, 2004a, b, 2007a, b). Some thought experiments are intellectual insights into a realm of properties that are not in space or time. These insights are like perceptions: they provide non-inferential *a priori* access to these properties and the lawlike relations between them.

This theory leaves the epistemology of thought experiments mysterious: how can minds get to know about things not in space and time? Brown makes a "companions in guilt" reply: it is equally mysterious how minds can get to know about things in space and time. Although it is relatively unmysterious how the external world acts on our nerve endings, it remains mysterious how changes in neurons produce changes in our beliefs (Brown 1991b, 65).

Even if this reply succeeds, the charge of mystery-mongering still has force. It is desirable to minimize the number of mysteries we admit. So a rival theory that does not harbour this mystery is, in that respect, a better theory.[1]

(3) *Thought experiments as arguments* (Norton 1991, 1996, 2004a, 2004b). Thought experiments are (inductive or deductive) arguments. The premises may be more or less explicit; the conclusion is the lesson that the thought experiment draws. The case for this theory is that various thought experiments can be represented as premise sets linked to conclusions by recognized forms of inference. Of course, the fact that thought experiments can be represented as arguments does not entail that thought experiments are arguments. But the fact that it is so illuminating and fruitful to represent thought experiments as arguments needs explaining, and the theory that they are identical provides a good explanation. For example, thought experiments can provide new knowledge because arguments can take us from familiar premises to surprising conclusions. The theory also makes thought experiments unmysterious. It is familiar and unmysterious that an argument can provide new and reliable information. An argument provides new information if its conclusion makes a claim that we do not already accept. The information provided is reliable if we have good reason to accept the argument's premise set. Now if a thought experiment is an argument, a thought experiment can provide new and reliable information in just the same way as an argument does.

Brown allows that some thought experiments are arguments, but denies that all are (Brown 1991b, 47). In particular, he denies that thought experiments such as Newton's bucket thought experiment are arguments. These are cases where the thought experiment establishes that there are certain phenomena (e.g., the states of the water before the bucket rotates and while rotating relative to the bucket), and we conjecture an explanation for the phenomena (here, the existence of absolute space) (Brown 1991b, 40–41).

---

1   For other criticisms of Brown's reply, see Norton (1993, 35–36), Sorensen (1992b, 1106–07), Cooper (2005, 333), and Häggqvist (2007).

But there is a straightforward way in which this kind of thought experiment can be construed as an argument: it can be construed as an inference to the best explanation. Newton thinks that certain phenomena need explaining; namely, the different states of the water in the bucket over time. He then selects what he takes to be the best potential explanation of this phenomena; namely, that in just one of these states the water and the bucket are rotating with respect to absolute space. Given the principle that it is warranted to believe that the best potential explanation of certain phenomena is the correct explanation, the thought experiment concludes that there is reason to believe that Newton's explanation is correct. (We discuss inference to the best explanation further in chapter 5, §5.)

Newton's thought experiment then has the following schematic argumentative form:

(1) Certain phenomena *p* need explaining.

(2) The best potential explanation of *p* is Newton's theory of absolute space.

(3) So probably Newton's theory of absolute space is true.

Brown writes that "absolute space is not the conclusion of an argument, it is the explanation for a phenomenon that Newton, in effect, postulates" (Brown 1991b, 48). But Brown makes a false opposition. The proposition *that absolute space exists* is both the conclusion of an argument — an argument that states an inference to the best explanation — and Newton's explanation of the behaviour of the water in the bucket.

Brown thinks that certain other thought experiments are not arguments. These are cases where the thought experiment starts with certain data and ends with a theory (Brown 1991b, 41–43). As an example Brown cites Galileo's thought experiment that all freely falling bodies fall at the same rate (Brown 1991b, 41). This is puzzling because earlier in his book Brown classifies this example as an argument; "it is a picturesque *reductio ad absurdum*" of Aristotle's theory of motion (Brown 1991b, 34). The thought experiment has the following schematic argumentative form:

(1) Heavier objects fall faster than lighter. (Assumption)

(2) Imagine two bodies, A heavier than B.

(3) Then A falls faster than B.

(4) So if A and B are united, then B will retard the fall of A.

(5) So the unit A + B falls slower than A.

(6) But the unit A + B weighs more than A.

(7) So the unit A + B falls faster than A. (Contradiction with 5.)

Since Aristotle's theory that heavier objects fall faster than lighter ones leads to a contradiction, similar reasoning shows that the theory that lighter objects fall faster than heavier ones also leads to a contradiction. But then it follows that freely falling bodies, whatever their weight, fall at the same rate. So Galileo's law of free fall is a corollary of his *reductio* argument against Aristotle. (Gendler [1998] claims that one of Galileo's thought experiments cannot be understood as an argument. For a reply, see Norton [2004b, §4.3].)

Another objection to the theory that thought experiments are arguments is that, since there are cases in which different parties reconstruct the same thought experiment as different arguments, such a thought experiment cannot be an argument (Bishop 1999 and Häggqvist 2009, 61). Notice, however, that there are also cases in which different parties reconstruct the same argument in Kant (his Transcendental Deduction) or in Wittgenstein (his anti-private language argument) as different arguments. That would not be a good objection to the claim that Kant and Wittgenstein offer arguments. In such a case, if none of the parties can be faulted on grounds of scholarship, it would be a misnomer to talk of *the* argument in the text. The author of the text was not sufficiently clear as to what his argument was, or perhaps different parties are sufficiently ingenious to read in lines of argument that did not occur to the author. A similar line can be taken with respect to thought experiments. In a case of the above kind, there is no unique thought experiment. There is an original statement that is suggestive of more than one thought experiment, each of which can be reconstructed as an argument.[2]

What we have seen so far is something of the versatility of the theory that a thought experiment is an argument. Although there may seem to be various kinds of thought experiments that are not arguments, this overlooks what forms an argument can take. As we have seen, an argument can be to the conclusion that a certain potential explanation is the best explanation of a phenomenon mentioned in the premise set. Given this, a thought experiment such as Newton's bucket can be readily accommodated as an argument.

Other objections to the theory are phenomenological. It has been claimed that running a thought experiment does not seem like giving an argument. "Thought experiments are often fun and easy, arguments are usually not" (Cooper 2005, 332). But "usually" is the giveaway. Why assume arguments are usually dull and difficult? (Bertrand Russell's were not.) And, that aside, why assume that thought experiments are like typical arguments? It is further objected that "when we perform a thought

---

2   Norton (2004b, 63–64) offers a similar reply.

experiment we imagine the situation unfolding in our mind's eye. We don't consider premises, modes of inference, and conclusions" (Cooper 2005, 332). Yet we are free to imagine a situation developing in any way we please. So why do we take it that an imagined situation would unfold (i.e., develop) in one way rather than another? The current theory offers an answer: given (a description of) an initial situation, and selected principles of development (certain inference rules), a certain further situation develops (a certain conclusion is inferred). Lastly, it is objected that a thought experiment such as Hume's one about the missing shade of blue "requires us to imagine what it is like to see blue, something that cannot be reduced to propositional form" (Cooper 2005, 332). Taken as an argument, Hume's thought experiment runs: "We can imagine a shade of colour if we perceive its neighbours in the colour spectrum. So we can imagine a colour shade if we perceive its neighbours, even if we have not perceived the shade being imagined." Let's grant that imagining what it is like to see the shade is not propositional. The argument does not assume otherwise. Instead, something propositional (the argument's premise) is used to represent something non-propositional (imagining what it is like to see the shade).

(4) *Thought experiments as genuine experiments* (Sorensen 1992a, Gooding 1990). The similarities between concrete experiments and thought experiments outweigh the dissimilarities. Both kinds of experiment can disconfirm theories, can identify interesting phenomena, and much else.

Nevertheless, emphasizing these similarities does not answer the principal question about thought experiments: how can imagining a situation tell us about what happens in actual situations? Since the theory at issue does not address that question, it is deficient. The theory can be supplemented with an epistemic account. Sorensen, for instance, claims that thought experiments are both experiments and arguments: they involve "a set of individually plausible yet inconsistent propositions" (Sorensen 1992a, 6). Given this combination of theories, it is unclear what work the "thought experiments are genuine experiments" theory does. Gooding talks of the "construction of experimental narratives that enable virtual or vicarious witnessing" (Gooding 1990, 204–05). Gooding does not develop those remarks and, as they stand, they can be interpreted in terms of any of the other theories of thought experiments. For example, on Kuhn's theory of thought experiments as triggers for memory, presenting a thought experiment can be understood as developing a story about an imaginary experiment, where hearing this story ("witnessing it") triggers a memory of that experiment actually being performed and producing a certain anomalous outcome.

(5) *Thought experiments as models of possible worlds* (Nernessian 1991, 1993, Miščević 1992, and Cooper 2005). Thought experiments pose "what if" questions. What would happen if bodies obeyed Aristotelian mechanics? What would happen if Mary saw something red for the first time? To answer such questions we predict how these objects would behave in the imagined circumstances. In some cases (such as the Aristotelian case), we know which laws would govern objects in the imagined circumstances, and we can thereby predict the objects' behaviour. In other cases, we can use our implicit understanding of laws that we cannot fully state. In both cases, what knowledge we have of these laws enables us to develop a model — a representation of various possible situations.

The theory that a thought experiment is a model of a possible world does not help answer any of the epistemological questions about thought experiments that have already been raised. Our key original question was: how does imagining something give new knowledge about the world? The present theory faces a variation of this question: how does devising a model give us new knowledge of the world? The fact that a given model is consistent (or impossible) tells us that it is consistent (or impossible) for the world to be that way only on the assumption that the model is an accurate model of the world. We cannot always tell from our armchairs, however, when that assumption is correct. For example, we cannot tell from our armchairs what laws of nature hold. Perhaps what the theory leads to is the view that a thought experiment articulates a counterfactual claim: if such and such a model were an accurate model of the world, then so and so would be the case.[3]

4. Scepticism about Philosophical Thought Experiments

Scepticism about thought experiments in philosophy stems from a number of quarters. We will review these criticisms in a series of sub-sections.

WHAT KIND OF REASONS DO THOUGHT EXPERIMENTS PROVIDE?

If both a concrete experiment and a thought experiment can provide epistemic reason to believe a scientific theory T, what kind of epistemic reason is this? A concrete experiment can show that T makes a correct prediction by testing of one of T's predictions. By contrast, a thought

---

3   For a similar view, see Williamson (2007, ch. 6), but see Ichikawa (2009) for criticisms.

experiment does *not* test the predictions of a theory. "[T]he function of thought experiments in science is to draw out the physical implications of our theories and to test their nonempirical virtues" (Bokulich 2001, 303). The theoretical (or "nonempirical") virtues of a theory include its explanatory power, its simplicity, its consistency, and its fruitfulness (its ability to suggest novel hypotheses). There is an issue about what the significance is of the fact that a given theory has a certain theoretical virtue. In particular, is it a reason to believe that theory? (We will take this issue up in the case of simplicity in chapter 4, §6.) Perhaps thought experiments provide no reason to believe (or disbelieve) a theory but play only a popularizing or heuristic role in presenting the theory, its commitments, and how it might be tested by actual experiments.

DO THOUGHT EXPERIMENTS GENERATE CONTRADICTORY CONCLUSIONS?

Jeanne Peijeneburg and David Atkinson claim that disagreement about the conclusion of a given thought experiment indicates that the thought experiment is a poor one (Peijeneburg and Atkinson 2003, 308–10). They think that this exposes many philosophical thought experiments as poor ones: "thought experiments in contemporary analytic philosophy often generate contradictory conclusions" (Peijeneburg and Atkinson 2003, 308). For example, one philosopher might conclude from the thought experiment about Mary the colour scientist that physicalism is false. Yet another philosopher might instead claim that it is psychologically impossible for someone to know all the physical facts about the working of the brain, and conclude that no lesson about physicalism can be drawn from the thought experiment. And still another philosopher might claim that were Mary to know all the physical facts about colour, then she *would* know what red things look like.

Peijeneburg and Atkinson admit, however, that this point also holds for certain scientific thought experiments, such as Newton's bucket thought experiment (Peijeneburg and Atkinson 2003, 306). Their response is to say that a scientific theory can provide reason to believe a particular conclusion of a scientific thought experiment (Peijeneburg and Atkinson 2003, 315). Their idea seems to be that if scientific theory T_1 is better than a rival T_2, then we should believe the conclusion that T_1 draws from a thought experiment rather than the conclusion that T_2 draws (if those conclusions differ). But then it seems that a similar principle can be used to select between conflicting conclusions drawn from philosophical thought experiments. Peijeneburg and Atkinson reject this, remarking that "[in] philosophy, however, the turn to theories is of little help. How should we decide between, say, the theories of Searle and Dennett on understanding, meaning and consciousness?" (Peijeneburg and Atkinson 2003, 315). Their argument can be reconstructed as follows:

(1)   There is no reason to believe one of those philosophical theories rather than the other except for the degree of support it gets from thought experiments.

(2)   The only reason to believe one conclusion of philosophical thought experiment rather than a rival conclusion would be because of a reason to believe one of these philosophical theories rather than another.

(3)   So there is no reason to believe one conclusion of a philosophical thought experiment rather than a rival conclusion.

It follows that we cannot work out which thought experiments are good ones (and so which philosophical theories are good ones) on pain of circularity.

The above argument is valid. The trouble with the above argument is that premise (1) is very contentious and Peijeneburg and Atkinson provide no justification for it. And if the premise itself states a philosophical theory — the philosophical theory that the only source of justification for such a theory is a thought experiment — then they cannot provide justification for it, on pain of contradiction.

Furthermore, what Duhem taught us about concrete experiments applies with equal force to thought experiments (Duhem 1914, 188-90, 204).[4] When a theory faces putative disconfirmation from a thought experiment or from a concrete experiment, it is always possible to modify the theory to avoid disconfirmation. For example, instead of taking the theory to be false, perhaps we should take some of the background assumptions used in testing the theory to be false. Or perhaps we wrongly assumed that certain potentially interfering factors were absent. Or again perhaps we wrongly assumed that certain factors were innocuous when in fact they interfered. If we made any of these revisions, we need not take the theory to be false. The issue then is whether the costs of the revision exceed the benefits: is the revision purely *ad hoc*, does it make the theory less simple, or does the theory make a more than compensating gain in explanatory power? Second, a thought experiment is always open to interpretation, and two rival theories may offer different interpretations of the same thought experiment. In this case, what the

---

4   See Bokulich (2001, 288–89) for the extension of Duhem's point to thought experiments.

best interpretation of the thought experiment is will be underdetermined. This issue also arises in the next sub-section.

ARE THOUGHT EXPERIMENTS QUESTION-BEGGING?

Peijeneburg and Atkinson also claim that another indicator that any given thought experiment is a poor one is if it assumes the very intuition that it is supposed to elicit (Peijeneburg and Atkinson 2003, 311). We will see an alleged illustration shortly. Their claim seems to be a special case of the general point that any argument that begs the question is defective. "The conclusions drawn from thought experiments beg the question: they hinge on intuitions of which the truth or falsity was supposed to be demonstrated by those very thought experiments" (Peijeneburg and Atkinson 2003, 310).[5] An argument begs the question when it contains at least one premise that would not be accepted by the target audience because they do not yet accept the conclusion of the argument. Or, more simply, anyone would have reason to accept all of its premises only if that person has independent reason to accept its conclusion (Walton 1989, 52 and Govier 1992, 85). Begging the question is a defect in any piece of reasoning. But is there any reason to think that philosophical thought experiments especially suffer from this defect?

Consider Quinton's thought experiment (see §2). Quinton imagines your having various experiences while awake in your humdrum life and various more exotic ones while asleep in your humdrum life. He interprets this as a situation in which you have experiences of two spatially unrelated worlds, the humdrum world and the exotic paradise. He concludes that it is not a necessary truth that every space is spatially related to every other space. But Quinton's interpretation assumes that it is possible for two worlds to be spatially unrelated — and that is the very conclusion to be established.

But just because Quinton's thought experiment has this failing, it cannot be supposed that every philosophical thought experiment does. A thought experiment does not beg the question just because it expresses an intuition in its conclusion. The premises of a thought experiment may give reason to accept the conclusion, and so give reason to accept the intuition. That is a perfectly reasonable way to proceed. Without building in the intuition as one of the premises of the argument, the argument shows that the intuition follows from a set of premises that there is independent reason to believe.

Peijeneburg and Atkinson also say that the conclusions of thought experiments beg the question because "they are embodiments of those

---

5   See also Ward (1995).

intuitions for the sake of which the entire thought experiment [*sic*] was conceived" (Peijeneburg and Atkinson 2003, 317). But this confuses the motivation for giving an argument with the question of whether the argument is question-begging. An argument may be given to show that *p* is true. It does not follow that the argument begs the question as to whether *p* is true. For example, suppose I want to persuade you that Pele is rich. I might argue as follows: all world class footballers are rich; Pele is a world class footballer; so Pele is rich. I gave that argument in order to persuade you that Pele is rich. But the argument did not beg the question as to whether he is rich.

Lastly, if Peijeneburg and Atkinson's claim that philosophical thought experiments beg the question were correct, their claim would apparently generalize so that all thought experiments beg the question. So scientific thought experiments would have the same defect. The authors think that this consequence can be avoided because concrete experiments can be performed in science to test the thought experiment's conclusion (Peijeneburg and Atkinson 2003, 317). But, first, even if the conclusion of a thought experiment can be tested, it is hard to see how that makes the thought experiment a good one. If argument *A* begs the question, the argument is not made a good one if a non-question begging argument *B* can also be provided for the same conclusion. Argument *A* remains a poor argument. Likewise, if thought experiment *C* begs the question, it is not made a good one if a concrete experiment can be conducted to reach the same result as the thought experiment predicted.

Second, the conclusions of some good scientific thought experiments cannot be tested in this way because they concern situations that are physically impossible. Einstein's thought experiment of what someone travelling at the speed of light would observe is one such example.

Third, the conclusions of some philosophical thought experiments can be tested by concrete experiments. Searle's Chinese room and Molyneux's example could all be carried out in real world experiments. Peijeneburg and Atkinson reply that such experiments "would not resolve the philosophical conundrum" (2003, 317). But now it seems that more is being required of a good thought experiment than that its conclusion is testable in a concrete experiment. Here it is being further required that the experiment resolves the philosophical dispute. The requirement seems unreasonable, however, given what was said above about Duhem's thesis and its implication for thought experiments. No concrete or thought experiment can be guaranteed to resolve a dispute between theories.[6]

---

6   See also the exchange between Cohnitz (2006) and Peijeneburg and Atkinson (2006).

We now have some sense of sceptical arguments against thought experiments in philosophy. There are further such arguments to address. As we have found in our two earlier chapters, the most profitable way to pursue a methodological issue is by examining how that methodology applies to a particular case study. To this end, we will consider a case study in §5. This will concern scepticism about thought experiments about personal identity. §6 will discuss whether philosophical thought experiments can be tested by empirical means. A recent movement, **Experimental Philosophy**, champions the view that it is very useful to do such empirical testing. Some of its findings have been especially interesting because they have been markedly negative.

5. Case Study: Thought Experiments about Personal Identity

One theory of personal identity identifies a person with his or her own body. The following brain transplant thought experiment is designed to challenge that theory. It is possible that a person's entire brain is transplanted into a new skull (or into a suitably prepared laboratory vat), and kept alive so that its brain functions continue as before. The brain would then remain conscious: it would produce experiences, thoughts, beliefs, apparent memories, and so forth. Indeed, there would seem to be psychological continuity between the brain's mental states before, and after, the transplant. This may prompt the intuition that where the brain goes, the person goes. Now let's assume that either the person is identical with the original body minus the brain, or the person is identical with the brain. Suppose that, perhaps thanks to the thought experiment, you have the intuition that the person is located wherever the brain is located. So, following the transplant, the person is not located where the original body is. It is a plausible principle governing identity that x is identical to y only if, at any time, the location of x is identical to the location of y (if x or y are located). It follows that the person is not identical to the original body. The brain transplant thought experiment is potentially a very powerful device. If successful, it would show that the theory that a person is identical to his or her body is false.

What should we make of such a thought experiment? Can it really undermine its intended target? One of the principal claims of Kathleen Wilkes's book *Real People* is that the practice of discussing personal identity in terms of what she calls "theoretically impossible" speculative cases is misguided (Wilkes 1988, ch. 1). Mark Johnston and Peter van Inwagen have similar views (Johnston 1987; van Inwagen 1997, 307–08).

Wilkes and Johnston each run the following line of argument. There is no background of theory against which such speculations can be evaluated. Consequently, either we run a thought experiment against the background of what we already believe about the world, or we run it against a quite different background of beliefs. On the first limb of the dilemma, we are running the thought experiment against a background that rules it out as "theoretically impossible," i.e., as conflicting with what we believe the laws of nature to be. On the second limb of the dilemma, we have an idle fantasy on a par with imagining that there are carnivorous rabbits on Mars, or that people can pass through mirrors.

Wilkes's positive proposal is that discussions of personal identity should consider only human beings and what actually happens to them. What occurs to some human beings is sufficiently puzzling and thought provoking that wildly speculative cases can be set aside without loss.

Let's consider the first limb of the above dilemma. James Robert Brown replies that:

> Too often thought experiments are used to find the laws of nature themselves; they are tools for unearthing the theoretically or nomologically possible. Stipulating the laws in advance and requiring thought experiments not to violate them would simply undermine their use as powerful tools for the investigation of nature. (Brown 1991b, 30)

Wilkes might reply that her claim is also consistent with Brown's view that thought experiments are epistemic tools for discovering laws of nature. Suppose that we make a series of thought experiments designed to find out the laws of nature. Suppose that our first thought experiment discovers that L is a law of nature. Wilkes's claim is that, given this discovery, no subsequent thought experiment should make a claim incompatible with L. The judgement that L is a law could not rationally be revised on the basis of a thought experiment.

Although this point shows that Brown's view is consistent with Wilkes's claim, it is itself open to objection. Some scientific thought experiments concern situations that are "theoretically impossible" in Wilkes's sense. Recall Einstein's thought experiment about what he would observe if he travelled at the speed of light. This thought experiment remains highly regarded despite the fact that it is theoretically impossible (i.e., incompatible with the laws of nature) for Einstein to travel at the speed of light — as Einstein himself recognized. Accordingly, Wilkes's claim flouts best scientific practice.

What seems right about Wilkes's claim is that, if we are given a description of a situation that we cannot make much sense of, anything further that we say about the situation will be guesswork. Consequently, anything further we might say will not count as evidence for, or against, any of our beliefs. This does not, however, license a blanket ban on philosophical thought experiments. To repeat: the ban applies only to descriptions of situations that we do not understand. And saying which descriptions these are should not be done in a casual matter. We have to think each description through on a case by case basis. If we fail to understand a description, we should at least have tried to understand it in the first place (Kitcher 1978, 105). None of the sample thought experiments given earlier seems to ask us to imagine the nonsensical. One point of some thought experiments might be to show that something that looks prima facie to be imaginable is actually impossible or incoherent.

Why is Wilkes sceptical about philosophical thought experiments? She has two arguments. Her first argument is as follows. If many philosophical arguments are judged against the world as we know it, they describe "theoretical" or "in principle" impossible situations. Therefore, they are no more than fantasy. Examples of "theoretical" impossible situations include gold not having atomic number 79, or water not being H_2O. Gold and water are examples of natural kinds: natural collections of natural things. Other natural kinds include tigers, spiders, and roses. According to Wilkes, thought experiments involving a natural kind are unsuccessful if they take instances of that natural kind to lack any of their essential properties. Gold is a natural kind, and its instances essentially have atomic number 79. Water is a natural kind and its instances are essentially composed of H_2O molecules. Hence thought experiments in which gold or water lack these, or any other, essential properties are unsuccessful. Wilkes further claims that human beings form a natural kind. Consequently, she claims that a thought experiment about human beings is unsuccessful if it takes a human being to lack any of its essential properties. The issue then is whether thought experiments such as the brain transplant thought experiment take a human being to lack any of its essential properties.

It might be thought that Wilkes's argument can be side-stepped. The response runs as follows. It seems possible that there are persons who are not human beings (as Wilkes [1988, 36] apparently concedes). If so, the philosophical thought experiments about persons that Wilkes objects to can be re-cast in terms of non-human beings who are persons. By re-casting the thought experiments in these terms, Wilkes's objection is circumvented (Madell 1991, 139). Thought experiments about persons who are not human beings are not thought experiments rooted in observation and experience. On the face of it, they are thought experiments about purely imaginary beings. This, however, takes us to Wilkes's second argument against philosophical thought experiments.

Her second argument runs as follows. All thought experiments make background assumptions. In scientific thought experiments, these background assumptions are made explicit. Many philosophical thought experiments, by contrast, leave their relevant background assumptions unspecified and only implicit. In this respect these thought experiments resemble fairy tales. But while, for the sake of an entertaining story, we may waive *how* Alice can pass through a mirror, philosophical thought experiments need to be more detailed and rigorous. Such thought experiments need to explain how, for example, a person's brain could be successfully transplanted from one body into another in a way that preserves that brain's mental and other functions. Again, the thought experiments need to explain how a person could be teletransported from one place to another.[7]

Taking the second of these examples, Madell replies that Wilkes's argument at most shows that we do not know how someone could be teletransported, but it does not show that the thought experiment is incoherent (Madell 1991, 139). Wilkes might respond that Madell's reply misses the point. The charge was not that the teletransporter thought experiment was incoherent. The charge was that, unless we are told how the thought experiment is possible, there is no more warrant for thinking that the thought experiment is coherent than that there is warrant to think that the fiction of Alice stepping through a mirror is coherent. Unless this challenge is met, there is no more reason to think that the thought experiment is coherent than there is to think that any fairy tale that does not contain an overt contradiction is coherent.

On which side does the burden of argument lie? Is Madell obliged to offer more justification for accepting the teletransporter thought experiment as coherent? Or is Wilkes obliged to offer more justification for questioning its coherence? Madell thinks that the onus is on Wilkes to "justify rejecting thought experiments [that are not overtly contradictory]" (Madell 1991, 139).[8] Lycan puts the point more generally:

> For any modal claim that something is a necessary truth, I would say that the burden is on the claim's proponent. A theorist who maintains of something that *is* not obviously impossible that nonetheless that thing is impossible owes us an

---

7   For related worries, see Cooper (2005, 345).
8   See also Snowdon (1991, 115).

argument. And since entailment claims are claims of necessity and impossibility the same goes for them....

... The proponent of a necessity, impossibility, entailment or incompatibility claim is saying that *in no possible world whatever* does it occur that so-and-so. That is a universal quantification. Given the richness and incredible variety of the pluriverse [i.e., the plurality consisting in every possible world], such a statement cannot be accepted without argument save for the case of basic logical intuitions that virtually everyone accepts. (Lycan 2003, 109)

To talk about "the richness and incredible variety of the pluriverse," however, does not settle matters. The issue is just how rich the "pluriverse" is. Granted the pluriverse contains every possibility. It is still up for argument what is possible and what is not.

Disputes about where the burden of proof lies often end in stalemate. When thought experiments describe fantastical situations, Madell and Snowdon take the default view to be that it is "Business As Usual." For Johnston and Wilkes, however, it is a case of "All Bets Are Off." Imaginative philosophers are free to dream up cases at will, and to stipulate that they are cases of (say) teleportation. Johnston and Wilkes warn that that does not make them cases of metaphysical discovery. For these critics, devising fantastical thought experiments "simply fails to make any contact with reality, and it is hard to see why discussions of such cases should be of any interest to [metaphysics]" (Maudlin 2007, 188).

These critics might run the following argument (Stroud 1977, 50). Some mathematical claims have been neither proved nor disproved. It is an open question which of these claims states something necessarily true, and which of them states something necessarily false. Goldbach's conjecture is the claim that every even number greater than two can be expressed as the sum of two primes. Now it seems that there is no overt contradiction in imagining proving the conjecture. Perhaps you imagine yourself working long and hard, scribbling down equations until you conclude that Goldbach's conjecture is true. There is also no overt contradiction in imagining disproving Goldbach's conjecture. Yet these thought experiments cannot both be successful. They cannot each reveal a genuine possibility because it is possible to prove Goldbach's conjecture only if it is impossible to disprove the conjecture. So a thought experiment that is not overtly self-contradictory may still describe something impossible.

Some philosophers think that mathematical claims that are neither provable nor disprovable are neither true nor false. We need not quarrel with these philosophers here. Even if Goldbach's conjecture is neither provable nor disprovable, the above point still holds. A thought experiment that describes you proving the conjecture and a thought experiment that describes you disproving the conjecture cannot both describe genuine possibilities. Perhaps neither thought experiment describes a genuine possibility because the conjecture can neither be proved nor disproved.[9]

The above line of argument can be challenged (McGrew and McGrew 1998, pt., 3). First, it is questionable whether, by imagining the above situations, you genuinely imagine Goldbach's conjecture being true or genuinely imagine it as false. Strictly what is imagined in the first situation is that you have written down a string of equations and form the belief that you have proved Goldbach's conjecture. That falls short of proving the conjecture: it is consistent with what you have imagined that the conjecture is false. Similarly, imagining your believing — even your justifiably believing — that the conjecture is false falls short of imagining that the conjecture is false. Notice that there is no contradiction between imagining your believing the conjecture *and* imagining your disbelieving the conjecture.

Madell and Snowdon might further reply that, when there is no evidence of any kind that a given thought experiment is impossible, the default view should be that the thought experiment describes a genuine possibility. If this suggestion is to be made tenable though, it would need to be formulated more carefully. Since some thought experiments, such as Quinton's, are unsuccessful, and so thought experimenting is not a fail-safe epistemic method, there is some evidence against any given thought experiment being successful. There is also a question of what counts as evidence against a given thought experiment. Does imagining that every attempt to build a teleportation device fails count as evidence that teleportation is impossible? Would that thought experiment conflict with Parfit's thought experiment much as the above pair of thought experiments about Goldbach's conjecture were conflicting thought experiments? It would not be helpful to suggest that, unless there is sufficient evidence against a thought experiment, the default view should be to take the thought experiment to describe a genuine possibility. We need to be told how much evidential support the default provides, and so what degree of counter-evidence would be needed to defeat it.

---

9   For further discussion of this issue, see Yablo (2000), Gendler and Hawthorne (2002, introduction), and Rosen (2006).

In fact, it is doubtful whether there is any methodological default for or against possibility claims. To say that it is possible that a donkey talks is to say that it is consistent with the nature of a donkey that it talks. To have a reason to believe such a claim, or to have a reason to believe such a claim is false, depends crucially on what one knows, or has good reason to believe, about that nature. So, in any given case, the key question to ask is what those reasons are. This was the point that Wilkes made in her emphasis on what natural kinds a given thing belongs to. Judgements about what is possible or what is impossible have to be assessed on a case-by-case basis, and not by some burden-shifting rule.

What is meant by a background assumption to a thought experiment? Do philosophical thought experiments leave their background assumptions unclear? If so, does this tell against those thought experiments? Can the background assumptions be made clear? If they are made clear, do any other difficulties face philosophical thought experiments?

It may be that philosophical thought experiments often leave their background assumptions unclear in the sense that they do not explain how those assumptions might come about, or they fail to explain all of the important consequences of those assumptions. But then the same goes for the scientific thought experiments (Snowdon 1991, 120). Take Einstein's thought experiment of what someone would observe if they travelled at the speed of light. Einstein does not seek to explain how the observer could travel at that speed, what the means of propulsion would be, how the observer could survive the resulting increase in mass, and so forth. What we have here is a "companions in guilt" reply to Wilkes. Wilkes makes a certain objection against philosophical thought experiments because they fail to explain how their assumptions come about, or what all their important consequences are. It is then replied that at least some scientific thought experiments have the same features. So either these scientific thought experiments are as bad as the philosophical thought experiments are claimed to be — both kinds of thought experiment are "companions in guilt" — or there is nothing objectionable about thought experiments having the features in question — both kinds of thought experiment are "innocent." Since Wilkes wants not to impugn scientific thought experiments, it seems that her current objection to philosophical thought experiments fails.

To sum up this section, there is no default assumption that a thought experiment describes a genuine possibility unless shown otherwise. Thought experiments need to be assessed on a case-by-case basis.

Particular attention needs to be paid to the (perhaps implicit) back-ground assumptions made and to their tenability.[10]

6. Experimental Philosophy

Suppose a thought experiment is devised in order to elicit a certain intuition. The thought experiment is successful only if it elicits that intu-ition in its audience. That raises the question: just how widespread is the intuition? Journal articles and conferences give some indication of how widespread the intuition is among philosophers. But we need to take into account the effect of authority figures in inculcating intuitions in their awestruck devotees and cowed students. Also the educational back-ground of academic philosophers is hardly typical of the wider popula-tion. They have undergone years of specialized learning that steeps them in weird and wonderful philosophical theories. As a result we can expect their intuitions to be shot through with theory and interpretation. Such theoretically biased data make the evidence less reliable than it would otherwise be for testing theories. This also has implications for the work-ing model of analysis presented in chapter 2, §3, since that model took intuitions about hypothetical cases to be tests for candidate analyses.

What needs to be done? Philosophers need to get out of their arm-chairs and into the field. They need to do concrete experiments. In particular, they need to conduct surveys on the general public to see what intuitions they have. Or so says a recent approach called "experi-mental philosophy" (or "x-phi," for short.) To date, researchers in this approach have conducted surveys to elicit intuitions about such topics as knowledge, reference, action, and moral responsibility (Alexander and Weinberg 2007, Kauppinen 2007, Knobe and Nichols 2008, pts. I-III, and Swain, Alexander, and Weinberg 2008). The results of these surveys have been very thought-provoking. Some results describe different responses from different groups to the same cases. Other results describe different responses by the same group to similar cases. To take a case of the first kind, Weinberg, Nichols and Stich (2008) claim that most Westerners surveyed judge a certain Gettier case not to be a case of knowledge, whereas most East Asians surveyed judge it to be a case of knowledge.

What should we make of experimental philosophy and its results? In presenting a thought experiment, a person is canvassing a response to a possible case: "What would you say about a case of the kind just described?" Take Locke's story of the prince and the cobbler (Locke 1694, bk. II, ch. 27, sec. 15). A person awakes. He has the prince's body but he

---

10 For further discussion of Wilkes, see Häggqvist (1996, ch. 2) and Coleman (2000).

lacks any memories of the prince's doings. He has, however, apparent memories of the cobbler's doings. Another person awakes. He has the cobbler's body but he lacks any memories of the cobbler's doings. He has, however, apparent memories of the prince's doings. Is this a case where the prince and the cobbler have swapped bodies? That question is a call for responses. It is a contingent matter knowable only *a posteriori* what those responses might be. This alone is enough to show that it is valuable for philosophers to make surveys of responses to possible cases. But some qualifications need to be made.

First, designing a survey, framing the questions to ask, conducting the survey, and replicating it all need to be properly carried out. Genoveva Martí thinks that at least one experimental philosophy survey has been badly designed. The survey's question is supposed to elicit intuitions about the reference of a name, but its formulation would instead elicit intuitions about theories of what determines the reference of names (Martí 2009).

Second, not all issues raised by thought experiments can be settled by survey (Jackson 2008). For instance, one lesson that Locke drew is that it is possible that one's bodily characteristics and one's psychological characteristics come apart. This is a surprising fact we learn whether or not Locke's story is a story of swapped bodies. Another lesson Locke drew is that it is useful to distinguish the concepts of being a person, of having a body, and of having a psychology.

Third, surveys do not tell us what lessons to draw from them, and it is perilous to draw definite conclusions on the basis of limited survey data. Weinberg *et al.* take the lessons to be that epistemic intuitions vary from culture to culture, and also that those intuitions vary from one socio-economic group to another (Nichols, Stich, and Weinberg 2003, 232). These lessons are controversial. Jackson suggests that the lesson might instead be that Westerners and East Asians have different concepts of knowledge (Jackson 2008).[11] Weinberg *et al.* have a number of responses (Nichols, Stich, and Weinberg 2003, 245). First, they respond that if Jackson is right, then perhaps philosophers (not to mention the folk) use different concepts when they debate. Yet that would threaten standard philosophical practice. Here Jackson should reply that the threat of talking past one another is always with us, and that his suggested lesson does not increase it. It helpfully points out one area where different groups talk past each other. As a practical measure, the level of threat in any debate can be evaluated by continuing the debate and seeing whether the partici-

---

11   See also Sosa (2008).

pants extensively disagree in their intuitions (which indicates difference in concepts) or whether the disagreement is relatively confined.

This also disarms a further query from Weinberg *et al.* They wonder whether it is plausible that *every* apparent disagreement traces back to a difference in concept. But the proposal is that only where there is *extensive* disagreement — disagreement about many Gettier cases, not just one or two — and that this disagreement remains after reflection, that the disagreement should be judged to lie in a difference of concepts. (Recall Rey's account of concept possession in chapter 2, §12.) Lastly, Weinberg *et al.* ask whether it is useful to have the Western (or East Asian) concept of knowledge. Major philosophical work, however, had already been done to explain the utility of at least the Western concept of knowledge (Craig 1990).[12]

Weinberg *et al.* talk of "intuition-driven romanticism" (Weinberg, Nichols and Stich 2008, 19–21). They think that the empirically discovered differences in intuition cast doubt on the reliability of intuitions about possible cases. At any rate, if the intuitions of one of the cultural groups are reliable, there is no saying which group it is. Jackson replies that this is

> [t]reating intuitions as if they were the deliverances of some kind of "intuition module" in the brain that's been shown to be unreliable with respect to, say, Gettier cases. But when we contemplate a Gettier case, we are asking whether or not the case as described counts as a case of knowledge. We don't introspect; we direct our attention to the case and ask what we believe about it. There is nothing more to having an intuition about a possible case then judging that the case is thus and so. (Jackson 2008)

It is unclear whether that addresses the charge. The charge is that intuition is unreliable. The fact that when we intuit we do not introspect, and that our attention is directed to the case at issue, is neither here nor there. Consider a parallel: wishful thinking is rightly charged with being unreliable. The fact that in wishful thinking we do not introspect, and that our attention is directed to the case at issue — the case that we wish obtains — does not meet the charge. (There is a large ongoing debate about the reliability of intuitions.)[13]

---

12 For other criticisms of Jackson's response, see Williamson (2009, 130).

13 For friends of intuitions, see Tidman (1994, 1996), Pust (2000a, 2000b), Levin (2004), Miščević (2004), Sosa (2006), Goldman (2007), and Liao (2008). For critics, see Hintikka (1999), Margolis and Laurence (2003), Kornblith (2002, ch. 1), Hales (2006, ch. 1), Kornblith (2006), Weinberg (2007), and Feltz (2008).

7. Conclusion

Despite any worries we might have about the reliability of intuitions, it might also seem that the appeal to intuitions is indispensable. Here is a tentative and speculative sceptical proposal. We need to test proposed philosophical analyses, and it might seem that the only means of testing them is by the method of hypothetical cases — the method of testing on the basis of our inclinations to apply words to certain imaginary cases. This last assumption, however, is questionable. In place of the method of hypothetical examples, we might think of an analysis as offering the best explanation of some antecedently known phenomena.[14] Take an example. Suppose that, however the circumstances otherwise vary, we find that cases of propositional knowledge and cases of reliably produced true belief are coextensive (i.e., our evidence is that anything is a case of knowledge if and only if it is a case of reliably produced true belief). We also learn from experience that having propositional knowledge enables us to navigate around our environment and to satisfy our desires. More or less independently, we learn which of our beliefs are true and have been produced by processes that more often produce true beliefs. These processes might be described in non-technical terms or in the specialized vocabulary of neurology or scientific psychology. Further investigation reveals that beliefs that are true and produced by reliable processes can be expected to help us to navigate around our environment and to satisfy our desires. This puts us in a position to explain why knowledge also has these same features, and why all recognized cases of knowledge are coextensive with cases of reliably produced true belief. The explanation is that knowledge is identical to reliably produced true belief. This explanation also explains why knowledge lacks certain other features. You can know that p without being certain that p or without knowing that you know that p. The explanation is that you can have a reliably produced true belief that p without knowing that you do or without being certain that p. Rival explanations might be devised, but this one is pleasingly simple and straightforward, and it follows a recognized scientific practice of advancing theoretical identifications to explain why certain phenomena have shared features and why they lack certain others. By an inference to the best explanation, we infer that knowledge is reliably produced true belief. No appeal to intuitions has been made.

The above example treated knowledge as an empirical phenomenon. Whether or not that is correct, the account can be applied to phenomena that are apparently knowable *a priori*. It can be known *a priori* that

---

14 This draws on some ideas in Melnyck (2008a, 284–85).

anything is an effectively computable function if and only if it is a Turing computable function. The hypothesis that these two kinds of function are identical has explanatory power by enabling us to prove various necessary truths about mechanical procedures and formal systems (Anderson 1990, 174–75).

The key point here is that the case for these illustrative examples of analyses does not rely on the method of hypothetical cases. Cases of knowledge are recognized through their behavioural effects. Cases of effectively computable functions are recognized through their formal properties. Intuitions are redundant. Or so our sceptical proposal says.

Questions for Discussion

1. At the end of §2 we noted the view that different thought experiments serve different roles. Are the listed roles exclusive? Are they exhaustive?

2. In §3 we considered five theories of what a thought experiment is. Which of those theories form consistent pairs? Which pairs are inconsistent?

3. Brown thinks that thought experiments provide knowledge of a Platonic realm. He admits that he has no explanation of how they do this, but says that the case of our knowledge of the physical world is no different. We lack an explanation of how brain changes produce changes in beliefs. Is Brown's defence effective?

4. If thought experiments are arguments, do they have a common structure? If so, what is that structure? (For some suggestions, see Sorensen [1992a, ch. 6] and Häggqvist [2009, 62–68].)

5. Can you imagine something glowing with a grey colour? If not, is that reason to believe that it is impossible for something to glow with a grey colour? More generally, is imagination a source of modal knowledge? And, if it is, is it our only source of modal knowledge?

6. Thought experiments sometimes concern far-fetched situations. Wilkes claims that the further a thought experiment is removed from everyday life, the more "dubious, uncertain and contestable" it is (Wilkes 1988, 47). Johnston says of intuitive judgements that "there will be reason to think that these judgements are more unreliable the more bizarre the cases in question are" (Johnston 1987, 63). Are these criticisms correct?

7. By seeking to describe cases far removed from everyday life, do thought experiments use words outside of their normal application (Coady 2007, 114)? Quine worries that:

> The method of science fiction has its uses in philosophy, but … I wonder whether the limits of the method are properly heeded. To seek what is "logically required" for sameness of person under unprecedented circumstances is to suggest that words have some logical force beyond what our past needs have invested them with. (Quine 1972, 490)

Are Quine's worries reasonable? How should his worries be met? (For some suggestions relevant to questions 6 and 7, see Sorensen [1992b, ch. 2 and 277–84].)

Core Reading for Chapter 3

Alexander, Joshua and Jonathan Weinberg (2007) "Analytic Epistemology and Experimental Philosophy."

Cooper, Rachel (2005) "Thought Experiments."

Gendler, Tamar Szabó (2000) *Thought Experiment: On the Powers and Limits of Imaginary Cases.*

Knobe, Joshua and Shaun Nichols (2008) (eds.) *Experimental Philosophy.*

Melnyck, Andrew (2008a) "Conceptual and Linguistic Analysis: A Two-Step Program."

Wilkes, Kathleen (1988) *Real People* ch. 1.

Williamson, Timothy (2007) *The Philosophy of Philosophy* chs. 6 and 7.

FOUR Simplicity

1. Introduction

Consider a spread of points on a graph. Each of the points represents a piece of data. Suppose that you want to draw a line through the points. Perhaps you would draw the smoothest curve that connects the points. But why draw a smooth line rather than a straggly one to connect the points? In fact, if there are finitely many points on the graph, infinitely many curves can be drawn through the points. Why privilege the smoothest curve?

Take a different case. Suppose that your apartment is burgled. The crime team identify one set of criminal fingerprints and one set of criminal footprints. How many burglars broke in? Given the evidence, you might well think that there was just one burglar. But why think that rather than that there were several burglars, one of whom was careless enough to leave fingerprints, and another of whom was careless enough to leave footprints, while all their accomplices were scrupulously careful? There are many hypotheses about the number of burglars that are consistent with the evidence given.

In both of the above examples, your thinking was presumably guided by considerations of simplicity. The same considerations are at work in science and in philosophy. They each treat simplicity as a theoretical virtue:

> Rule I: We are to admit no more causes of natural things than such as are both true and sufficient to explain their appearances. (Newton 1686, bk. III)

> Entities are not to be multiplied without necessity. In other words, in dealing with any subject matter, find out what enti-

ties are undeniably involved, and state everything else in terms
of these entities. (Russell 1914, 107)

The principle of simplicity that Newton and Russell appeal to is called
Ockham's Razor. The razor owes its name to William of Ockham and to
the medieval practice of scrapping excess ink or errors off vellum with
razors. There is an interpretative issue about how Ockham intended his
razor (or, more properly, his eraser) to be used, but this chapter will be
concerned with only modern uses of the razor. One way of formulating
the razor concerns the number of entities posited: this formulation says
that entities should not be posited without necessity. Ockham's Razor and
its various formulations will be the topic of this chapter.

2. Varieties of Simplicity

Ockham's Razor raises a number of questions:

> (Q1) How should any principle of simplicity be further
> understood?
> (Q2) Is simplicity a good feature of a scientific or
> philosophical hypothesis?
> (Q3) If it is a good feature, what accounts for its goodness? Is
> its goodness primitive or can it be understood in terms
> of other features of a hypothesis?

The present section will be concerned with (Q1). That question concerns
any principle of simplicity. (There may be more than one.) A simplicity
principle is a principle governing hypothesis selection. Such a principle
says:

> If hypothesis H_1 is simpler than hypothesis H_2, then, other
> things being equal, H_1 is a better hypothesis than H_2, and we
> should accept H_1 rather than H_2.

There are some points to note about this. First, simplicity is not an all-or-
nothing matter. The simplicity of a hypothesis admits of degree.

Second, the simplicity of a hypothesis is a comparative matter. One
hypothesis may be simpler than a second, but less simple than a third.

Third, whether one hypothesis is simpler than a second hypothesis
partly depends upon what the hypotheses are about. The comparative
simplicity of a pair of hypotheses is informed by the subject matter of
these hypotheses.

Fourth, simplicity is just one among a number of what are called "theoretical virtues." These are desirable properties that a given hypothesis may have. They include compatibility with the data, compatibility with background theory, explanatory power, fruitfulness (how many new ideas and applications the hypothesis suggests), and avoidance of intractable problems.

Fifth, the role of the clause "other things being equal" is that the simplicity of a hypothesis is weighed along with the other theoretical virtues. A simpler hypothesis may be preferable to another despite the fact that the other is slightly preferable in terms of some of the other virtues. Simplicity is, however, a defeasible reason for accepting a hypothesis. A less simple hypothesis may be preferable to another if the first hypothesis has many of the other theoretical virtues to a much higher degree. For example, if a hypothesis is much more explanatory and fruitful than its simpler rival, then this may make the hypothesis preferable to its rival.

IDEOLOGICAL AND ONTOLOGICAL SIMPLICITY

We have left it open whether there is more than one kind of simplicity, and it seems that there is. There is a distinction between what we might call ideological and ontological simplicity. Ontological simplicity concerns (roughly) how simple a hypothesis says the world is. Ideological simplicity concerns the number of extra-logical terms that a hypothesis takes as primitive, i.e., as undefined (see Quine 1951). The degree of ideological simplicity of a hypothesis is determined by the number of primitive terms needed to formulate the hypothesis. Perhaps you have a mathematical theory that contains the terms "set" and "number" among its primitive terms. You then find a way to define "number" in terms of "set," and so your theory no longer needs to take "number" to be one of its primitive terms. Your theory still has the same expressive resources as before; your theory can still generate as many sentences as before. But your theory has become ideologically simpler by taking one less term as a primitive.

Ontological simplicity admits of three distinctions: qualitative and quantitative simplicity; anti-quantity and anti-superfluity; and hypothesis-relative and absolute simplicity. These distinctions do not exclude one another, and something's falling on one side of one distinction leaves open what side it will fall on in another of the distinctions.

QUALITATIVE AND QUANTITATIVE SIMPLICITY

Qualitative simplicity concerns the number of types of thing taken as basic by a given hypothesis. Quantitative simplicity concerns the number of instances posited by the hypothesis for each of the types it takes as basic. For example, in the nineteenth century astronomers had observed perturbations in the orbit of Uranus and sought to explain them. In 1845–46 Leverrier and Adams posited an unobserved planet (Neptune) with a certain mass and orbit that would cause the observed anomalies in Uranus's orbit. By positing a planet, they were positing something belonging to a type already taken by astronomy to be a basic type. So their hypothesis was qualitatively simple. By positing only one thing of that type, their hypothesis was quantitatively simple. Consider an imaginary rival hypothesis that seeks to explain Uranus's orbit by positing a dozen planets, where each of the planets has a greater mass than Leverrier and Adams take Neptune to have (Schlesinger 1963, 24). These planets are taken to be so located that they partly cancel out each other's gravitational influence on Uranus, although their combined influence produces the observed anomalous movements of Uranus. This "many planets" theory is qualitatively simple: it posits only things of a type already admitted as basic by astronomy. But it is quantitatively less simple than Leverrier and Adam's theory. (For a similar example, see the discussion of neutrino theory in Baker [2003, 245–46].)

Differences in qualitative simplicity between two hypotheses match differences in their ideological simplicity. A hypothesis posits a new basic type of thing K if and only if the hypothesis introduces a primitive predicate "κ." The left-to-right reading of this biconditional seems uncontroversial: a hypothesis posits a new basic type K only if it introduces a primitive term to describe its new posit. The right-to-left hand reading of the biconditional is controversial. This is the reading that says that a hypothesis introduces a primitive predicate "κ" only if it posits a new basic type of thing K. An alleged counter-example is provided by non-sortal terms such as "red" and "hot" (see Weintraub 1997, 115). Unlike a sortal term such as "frog" or "toaster," a non-sortal term does not provide a principle for individuating and counting the things that it applies to. For example, we cannot sensibly ask whether one given thing is the same hot as another given thing.

Nevertheless, non-sortal terms do not provide a counter-example. A hypothesis introduces a non-sortal primitive predicate "κ" if and only if it posits a basic type of thing K such that "κ" applies to all and only things of that type. By introducing "hot" as one of its primitive predicates, a hypothesis would be positing a basic type of thing — the hot things. It is irrelevant that the predicate does not also provide a way of individuating and counting things of that type.

ANTI-QUANTITATIVE AND ANTI-SUPERFLUOUS SIMPLICITY
Ontological simplicity can be further distinguished in terms of anti-quantity and anti-superfluity (Barnes 2000). The anti-quantity principle

tells us to posit as few hypotheses as possible to explain phenomena. The anti-superfluity principle tells us not to posit hypotheses not needed for explaining data. Here is an illustration of this distinction.

Suppose that rival theories T_1 and T_2 each fit the available data equally well, but T_1 contains more hypotheses than T_2. Then the anti-quantity principle says that T_1 is less simple than T_2. Nevertheless, every hypothesis in T_1 may be required for T_1 to explain the data, whereas T_2 contains some hypothesis that it does not need to explain the data. Then the anti-superfluity principle says that T_2 is less simple than T_1. To return to the Uranus example, Leverrier and Adams's theory consists of a single hypothesis — the Neptune hypothesis. The many planets theory consists of a dozen hypotheses, with each of the hypotheses describing the mass and path through space and time of one of the planets posited. The anti-quantity principle says that the Neptune theory is simpler than the many planets theory. Nevertheless, none of the twelve hypotheses in the many planets theory is redundant for explaining the observed movement of Uranus. They are all needed for the theory to provide the explanation. So the anti-superfluity principle does not say that the Neptune theory is simpler than the many planets theory.

When there is evidence against a theory, one bad way of trying to save the theory is by modifying it just in such a way that the evidence no longer tells against the theory. This is known as an *ad hoc* modification of the theory. It is a bad way of modifying the theory because there is no independent reason to modify the theory other than to protect it against the evidence. Counter-evidence is a legitimate reason for modifying a theory only if the modification would lead the theory to make predictions that it did not previously make. If these new predictions are successful, they provide reasons to accept the theory that it did not previously have. Whenever a theory is *ad hoc*, it is vulnerable to the anti-quantity principle. Suppose that a theory T_1 faces some counter-evidence. A new hypothesis is added to T_1 to make the theory consistent with the data. But if there is a rival theory T_2 that is consistent with the data, and that consists in fewer hypotheses than the modified version of T_1, the anti-quantity principle will select T_2 over T_1.

ABSOLUTE AND HYPOTHESIS-RELATIVE SIMPLICITY
Simplicity may be absolute or hypothesis-relative. We can see this with both the anti-quantity and anti-superfluity principles. Consider the anti-quantity principle. Suppose that H_1 and H_2 are rival hypotheses each of which would explain the same phenomena. The anti-quantity principle tells us to posit as few hypotheses as possible to explain phenomena. So, relative to each hypothesis, the rival hypothesis should not be accepted.

In that sense simplicity can be hypothesis-relative. Simplicity can be absolute in the sense that, given established background beliefs, a given hypothesis should not be accepted because it need not be accepted. This absolute sense of simplicity can be understood as a special case of hypothesis-relative simplicity, where the established background beliefs are well-confirmed hypotheses.

Explanatory superfluity can also be hypothesis-relative or absolute. Suppose that H_1 and H_2 are rival hypotheses that would explain the same data. Relative to each hypothesis, the other hypothesis is explanatorily superfluous. Consequently, every hypothesis is relatively superfluous if there is a competitor hypothesis. In this sense superfluity can be hypothesis-relative. Superfluity can instead be absolute in the sense that, given established background beliefs, a given hypothesis is superfluous for explaining certain data.

Having established different kinds of simplicity, there is a question about how we should consider a hypothesis that is less simple than one that fits the data equally well. We can distinguish between what we might call "atheistic" and "agnostic" construals (Sober 1981, 145–46).

On the atheistic construal, if there is no reason to believe that there are Ks, simplicity provides reason to believe that Ks do not exist. On the agnostic construal, simplicity provides reason to suspend judgement about whether Ks exist. (Sober argues for the atheistic construal on the basis of some scientific examples.) These treatments need not apply only to principles of ontological simplicity. Suppose that hypotheses H_1 and H_2 otherwise share the same primitive terms except that H_2 uses in addition the primitive term "K." Then H_1 is ideologically simpler than H_2. There is no reason to believe that there are Ks if and only if there is no reason to believe that the term "K" applies to anything. So if there is no reason to believe that "K" does apply to anything, ideological simplicity provides reason to believe that Ks do not exist (on the atheistic treatment) or reason to suspend judgement about whether Ks exist (on the agnostic treatment).

To sum up, simplicity is marked by the following distinctions. First, there is a distinction between ontological and ideological simplicity. The ideological simplicity of a hypothesis concerns the number of terms it takes as primitive. The ontological simplicity of a hypothesis concerns how simple it takes the world to be. Ontological simplicity can itself be understood in terms of a battery of distinctions. There is a distinction between qualitative simplicity — the number of basic kinds a hypothesis posits — and quantitative simplicity — the number of instances the hypothesis posits for each of those basic kinds. There is a distinction between anti-quantitative simplicity — positing as few hypotheses as possible — and anti-superfluous simplicity — positing only hypotheses that do explanatory work. (This looks ahead to chapter 5.) Finally, there is a distinction between hypothesis-relative simplicity — what is simple by the lights of a certain hypothesis — and what is simple in an absolute respect — what is simple against a background of well-established beliefs.

3. Is Simplicity a Theoretical Virtue?

(Q2) asked whether simplicity is a good feature (a "theoretical virtue") of scientific or philosophical hypotheses. Since we have distinguished different kinds of simplicity, (Q2) can be taken as asking which (if any) of them are significant features of hypotheses. Even if simplicity is a significant feature of scientific hypotheses, we cannot automatically assume that it is also a significant feature of philosophical hypotheses. For one thing judgements of simplicity in science are highly context-dependent:

> The most reasonable way to look at simplicity, I think, is to regard it as a highly relevant characteristic, but one whose applicability varies from one scientific context to another. Specialists in any given branch of science make judgements about the degree of simplicity or complexity that is appropriate to the context at hand, and they do so on the basis of extensive experience in that particular area of scientific investigation. Since there is no precise measure of simplicity as applied to scientific hypotheses and theories, scientists must use their judgement concerning the degree of simplicity that is desirable in the given context. The kind of judgement to which I refer is not spooky; it is the kind of judgement that arises on the basis of training and experience. This experience is far too rich to be the sort of thing that can be spelled out explicitly. (Salmon 1990, 563)

Salmon's point is that the use of simplicity considerations in science depends on highly specific features of the situation in question. Remove these features and you remove the basis for applying those considerations.

Furthermore, Sober argues that there are grounds for distinguishing between the comparative simplicity of scientific hypotheses that make conflicting predictions, but that these grounds do not extend to hypotheses that match in their predictions. Since philosophical hypotheses typically do not make predictions, it is trivially the case that they match in their predictions. Sober's argument entails that there are no grounds for applying simplicity considerations to these hypotheses (see Sober 1990; 1996; Forster and Sober 2004; and Vahid 2001, §3).

We will consider two areas where considerations of simplicity have been applied to philosophical hypotheses. The first is the philosophy of mind. The issue here is whether Ockham's Razor supports the **mind-brain identity theory** (§4). The second area is modality. The issue here is whether Ockham's Razor tells against David Lewis's **modal realism**: the view that other possible worlds exist and are things of the same kind as the actual world (§5).

4. Case Study: The Mind-Brain Identity Theory

The mind-brain identity theory was notably defended by J.J.C. Smart (1959, 1984). Smart's chief argument for the theory appealed to Ockham's Razor. More recently, Smart's theory and his argument have both been defended by Christopher Hill (1991, 35–40). We will consider the theory itself, and then evaluate Smart's argument from Ockham's Razor.

The mind-brain identity theory is a physicalist theory. It claims that the mind is identical to the physical brain. More fully, the theory is that every mental property (or type) is identical to some physical property. Having a pain, or thinking that Vienna is a capital city, or wanting a drink from the fridge are each mental properties, and different people, or the same person at different times, can have the same mental property. The identity theory claims that a person's having a certain mental property is identical to that person's having a certain physical property — a physical property of their central nervous system. (In fact, Smart never originally intended to claim that *all* mental properties are identical with physical properties, although that is the theory that many philosophers have attributed to him.) Although the theory that mental properties are identical to physical properties of the brain is a philosophical theory, the theory further claims that it is for science to discover just which physical properties are identical to which mental properties. The theory is presented as a **contingent truth** about mental properties, as opposed to a necessary truth about them. It is also taken to be a theory that needs to be supported by empirical evidence. The identity theory is opposed to dualism, the theory that mental and physical properties are fundamental and distinct properties.

The argument from Ockham's Razor for the identity theory runs as follows. There is inductive evidence for the claim that instances of each mental property are correlated one-to-one with instances of some physical property. So, for instance, there is inductive evidence that any person has severe pain (a certain mental property) when and only when that person has a certain physical property of the brain. On this much, dualists and physicalists can agree: instances of each mental property are correlated one-to-one with instances of some physical property. For the dualist this correlation will be a brute fact. But whereas the dualist posits both mental properties and physical properties as fundamental properties, the identity theorist posits only physical properties as fundamental properties. Recall that one formulation of Ockham's Razor says that if hypothesis H_1 is simpler than hypothesis H_2, then, other things being equal, H_1 is a better hypothesis than H_2, and we should accept H_1 rather than H_2. In particular, other things being equal, we should prefer the hypothesis that posits fewer coincidences — fewer brute facts — than its rival (Maudlin 2007, 179–80). Therefore, the identity theory is a better theory than dualism, and we should accept the former theory. Schematically, the argument runs:

(P1) *Correlation*: for every mental property M, there is some physical property P such that instances of M are correlated 1-1 with instances of P.

(P2) *Simplicity*: other things being equal, taking M to be identical to P is simpler than taking M to be non-identical to P.

(C) ∴ *Identity theory*: So M is identical to P.

Premise (P1) has been questioned on the ground that creatures of different species can have the same mental property although they differ in their brains' physical properties.[1] Perhaps for humans to have pain is for C-fibres in their brains to fire, for dolphins to feel pain is for D-fibres in their brains to fire, and for octopi to feel pain is for their brains to have yet another physical property again. Mental properties, so the claim goes, are multiply realized by different physical properties.

In response to this, the identity theorist may claim that the identities between mental and physical properties are "restricted." It is not the property of pain that is identical with C-fibres firing. It is the property of pain-in-humans that is identical with C-fibres firing. It is the property of pain-in-dolphins that is identical with D-fibres firing. And so on. In each case a (restricted) mental property is identified with some physical property (Jackson and Braddon-Mitchell 1996, 99–100).

Even if dualists grant that there is a one-to-one correlation between instances of every mental property and instances of some physical property, typically they will challenge the application of Ockham's Razor to

---

1 See, for example, Mucciolo (1974).

this correlation. They will raise the issue of how a mental property could be identical with a physical property. They will claim that there is an "explanatory gap" between whatever physical properties a creature has and whatever mental properties it has, and that this gap excludes the identification of mental properties with physical properties (Chalmers 1996, 169). Dualists have two ways of making the case for this explanatory gap. First, many mental properties have intentionality: they purport to represent how the world is. Although some physical things represent, such as signposts and words on a page, their representational powers are derived from our use of them. The representational powers of mental states, by contrast, are intrinsic. To think of Alberta, or to wish for a sunny day, is to represent certain objects or situations. These states do not have these representational powers because we use them in certain ways, much as we use a signpost or a diary. Dualists conclude that this difference in kind between representational mental properties and physical properties rules out their being identical. Second, many mental properties have an experiential "raw feel": there is something it is like to have an itch, or to feel scared, or to have an orange after-image. These mental properties have distinctive experiential qualities ("qualia"). No physical property has such an experiential quality. A simple thought-experiment tells us as much: we can imagine a race of beings who are physically indistinguishable from us and who behave as we do, but who have no inner mental life and no experiences. In that sense, they are "zombies." (This thought experiment was outlined in chapter 3, §2.) Dualists conclude that this difference in kind between experiential mental properties and physical properties rules out their being identical.

It may be that the identity theory can solve these and any other problems facing it. We will not pursue the issue further here. (Rey [1997, chapter 2] discusses what he calls such "temptations to dualism.") The key point is that until there is general agreement that the theory can solve these problems, it would be unwarranted to use Ockham's Razor to argue for the identity theory. Smart would agree (1966, 381):

> ... if the view that experiences just are brain processes can be defended against a priori objections it should be preferred, as against dualism, as a more simple, elegant, and economical hypothesis.

The above response by dualists to Smart's argument from Ockham's Razor is representative of the response that many philosophers have when objections from Ockham's Razor are made against their theories. The response is to deny that other things are equal between the rival hypotheses. Moreover, if the only reason for selecting hypothesis H_1 as opposed to H_2 is that H_1 is simpler than H_2, the defender of H_1 would be conceding that in all other respects H_2 is a good hypothesis. That would be a substantive concession, and perhaps one that the defender of H_1 should review. For example, the identity theory of mind is a physicalist theory of mind. That theory then coheres better with a physicalist theory of (say) life than does dualism and that seems to be a further good feature of the identity theory.

(Q2) asked whether simplicity is a good feature of a philosophical or scientific hypothesis. The present section has not given a direct answer to that question, but two relevant points have emerged. First, faced with the charge that a hypothesis is not simple, a defender of the hypothesis can be expected to claim that other things are not equal and that the charge is unwarranted. Second, where a hypothesis is a simple one, we should expect it to have other good features not shared by its rivals.

5. Case Study: Modal Realism

Modality (or, more accurately, *alethic* modality) is concerned with what is possibly true (or possibly false) and what is necessarily true (or necessarily false). Al Gore lost the 2000 US presidential election. But the course of US political history could have taken a different turn. If various political and social factors had been different, Gore would have won the election. In that sense, it is possible that Gore won the 2000 US presidential election. This can be expressed as follows: in a possible world Gore won the 2000 US presidential election. By contrast, Al Gore must either have won the 2000 US presidential election or have not won the election. In that sense, it is necessary that either Gore won the 2000 US presidential election or Gore did not win the 2000 US presidential election. We might put this by saying: in every possible world Gore won the 2000 US presidential election or Gore did not win the 2000 US presidential election. But how should this talk of things in possible worlds be further understood?

David Lewis's thesis of modal realism is a thesis about the nature of modality and about what exists (Lewis 1973, ch. 4 and 1986, ch. 1). The thesis says that there exists an infinite number of spatio-temporal universes in addition to our own universe. More fully, according to Lewis's thesis, (1) modal claims are to be understood as claims about possible worlds, (2) a possible world is a thing of the same kind as the actual world, and (3) other possible worlds besides the actual world exist.

Claim (1) says that modal claims — claims about what is possible or about what is necessary — are to be understood as claims about what is true at some possible world or worlds. In particular, it is possible that *p* if and only if the proposition that p is true at some world, and it is necessary that p if and only if the proposition that p is true at all worlds. So, for example, it is possible that swans are three-legged if and only if the proposition that swans are three-legged is true in some world, and it is necessary that swans are birds if and only if the proposition that swans are birds is true in all worlds.

Claim (2) is a claim about what possible worlds are. Our universe is a possible world, where our universe is the largest connected spatio-temporal system of objects that includes us. Every other possible world is also a spatio-temporal system of concrete objects (or at least a system of objects in something like spatio-temporal relations). On Lewis's theory, no world is spatio-temporally connected to any other world, and no object exists in more than one world.

Claim (3) says a plurality of possible worlds exist. According to modal realism, there are at least as many worlds as are formed by the principle of recombination. This principle says that, for any collection of objects from any number of worlds, there is a world populated by any number of duplicates of those objects (providing that there is a space-time large enough to contain them). The world we call "the actual world" is the world in which we exist.

Because of claims (2) and (3), modal realism seems to be an extremely non-simple hypothesis. For every proposition that is possibly true, there exists some world at which that proposition is true. So for every existential proposition that is possibly true, there exists some world at which that proposition is true. For example, although Martians and the Yeti do not exist in the actual world, the existential propositions that Martians exist and that the Yeti exists are each possibly true. So, according to modal realism, there exist worlds in which each of these propositions is true. Since these worlds exist, what inhabits them exists as well. A world in which it is true that Martians exist is a world in which Martians exist. Similarly, a world at which it is true that the Yeti exists is a world in which the Yeti exists. So Martians and the Yeti exist. In general, if the proposition that Ks exist is possibly true, then, according to modal realism, there is a world in which Ks exist, and that is to say that Ks exist. Modal realism is thereby committed to the existence of Ks.

Lewis has a reply to this concern about simplicity and modal realism. Recall the distinction between qualitative and quantitative simplicity. Lewis concedes that modal realism is quantitatively non-simple because it is committed to the existence of a plurality of possible worlds. But he denies that modal realism is qualitatively non-simple. His reason is that modal realism is not committed to the existence of many different types of thing. Lewis argues as follows. You admit the existence of the actual world. That is an instance of a type of thing. The type of thing in question is the type *possible world*. That is the only type whose existence modal realism is committed to. So modal realism is as qualitatively simple as your view that the actual world exists. Modal realism is committed to the existence of a plurality of possible worlds. That is a commitment to the existence of a plurality of instances of one type of thing, namely the type *possible world*. Lewis further claims that, of the two kinds of ontological simplicity, only qualitative simplicity is theoretically important. It follows that the quantitative non-simplicity of modal realism is not theoretically significant. As Lewis puts it:

> I subscribe to the general view that qualitative parsimony is good in a philosophical or empirical hypothesis; but I recognize no presumption whatever in favour of quantitative parsimony. My realism about possible worlds is merely quantitatively, not qualitatively, unparsimonious. You believe in the actual world already. I ask you to believe in more things of that kind, not in things of some new kind. (Lewis 1973, 87)

There is reason, however, to query Lewis's assumption that qualitative simplicity is theoretically significant whereas quantitative simplicity is not. Qualitative simplicity can be understood in terms of quantitative simplicity. Each type of thing is itself an instance of a higher-order type. It is an instance of the following type: *a type of thing*. If hypothesis H_1 posits more types than hypothesis H_2, then H_1 posits more instances of this higher-order type than H_2 does. That is, qualitative simplicity is a species of quantitative simplicity. So the claim that qualitative simplicity is theoretically significant whereas quantitative simplicity is not, is untenable. To accommodate this line of argument, Lewis's assumption might then be restated as the claim that the only kind of quantitative simplicity that is theoretically significant is that of qualitative simplicity. But the restated view seems less obvious than Lewis's originally stated assumption. If qualitative simplicity and quantitative simplicity are distinct considerations, then there is some plausibility to the view that only one of them is an important consideration in hypothesis selection. But if they are not distinct considerations, and are related as species and genera, then that view seems less plausible.

That aside, modal realism seems to be qualitatively complex. It is committed to the claim that, for every possible type of thing, there exist things of that type. For instance, green dragons form a possible type of thing, and so do talking donkeys. Modal realism is committed to the claim that there exist things of each of these types. In general, it is committed to the claim that there exist things of every type that there could possibly be (Melia 1992).[2]

Note that whereas Lewis took the relevant type of thing to be a world, the objection is much more liberal about what counts as a type. It takes any class of thing to form a type. Lewis might defend his classification by claiming that a hypothesis's qualitative simplicity is measured by the number of types it takes as basic. According to modal realism, a world is a basic type of thing, whereas such types as green dragons or talking donkeys are not. They are types of thing formed out of space-time regions of worlds. In that sense, they are derivative, not basic, types.

Let's review the issue. Lewis's modal realism says there are worlds other than the actual world. That view seems to be qualitatively complex. Lewis denies this. He says that everyone agrees that at least one possible world exists (namely, the actual world), and he believes merely that there exist more things of the same type. Here Lewis tries to meet the criticism that his theory is qualitatively complex by telling us that the relevant type with which to assess his theory is the type *possible world*. This is a crucial claim. It suggests a general procedure for defending any philosophical theory against the charge of being qualitatively complex.

Consider again the debate between dualism and physicalism. Dualism admits two fundamental types of thing, physical objects and minds, whereas physicalism admits only one fundamental kind of thing, physical objects. So dualism seems to be qualitatively complex. But, following Lewis's example, the dualist can reply to this criticism as follows: "You, the physicalist, admit that at least some substances exist (namely, physical substances). I merely admit more things of the same type."

The general procedure suggested by Lewis amounts to a "get-out-of-jail-free" card. Suppose a given philosophical theory T is criticized for being qualitatively complex, because T posits both As and Bs whereas a rival theory T^* posits only As. Now there is a general way of characterizing both As and Bs. If need be, they can simply be characterized as both belonging to the type *being either an A or a B*. On this characterization, T is not more qualitatively complex than its rival T^*. Each theory posits things of only one type, the type *being either an A or a B*. The difference between the two theories is then not qualitative, but only quantitative. T posits only more instances of that single type than its rival T^* does.

If correct, this general procedure would show that no theory is more qualitatively complex than its rivals. Presumably, Lewis would have found this an unwelcome consequence, but that suggests that there is

---

2   For other uses of Ockham's Razor against modal realism, see Forrest (1982), (2001), and Divers (1994).

something wrong with the general procedure. To block this consequence, we might introduce the following methodological principle. When a pair of theories disagree about what there is, we should frame the disagreement between them in terms of a disagreement about what types of thing there are. Dualism and physicalism disagree about what there is. So we should frame the disagreement between them in terms of what types each of them posits. Here is how the disagreement should then be framed: dualism posits two fundamental types, whereas physicalism posits just one fundamental type. Dualism thereby counts as a qualitatively more complex theory than physicalism. Actualism and modal realism also disagree about what there is. So we should frame the disagreement between them in terms of what types each of them posits. One way of framing the disagreement between them is that modal realism posits things of two types, *actual things* and *non-actual things*, whereas actualism posits things of only one type, *actual things*. Modal realism thereby counts as a qualitatively more complex theory.

Lewis says the term "actual" is an indexical like the word "here" (Lewis 1986, 92–96). Wherever you are, your use of "here" picks out your location. Similarly, whichever world someone is at, their use of "actual" picks out the world they are at. For any world w, relative to w, w is actual. We need not argue with this. Lewis's view that "actual" is indexical means that which world is actual and which worlds are non-actual is world-relative. Nevertheless, this still leaves modal realism with things of two types, *actual things* and *non-actual things*. It is just that which things belong to which type is relative to a world. The actualist does not posit things of both kinds relative to a world. Nor does the actualist posit things of both kinds in a respect that is not relative to a world. Actualism still comes out as a qualitatively more simple theory.

There may be other ways of framing the disagreement between modal realism and actualism in terms of the types that they posit. As we have seen, Melia (1992) suggests another such way. But, on every one of these other ways of framing the disagreement, modal realism will emerge as a qualitatively more complex theory than actualism.

Notice too that any quantitative difference between what theories posit can be re-formulated as a qualitative difference between them. For example, suppose that theory T_1 posits 20 instances of type A, whereas theory T_2 claims that there are 30. There will always be some differences between any two items in type A, and those differences can be reframed as a difference of type. For instance, suppose that none of the As posited by T_1 have some certain feature, but that 10 of the As posited by T_2 have that feature. We can then classify As in terms of this feature. Call all and only As that have that feature, Bs. So the quantitative difference between the theories can be recast in terms of T_1 claiming that there are 20 As but no Bs, and T_2 claiming that there are 20 As and 10 Bs. It follows that, because T_1 is quantitatively more simple than T_2, T_1 is also qualitatively more simple than T_2. One consequence of this point is that Lewis is mistaken in claiming that quantitative differences between what theories posit are irrelevant whereas qualitative differences between them are relevant.

Still, even if the objection from qualitative simplicity has force against modal realism, how much force it has depends upon the standing of rival hypotheses. These rivals differ in their positive accounts of modality, but they agree that modal truths are not truths about Lewisian worlds, spatio-temporal universes distinct from the actual world. They agree that the only world is the actual world. Hence these rival hypotheses are called "actualist." Lewis thinks that modal realism has the benefits of account-ing for a wealth of sentences — sentences about possible and necessary truth, counterfactuals, sentences about propositions, properties, super-venience, causation and approximate truth — in terms of sentences about possible worlds, and that understanding possible worlds as Lewisian worlds reduces all modal truths to non-modal truths (Lewis 1986, ch. 1). In contrast, Lewis argues, actualist hypotheses either cannot account for the same range of sentences or they fail to reduce all modal truths to non-modal truths (Lewis 1986, ch. 3). Lewis thinks that these failings make modal realism superior to actualist hypotheses. This superiority is so marked that, even if modal realism is qualitatively complex in com-parison to the actualist hypotheses, it is still a better hypothesis than its rivals. If this is correct, the argument from Ockham's Razor fails against modal realism.

This last point offers another illustration of how an objection from Ockham's Razor against a given theory can be countered by the reply that other things are not equal. In the case of modal realism, Lewis in effect replies that the actualist rival theories to modal realism are explanatorily inferior to it, so the alleged greater simplicity of these actualist theories as compared with modal realism is not a reason to reject modal realism. The case of modal realism also illustrates how objections from qualitative simplicity crucially turn on what the relevant types of thing are taken to be, and that this is often open to debate. Philosophers may disagree about whether hypothesis H_1 is qualitatively simpler than H_2 because they dis-agree about what the relevant types of thing are in terms of which these hypotheses should be compared.[3]

---

3   For an assessment of the role of Ockham's Razor in the debate on whether mathematical objects exist, see Burgess and Rosen (1997, 214–25), Burgess (1998), and Dieterle (2001, §1).

6. Why Be Simple?

(Q3) asks why we should take the simplicity of a hypothesis to be a good thing. Furthermore, since the simplicity of a hypothesis is often taken to be a reason for believing that hypothesis, (Q3) asks what justification there is for that attitude. The worst case scenario is that simplicity is not a significant feature of a hypothesis, and that it provides no basis for accepting a hypothesis.[4] John P. Burgess has dismissed Ockham's Razor as an example of "medieval superstition" (Burgess 1983, 99).[5] He appears to have in mind here an anti-quantity principle of simplicity. In a later paper, he considers whether Ockham's Razor is a rule of scientific method (Burgess 1998, 197). He concludes that in science "purely gratuitous assumptions of *whatever* category [i.e., ontology or ideology] are to be avoided" (Burgess 1998, 211, his italics). He appears to have in mind here an anti-superfluity principle. But it is not clear why he has contrasting attitudes to the anti-quantity and anti-superfluity principles. Furthermore, principles of simplicity should be dismissed only if they lack justification. Whether they lack it or not needs to be argued for.

It is questionable whether such principles can be justified on the ground that nature itself is simple. For example, ancient Greek science posited exactly four elements (earth, air, water and fire) whereas the modern periodic table posits more than 100 elements (Hales 1997, 357). In this respect, modern science takes nature to be less simple than ancient Greek science did, and so it takes nature to be less simple than nature conceivably could be. (More radically still, the theories of Thales and Anaximenes each posited only one element, water and air respectively.)

Simplicity is not an end in itself. It is presumably a means to something else. But what would this be? The justification for appeals to ideological simplicity partly consists in the practical advantages that it confers. The more elegant a hypothesis is, the more perspicuous it is, and the easier it is to use it. More importantly, as was claimed in §2, since the ideological simplicity of a hypothesis matches its qualitative simplicity, whatever justification attaches to the principle of qualitative simplicity will also attach to the principle of ideological simplicity.

Does ontological simplicity matter in science or philosophy? A sceptic might challenge the appeal to ontological simplicity in the following way: "Of all the examples given here, the most persuasive appeal to the Razor was given in the example of Uranus. But if that is the best case that can be

---

4   Newton-Smith (1981, 231) and Brown (1991, 78) think that simplicity has no evidential bearing on scientific hypotheses. See Swinburne (2001, 99–102) for a reply. Hales (1997) and Huemer (2008) argue that simplicity has no evidential bearing on philosophical hypotheses.

5   See also Gunner (1967, 5).

provided for the Razor, and if the best case fails, then the use of the Razor is unwarranted. But the Uranus example *does* fail. To see this, consider a variation of the example. Suppose we know little about the physical layout of the White House. Should we give higher credence to the White House having 70 rooms rather than to its 71? No. Given the state of our knowledge, we should suspend judgement about what the number of the White House's rooms is. Likewise, given Leverrier and Adams's state of knowledge in 1846, they should have suspended judgement about the number of planets putatively affecting Uranus's orbit."

Considerations of ontological simplicity, however, are not a matter of merely preferring one number to some other because the former is smaller. Our earlier example of drawing a line through a series of points shows how simplicity may involve uniformity considerations. In the planet case, we consider the class of hypotheses about extra planets that would explain Uranus's orbit. In that class, the hypothesis that the spacing and number of the planets is uniform is simpler, and so more plausible, than any hypothesis that takes the spacing and number of planets not to be uniform. What we already know about the spacing and number of planets, in conjunction with the uniformity hypothesis, tells us that only one planet is affecting Uranus's orbit. Similar considerations do not apply to the White House case, and so here is the disanalogy between the two cases. We already know that the number of rooms in a building differs between buildings, and that buildings we have examined are importantly structurally dissimilar to the White House. So we cannot use considerations of uniformity to infer what the number of rooms in the White House is.

Does quantitative simplicity matter in philosophy? Lewis does not say why he thinks that quantitative simplicity is not a significant feature of a hypothesis. It has been argued against him that it is a significant feature of scientific hypotheses (Nolan 1997). Even so, a Lewisian might concede that quantitative simplicity is a significant feature of scientific hypotheses, but not of philosophical hypotheses. A supporting reason might be as follows.[6] Metaphysics is concerned with the classification of entities into basic types. So metaphysics will be concerned with such questions as: Are there *K*s? Are *K*s ontologically basic? If not, how are *K*s related to things of the basic types? Considerations of qualitative simplicity are relevant to answering these questions. Considerations of quantitative simplicity are not. So considerations of the latter kind are irrelevant to metaphysics. It is for science to discover *a posteriori* how many instances each of these basic types has. So it is for science alone to ask: how many *K*s are there?

---

6   This reason draws on Brock and Mares (2007, 18).

Considerations of quantitative simplicity are relevant to that question, but then they are relevant only to science.

The above line of reasoning is questionable. If considerations of quantitative simplicity were irrelevant to metaphysics, then infinite regress arguments would be irrelevant in metaphysics as well. Consider the KK principle: the principle that if you know that *p*, you know that you know that *p*. According to this principle if Moore knows the proposition *that he has hands*, he also knows the proposition *that he knows that he has hands*. So far the principle may seem plausible to some people. But the principle also entails that if Moore knows the proposition *that he knows that he has hands*, then he knows the proposition *that he knows that he knows that he has hands*. And the KK principle applies once again: if Moore knows the proposition *that he knows that he knows that he has hands*, he knows the proposition *that he knows that he knows that he knows that he has hands*. An infinite regress has been generated. If Moore knows that he has hands, the KK principle entails that he knows infinitely many propositions, each one of increasing complexity. The KK principle is ontologically extravagant since it is committed to Moore knowing infinitely many propositions if he knows any proposition. But this is just to say that the principle's lack of quantitative simplicity counts against it. (See Nolan 2001, esp. 534–36.)

Here in summary form is how the regress is generated:

1. *KK principle*: if someone knows a proposition, that person knows that they know that proposition.
2. If Moore knows that *p*, he know a proposition.
3. So if Moore knows that p, he knows that he knows that *p*. [By (1) and (2)]
4. If Moore knows that he knows that *p*, he knows a proposition.
5. So if Moore knows that he knows that *p*, he knows that he knows that he knows that *p*. [By (1) and (4)]
6. If Moore knows that he knows that he knows that *p*, he knows a proposition.
7. So if Moore knows that he knows that he knows that *p*, then he knows that he knows that he knows that he knows that *p*. [By (1) and (6)]

The lesson of the above paragraph is that considerations of quantitative simplicity are relevant to metaphysics. We can explain why this is so as follows. All parties to the current debate agree that considerations of qualitative simplicity are relevant to metaphysics's attempt to discover what basic types of thing there are. One way of arguing that there is no type of thing K is by arguing that there are no Ks. And one way of arguing that there are no Ks is to present an infinite regress argument against the existence of Ks. The argument shows that if there is one K, then there are infinitely many Ks, although there is no independent reason to believe that there are infinitely many Ks. The quantitative complexity of this consequence is taken to show that there are no Ks.

What justification can be offered for principles of ontological simplicity? Sober (1981, 151) offers the following justification:

> Consider two existence claims, each of which, if true, would explain a particular phenomenon P.... [The] razor demands that a postulate be rejected if it, unlike its competitors, is not needed to explain *anything*; its superfluity in a particular case is not what matters. Thus, where the two existence claims would each explain P, the one to be rejected is the one which is not needed to explain *any other phenomenon*. If only one of the existence claims is thought to be the explanation of other phenomena, the razor bids us conjecture that this claim is also the explanation of P; where the other existence claim is thought to explain no other phenomenon, the razor says that this claim is not the explanation of P either. The razor is thus nothing more than a principle of induction which focuses on existence claims. In Quine's words, it embodies a taste for old mechanisms. When it comes to explaining a new phenomenon, existence claims which already have played an explanatory role are preferable over ones which lack such credentials, even when the new existence claim seems to be quite capable of explaining the novel phenomenon.

Two points should be noted. First, the above passage concerns two distinct factors. One is explanatory: it says that if H_1 and H_2 are rival explanations of phenomenon P, then, other things being equal, we should accept whichever hypothesis has the wider explanatory scope (and reject its rival). The other consideration is a species of epistemic conservatism: this says that if H_1 and H_2 are rival explanations of phenomenon P, then, other things being equal, we should accept whichever hypothesis has already been used in giving explanations (and reject its rival).

The second point is that some applications of simplicity principles are supported neither by considerations of wider explanatory scope nor by conservatism. Consider once more the case of Uranus. The example supposed that the Neptune hypothesis and the many planets hypothesis have equal explanatory scope: they explain only the movements of Uranus. Nevertheless, considerations of simplicity eliminate the many planets hypothesis in favour of the Neptune hypothesis. What we lack is a rationale for these considerations.

It seems that explanatory power and simplicity can conflict. On the face of it, a hypothesis H_1 that posits more types of thing, or more things of some type, can gain in explanatory power what it loses in simplicity as compared with another hypothesis H_2 (Brock and Mares 2007, 178). Likewise, it seems that conservatism and simplicity can conflict. H_3 may be a well-established hypothesis whereas H_4 is not, despite the fact that H_3 is qualitatively and quantitatively less simple than H_4.

In the case of the mind-brain identity theory, considerations of simplicity and of explanatory power seem to work in tandem rather than in opposition. Dualism takes it to be a brute fact that there are certain correlations between mental states and brain states. By not explaining those correlations, it admits a high number of brute correlations. In contrast, the mind-brain identity theory seeks to explain those correlations between mental and brain states in terms of identities between those states. By explaining those correlations, the theory decreases the number of brute correlations it admits.

This case raises the possibility of justifying principles of simplicity in terms of other theoretical virtues. Qualitative and quantitative simplicity might each be justified by appeal to **epistemic conservatism**. We seek to explain as much as we can in terms of types of thing that we already posit. So if H_1 and H_2 are rival hypotheses that would explain the same phenomena, and H_1 alone posits only types of thing that our established background beliefs already posit, then we should accept H_1 rather than H_2. The less simple of the two hypotheses departs furthest from what we already believe, and for that reason should be rejected.

Simplicity tracks conservativeness, however, only in cases where a hypothesis says there are *more* things than we currently believe that there are. Consider a hypothesis that says there are *fewer* things than we currently believe there are. That hypothesis will be simpler but revisionary of what we believe. Here simplicity and conservativeness conflict. So conservativeness cannot provide a general rationale for simplicity.

Qualitative and quantitative simplicity might also be justified by appeal to explanatory power. The above case for the mind-brain identity theory provided an illustration of this. The example of Uranus provides another. Although the Neptune hypothesis and the many planets hypotheses each explain the observed movement of Uranus, it remains an open question whether these hypotheses match in explanatory power. The likelihood of not observing an extra planet if there are twelve extra planets is much lower than the likelihood of not observing an extra planet if there is only a single extra planet. So the fact that we have not observed an extra planet makes the many planets hypothesis more improbable than the Neptune hypothesis. Because of its high improbability, the failure to observe twelve extra planets requires explanation. The Neptune hypothesis helps provide a better explanation of this non-observation than the many planets hypothesis. Its explanation is simply that there are not twelve extra planets in our solar system. This is just a sketch of the idea that quantitatively simple hypotheses provide better explanations than their less simple rivals.[7] The guiding thought is that the less quantitatively simple a hypothesis is, the more puzzling it is if we do not have independent evidence for the extra things posited.

7. Conclusion

Simplicity considerations are prevalent and apparently powerful devices for hypothesis selection. Yet many philosophers think that their use is undermined by the difficulty in giving a justification for them. For instance, despite using the Razor, Hill despairs of justifying it by anything more than "aesthetic intuitions" (Hill 1991, 40).[8] These concerns seem unduly pessimistic. At any rate, simplicity considerations are not worse placed than other non-demonstrative forms of inference and hypothesis selection. There is a general question about how any non-demonstrative principle can be justified (Hume 1739–40, bk. I, pt. III, §§vi–vii). A more pressing concern is that simplicity considerations select between hypotheses only if other things are equal between those hypotheses. We saw that the dualist will claim that mental properties have features (such as intrinsic intentionality or qualia) that no physical property can have, and so that the Razor should not be used to identify mental and physical properties. We also saw that the modal realist will claim that his theory has substantial benefits that all of the rival actualist hypotheses lack, and so that the Razor should not be used to eliminate his posited possible worlds. Given that relatively few pairs of hypotheses are such that all other things are equal between them, this suggests that simplicity considerations are quite restricted in applicability.

---

7   Baker (2003) gives a restricted defence of this claim.
8   See also Walsh (1979), Foley (1993) and White (2005).

Questions for Discussion

1. Imagine that we are in an early stage of astronomy. Suppose that we can observe only one other planet. What causes that planet's particular orbit? Hypothesis H_1 says that there is no god but there are many planets that are not observed and they cause the orbit. Hypothesis H_2 says that there are no other planets, but a god causes the planet's orbit. Which hypothesis is simpler? (This is an example by Yafeng Shan.)

2. Berkeley believes that there exist only minds and ideas. Moore believes that there exist mind, ideas, and physical objects. Moore explains why we have certain ideas in terms of their being caused by physical objects. Berkeley explains why we have those ideas in terms of their being caused by God. Which is the simpler theory?

3. In §2 we distinguished between qualitative and quantitative ontological simplicity. Suppose T_1 and T_2 are rival theories. T_1 posits 2 fundamental kinds of thing and says that there are 10 instances of each of those kinds. T_2 posits 4 fundamental kinds and says that there are 4 instances of each of those kinds. Is one of these theories more ontologically simple? Can we choose between these theories solely on ground of simplicity?

4. In §2 we also distinguished between ontological and ideological simplicity. Suppose T_3 and T_4 are rival theories. T_3 is more ontologically simple than T_4, but it is less ideologically simple than T_4. Is one of these theories overall more simple? Can we choose between these theories solely on ground of simplicity?

5. In §6 we explored whether simplicity can be justified in terms of other theoretical virtues, such as conservativeness and explanatory power. Since simplicity can conflict with each of these other virtues, does it follow that simplicity cannot be justified in terms of any of them or any combination of them?

Core Reading for Chapter 4

Baker, Alan (2003) "Quantitative Parsimony and Explanatory Power."
Barnes, E.C. (2000) "Ockham's Razor and the Anti-Superfluity Principle."
Hill, Christopher S. (1991) *Sensations: A Defense of Type Materialism* pp. 35–40.
Huemer, Michael (2008) "When is Parsimony a Virtue?"
Lewis, David (1973) *Counterfactuals* p. 87.

Smart, J.J.C. (1959) "Sensations and Brain Processes."
Smart, J.J.C. (1984) "Ockham's Razor."
Sober, Elliott (1981) "The Principle of Parsimony."

FIVE Explanation

1. Introduction

Understood informally, a theory is a systematic set of claims. It is second nature for philosophers to talk about philosophical theories — there is Descartes's theory of the mind, Aristotle's theory of the good, Rawls's theory of justice, and there are many others besides. Something that theories do is to attempt to explain some of the phenomena that they are theories of. For example, a theory of evolution attempts to explain why species change and proliferate. A theory of matter seeks to explain why matter behaves as it does under different conditions. And so on. Philosophical theories seem to be in the same business. A theory of the good seeks to explain why people pursue good things. A philosophical theory of the mind seeks to explain how the mind changes, and is changed by, the body. And so on.

There are at least three ways that philosophical theories can be evaluated, each of which is concerned with the issue of explanation.

First, there are arguments for the truth of some philosophical theory on the grounds that it explains certain phenomena. Various arguments for the existence of God are of this sort. Cosmological arguments seek to explain why there is a universe, or of why there are any contingent things, by appeal to God's existence. Similarly, design arguments seek to explain why there is order in nature by appeal to God's existence. In each case there are rival hypotheses and the issue is then to establish which one provides the better explanation.

Second, in the previous chapter we saw that philosophical and other theories are assessed in terms of their simplicity. At the close of the chapter we noted that one possible rationale for choosing the qualitatively simpler of two otherwise matched theories is that it is the more explanatory theory (chapter 4, §6).

Third, the process of reflective equilibrium involves judging data against theory in order to reach a coherent balance between them (chapter 2, §3). This process involves finding the simplest and most comprehensive explanation of the data that theory can provide, even as we evaluate the validity of data by its coherence with a preferred theory. Insofar as reflective equilibrium is an appropriate model of philosophical method, explanatory power has a key role in philosophical theory selection.

The role of explanatory power in theory selection is captured by the following methodological maxim:

> If hypothesis H_1 explains phenomena better than a rival hypothesis H_2, then, other things being equal, we should accept H_1 rather than H_2.

Some terminology is helpful here. In an explanation, the *explanandum* is what is to be explained; the *explanans* is what provides the explanation.

The role of explanatory power as a desirable feature of philosophical theories (a "theoretical virtue") gives rise to some inter-related questions:

(Q1) Do philosophical theories really give explanations?

(Q2) Insofar as a philosophical theory differs from a scientific theory, how can a philosophical theory be genuinely explanatory?

(Q3) What would make a philosophical theory genuinely explanatory?

(Q1) asks whether philosophical theories purport to give explanations. Perhaps this is a correct and useful way of thinking about these theories. Or perhaps it is a misconception about philosophical theories. Scientific theories evidently try to explain things. (In other intellectual climates this was not evident. Some late nineteenth and early twentieth century figures, such as Kirchhoff and Duhem, claimed that science did not attempt to explain anything, and that it merely described observable things [see Duhem 1914, ch. 1].) Since there are some differences between scientific and philosophical theories, (Q2) asks whether these differences prevent philosophical theories from being explanatory. Lastly, assuming that philosophical theories are in the business of giving explanations, (Q3) asks what kind of explanations they give, and what it is about a given philosophical theory that would make it explanatory.

2. Do Philosophical Theories Give Explanations?

The first issue we need to consider is whether there is any reason to link philosophical hypotheses with the role of explanation. In addition to the considerations already canvassed, there are two reasons. One concerns the nature of philosophical problems. The other concerns the link between the problem-solving ability of philosophical theories and explanatory power.

Robert Nozick thought that philosophical problems can be presented as problems about how something is possible, given certain facts (Nozick 1981, 8–11). These problems take the following form:

> Given that r, how is it possible that p rather than that q?

Here are some illustrations of how familiar philosophical problems take this form:

> There is the free will problem: Given that determinism (or: indeterminism) is true, how is it possible that we have free will (rather than lack it)?

> There is the problem of our knowledge of the external world: Given that our sensory experience is consistent with our being brains in vats, how is it possible that we know that there is an external world (rather than not know this)?

> And there is the problem of identity over time: Given that a concrete thing changes, how can it be the very same thing over time (rather than fail to be the same thing over time)?

In the above schema, we want an explanation of how it is possible that p is the case rather than that q is the case. Typically, the proposition that q is simply the negation of the proposition that p. What is then wanted is an explanation of how it is possible that p is the case rather than that not-p is the case. Our explanation is constrained by having to show how this is possible despite its being the case that r. The proposition that r apparently entails that p is false. For example, the proposition that the world is deterministic apparently entails that it is false that we have free will. Our task is then to explain how it is possible that we have free will despite the world's being deterministic. The proposition that r need not be a well-established truth. It might only be a tentative theory or merely something assumed or taken for granted. Whatever the degree of support for r happens to be, the problem is one about mutual consistency: how could the propositions that p and that r both be true? The proposition that r is apparently incompatible with the proposition that p.

Two ways of solving a philosophical problem present themselves. We may provide the needed explanation by showing that the propositions that p and that r are compatible, or by showing that, although they are incompatible, the proposition that r is false. A philosophical debate may then consist in one party seeking to show that r entails that not-p, whereas a rival party seeks to show that p and r are compatible, and so that r does not entail that not-p. (Other views about the debate are possible. For example, someone might question whether there are such propositions as the proposition that p or the proposition that r, and whether the sentences that appear to express these propositions are intelligible.)

There is currently a tendency among some philosophers to talk of a philosophical problem as consisting of various sentences or propositions being in "tension" with one another. Beware: "tension" is a weasel word. Either it means that the sentences are (apparently) mutually logically incompatible or mutually highly improbable, in which case those philosophers should simply say that, or it is obscure what is being meant, in which case there is no reason why we should think that a problem has been stated.

In chapter 1, §6 we discussed G.E. Moore's so-called proof of an external world and found it unsatisfactory. Moore's argument is apparently question-begging. Another unsatisfactory feature of his argument is that even if Moore had proved that there is an external world, and shown that he knew that there was one, he would not thereby have solved the problem of the external world. The problem does not consist only in the problem of showing that there is an external world or only in the problem of showing that someone knows that there is an external world. The problem consists in showing how anyone can know that there is an external world, given that all of our sensory experiences are consistent with our not perceiving an external world (Vogel 1993, 242). In one sceptical scenario we have the same flow of sensory experiences as we actually have, but we are brains in vats in the control of a mad scientist. In that scenario we do not have sensory experience of an external world. Moore does nothing to solve this problem. Proving that p is true does not thereby explain how it is possible that p is true given that r is true, where p and r are apparently incompatible (Nozick 1981, 10). Take an example from science. A proof (if we could have one) that the same side of the moon always faces the Earth (p) does not explain how it is possible that the same side of the moon faces the Earth, given that (r) the moon rotates on its own axis and orbits the Earth. Likewise, a proof that there is an external world (p) does not explain how it is possible that we know that there is an external world, given that (r) our only evidence that there is one is apparently compatible with our not knowing that there is an external world.

Let's turn to a second reason for linking philosophical hypotheses with the notion of explanation. How do you argue for a philosophical hypothesis? According to Russell, the success of a philosophical theory in solving problems that cannot otherwise be solved counts as evidence for that theory (Russell 1905, 45). Now if a philosophical problem is something that calls for an explanation, a theory that solves that problem thereby answers that call. That is, the theory provides an explanation. So the problem-solving ability of a philosophical hypothesis testifies to its explanatory power. Humphreys (1984, 173) explicitly contrasts philosophical explanations with philosophical puzzle solving. Yet even if puzzle solving is understood only in the sense in which conceptual analysis practises it, conceptual analysis can itself be seen as an exercise in explanation giving. An analysis of a concept would help explain why that concept has the extension that it does.

Some philosophers (chiefly Wittgensteinians and ordinary language philosophers) have denied that philosophy provides explanations. (Wittgenstein wrote that "philosophy really *is* purely descriptive" [1964, 18], that "we must do away with all *explanation*, and description alone must take its place" [1953, §109], and that "if one tried to advance *theses* in philosophy, it would never be possible to question them, because everyone would agree to them" [1953, §128].) This comes as no surprise since those philosophers deny that there are any philosophical problems, and they think that the proper business of philosophy consists in providing humdrum reminders about how words in natural languages are ordinarily used. If there are no philosophical problems, there is nothing to explain and no need to theorize. As always, the best way to evaluate such a metaphilosophical view is to examine in detail its application to particular cases. Take as an example Hume's problem of induction: the problem of showing that our practice of inferring from the observed to the unobserved is reliable. Philosophers of the above stripe have sought to "dissolve" this problem on the ground that it is generated by a failure to understand how terms such as "evidence," "knows," "reasonable" and the like are used in everyday contexts. But such attempted dissolutions of the problem of induction have suffered a heavy critical drubbing (Salmon 1957; Skyrms 1966, ch. 2; and Blackburn 1973, ch. 1). To date, these criticisms have not been met. Unless debunking treatments of such test cases can be made good, there seems no merit in blanket scepticism about the genuineness of philosophical problems and the point of philosophical theorizing. Perhaps some philosophical problems are pseudo-problems, but which problems these are needs to be argued for on a case-by-case basis. It cannot be established by an across-the-board dictate.

Given that philosophical hypotheses purport to offer explanations, what kind of explanations do they offer? There are two routes philosophers might explore. Philosophers might devise explanations that emulate forms of explanation found outside philosophy, and especially in science. Alternatively, they might strike out on their own and produce a form of explanation peculiar to philosophy.

Taking this second route would be understandable. If only philosophy can solve philosophical problems, and those problems are requests for explanations, then perhaps their solutions require a form of explanation peculiar to philosophy. A disadvantage with taking this route is that it leaves philosophers to their own devices in answering such questions as: What would make different philosophical explanations of the same phenomena rival explanations? How should we choose between rivals? What would count as a good or a bad explanation in this sense? Having resolved to devise a novel form of explanation, one peculiar to philosophy, philosophers cannot draw upon the criteria used in forms of explanation found outside philosophy. The status of this alleged form of explanation is left unclear. It will not be obvious that philosophical hypotheses are genuinely explanatory.

An example of this predicament is given by the "two worlds" interpretation of a metaphysical thesis that Kant calls "transcendental idealism" (Strawson 1966). We will not take up the exegetical issue of how accurate or defensible this interpretation is. Our interest here is in its supposed explanatory content. Kant sought to explain how it is possible to have experience of a world of objects in space and time that fall under Newtonian laws of mechanics and gravitation. According to the two worlds interpretation of Kant's metaphysics, there is a world of things-in-themselves ("noumena") including our noumenal selves, and there is a world of things-as-appearances ("phenomena") including our selves as they appear to us. Phenomena are objects in space and time that are acted on by Newtonian laws; noumena are not. We perceive phenomena; we do not perceive noumena. Noumena act on our noumenal selves to produce a phenomenal world. This last claim contains the crucial explanatory claim in the two worlds interpretation. But what kind of explanation does it involve? Noumena do not *causally* act on our noumenal selves to produce the phenomenal world. Kant is explicit that causal relations hold among only phenomenal objects. It is then utterly mysterious what these noumenal relations are, and so what kind of explanation, if any, Kant is giving.

Given the difficulties facing the ambitious route of devising a peculiarly philosophical form of explanation, let's turn to the route that emulates forms of explanation found outside philosophy, and particularly in science or mathematics. By taking this route, we need to address (Q2): Insofar as a philosophical theory differs from a scientific theory, how can a philosophical theory be genuinely explanatory?

3. Differences between Philosophical and Scientific Theories

At one stage in his philosophical career, Russell advocated modelling philosophical explanations on successful forms of scientific explanation (Russell 1918, 96):

> What I wish to bring to your notice is the possibility and importance of applying to philosophical problems certain broad principles of method which have been found successful in the study of scientific questions.

A difficulty facing this approach is that there is no widely agreed view about the nature of scientific explanation. No account of scientific explanation is both completely general and free of difficulties. There is not even agreement about which is the promising account to work on. This need not, however, wreck the approach. Sometimes we can correctly identify some things as Ks and identify other things as non-Ks, even if we cannot say what a K is. For example, people without expert biological knowledge can correctly identify some things as dogs and other things as non-dogs, even if they cannot say what a dog is. (What is the difference between a dog and a wolf? Is a hyena a dog?) Similarly, there is large measure of agreement about certain scientific theories that they are explanatory (or at least they would be explanatory if they were true) and that certain other theories purport to explain but fail to do so (van Fraassen 1989, 31 and Swoyer 1999, 127). Paradigms of explanatory scientific theory include Galileo's theory of the pendulum, Newton's theory of planetary motion, and Maxwell's theory of electromagnetism. An example of a theory that tried to provide an explanation but failed is Aristotle's theory of the shape of what he called "the heavens." He wrote that "The shape of the heavens is of necessity spherical; for that is the shape most appropriate to its substance and also by nature primary" (Aristotle *De Caelo*, bk. II, ch. 4). (There is no agreement about which philosophical theories are explanatory so it would be no good looking in *that* quarter.)

If philosophy is to emulate scientific explanatory practice, we need to consider what kind of objects a philosophical or scientific hypothesis may posit. It may posit objects of two kinds: abstract objects or concrete objects. The distinction between concrete and abstract objects is supposed to be exhaustive (every object is either abstract or concrete) and exclusive (no object is both abstract and concrete). But exactly how (if at all) the distinction between these two kinds of object should be drawn remains controversial. It is enough for our purposes to introduce the distinction by means of some paradigm examples and a somewhat stipulative definition that classifies at least the paradigms correctly. Paradigm examples of abstract objects include Platonic Forms, numbers, pure sets, and propositions. Paradigm examples of concrete objects include cabbages, squirrels, and mountains. Let us define "abstract object" as *an object that is not located in space-time and that does not stand in causal relations to anything*, and "concrete object" as *an object that is located in space-time and that stands in causal relations*. This definition leaves unclear the status of, for example, Lewisian possible worlds (Lewis 1986, 81–86). The inhabitants of such worlds are in space-time and they stand in causal relations to one another. We will stipulate that Lewisian worlds are abstract objects if only because they (and their inhabitants) are not located in actual space-time and they are not causally connected to anything in the actual world. Another issue is that contemporary physics takes seriously the suggestion that space-time is the product of some more fundamental structure (Ladyman and Ross 2007, 23). The definition may need revision in the light of this.

It is tempting to think that the distinction between philosophical and scientific theories corresponds to the distinction between theories that posit concrete objects and those that posit abstract objects. This is not so. First, the philosophical hypothesis that there is an external world posits concrete objects (namely, objects in the external world). Second, Quine claims that the canonical formulation of current scientific theory quantifies over sets, and thereby posit these objects (Quine 1981c, 149–50). Other philosophers dispute whether scientific theories posit such objects. Entering this debate would take us too far afield. For the sake of argument, let's assume that Quine is right. Our task in this section is to compare (1) scientific theories that posit concrete objects (such as electrons, viruses or continental shifts) with (2) philosophical theories that posit concrete objects (such as the external world hypothesis), and also with (3) philosophical theories that posit abstract objects. Theories in class (1) undoubtedly have explanatory power. But how similar to them are the theories in classes (2) or (3)?

Scientific theories explain phenomena by citing laws of nature, yet philosophical theories do not attempt to explain phenomena in that way. Nevertheless, philosophical theories often attempt to explain by citing various general metaphysical principles. These principles include the indiscernibility of identicals (an object picked out one way is the same object as one picked out in another way only if what is picked out in the first way has the same properties as what is picked out in the other way), the necessity of identity (that identical things are necessarily identical), and the supervenience of the mental on the physical (that objects do not differ mentally unless they differ physically). For example, Saul Kripke explains why it is necessary that heat is identical to mean molecular motion by deducing it from the conjunction of the scientific discovery that heat is identical to mean molecular motion with the principle of the necessity of identity (Kripke 1971, 84–85). Although the epistemology and metaphysics of these metaphysical principles may differ in various respects from those of laws of nature, they have a common role in serving as general principles that subsume the phenomena they are invoked to explain. (Humphreys [1984, 174, 179] thinks that there are no analogues in philosophy to laws of nature, and seeks to meet the difficulty another way.)

Scientific theories often explain phenomena by citing their causes, but philosophical theories typically do not attempt to explain by citing causes (Humphreys 1984, 174). David Armstrong has tried to exploit this consideration (Armstrong 1978, 130):

> A spatio-temporal realm of particulars certainly exists (it includes our bodies). Whether anything else exists is controversial. If any entities outside this realm are postulated, but it is stipulated further that they have no manner of causal action upon the particulars in this realm, then there is no compelling reason to postulate them. [Ockham's] Razor then enjoins us not to postulate them.

Armstrong is arguing that we should not accept hypotheses that posit abstract objects (in the sense defined above). He argues as follows: (1) Unlike concrete objects such as cabbages and electrons, abstract objects such as Platonic Forms, numbers, and propositions (if they exist) would not exist in space and time. (2) Objects are causally related only if they are in space and time. (3) So, even if abstract objects exist, they would not make a causal difference to concrete objects: "... they do not *bring about* anything in the realm of Nature in the way that genes and electrons do" (Armstrong 1978, 131, his italics). (4) So, even if abstract objects exist, they would not help causally explain the behaviour of any concrete objects.

(5) So there is no reason to believe that abstract objects exist. (6) So, by the atheistic construal of Ockham's Razor, there is reason to believe that no abstract objects exist. (For this construal, see chapter 4, §2.) A corollary of this argument is that philosophical hypotheses that posit abstract objects are not explanatory and should be rejected.

The following thought experiment is often deployed to support premise (2). Consider the question: Do numbers exist? To answer this question, we might first think about what kind of thing numbers would be if they existed. Well, if numbers exist, you would not expect to find them under your kitchen table or down a mineshaft or somewhere in deep space. You would not expect them to be located anywhere, even across some scattered region of space. Similarly, you would not expect numbers to have come into existence at a particular time — say, at noon on 4 June 1564. More generally, if numbers exist, they would not be located anywhere in space or time. What difference would the existence of numbers, or their non-existence, make to the behaviour of any object in the concrete world? Since numbers are not in space or time, they would not affect any cabbage or electron. More generally, even if numbers were to exist, they would not exert a causal influence on any concrete object, including our measuring devices and our sense organs. But then it is difficult to see what explanatory work numbers could do, even if they existed. Numbers would be explanatorily idle entities, and positing them would be explanatorily superfluous (Armstrong 1978, 128–29).[1]

A crucial step in Armstrong's argument is the step from (3) to (4): from the existence of numbers not being causally explanatory to there being no reason to believe that numbers exist. This step apparently assumes that the only form of explanation is causal. But not every scientific explanation is causal: science also explains phenomena in geometrical terms or by non-causal statistical principles such as regression to the mean. Here is an example. Throw a bunch of sticks in the air, and take a snapshot of the sticks as they fall. In the snapshot, more of the sticks will be near the horizontal axis than the vertical axis. Why is this? There is a simple non-causal explanation of this phenomenon: there are two horizontal axes and only one vertical axis.[2] So science itself uses forms of explanation other than causal ones, and it is not valid to infer from an object's being causally idle to its being explanatorily idle. So philosophers who posit abstract objects can admit that those objects are causally idle

---

1   Van Fraassen (1975, 39) gives this thought experiment an added twist.
2   See Lipton (2004, 31–32) for this and other examples of non-causal explanations. Colyvan (2001, 47–51) offers yet more.

but still claim that they have an explanatory role without thereby radically departing from scientific practice.[3]

Furthermore, some philosophical hypotheses posit causally active objects. The hypothesis that there is an external world has been put forward as a causal explanation of our experiences (Armstrong 1978, 131–32). The hypothesis that there are other minds has been put forward as a causal explanation of the behaviour of other human beings. And the hypothesis that God exists has been put forward as a causal explanation of the order found in nature.

These rejoinders leave two issues open. First, are any non-causal philosophical hypotheses good explanations? These include hypotheses that posit only abstract objects. These hypotheses were the target of Armstrong's argument. We have criticized that argument, but can any positive case be made for claiming that such hypotheses are explanatory? We will consider two answers: an appeal to theoretical unification (§4) and an appeal to inference to the best explanation (§5). We will then consider as a case study the mind-brain identity theory as providing non-causal explanation of correlations between mental and physical properties.

The second issue left open is whether any causal philosophical hypotheses are good explanations. In §7 we will consider as a case study whether the external world hypothesis is a good explanation of the flow of our experiences.

4. Theoretical Unification and Philosophical Explanation

Some philosophers suggest that a scientific explanation consists in a theory's describing a variety of apparently diverse and independent types of phenomena using the same small set of terms. This enables many apparently independent types to be reduced in number. By unifying these types of phenomena, the theory thereby explains them (Friedman 1981). For example, prior to Newtonian mechanics, the behaviour of planets, tides, terrestrial projectiles and celestial bodies seemed to be independent types of phenomena, each requiring their own explanation (if they had an explanation at all). Newtonian mechanics describes the behaviour of each of these types in terms of their masses, velocities and the gravitational forces acting on them. Newtonian mechanics unified what had otherwise seemed to be a heterogeneous collection of types of thing. By achieving this unification, Newton's theory reduced the number of independent types of thing, and it thereby explained the behaviour of things of each type in the collection.

---

3   See Oddie (1982) and Colyvan (2001, ch. 3) for further discussion.

Despite the intuitive appeal of this view of scientific explanation, it has proved hard to make precise the crucial notion of "independent type of phenomena." Moreover, the closeness of the connection between unification and explanation is open to question (Barnes 1992, Humphreys 1993). Bearing these reservations in mind, let's consider whether philosophy can emulate this practice of **explanation by unification**. Various philosophers have seen themselves as explaining phenomena by unifying them. It seems that Plato did so (Cherniss 1936). More recently, Swoyer sees theories of properties as offering "unified and integrated accounts" of certain mathematical, semantic and scientific phenomena (Swoyer 1999, 126). We saw in chapter 4, §5 that David Lewis claims that there exists a plurality of possible worlds, where a possible world is a thing of the same type as the actual world. Lewis seeks to explain the content of sentences, and much else besides, in terms of possible worlds (Lewis 1986, ch. 1). Part of his case for his theory of modal realism is the theoretical unification that he thinks that it achieves (Lewis 1986, 3–5). Modal realism has even been described as "offering the best account of the nature of science and of the world" (Bigelow and Pargetter 1990, 345).

The explanatory credentials of Lewis's theory, however, have been challenged. Michael Friedman has levelled the following objection (Friedman 1981, 13-14, his italics):

> It must be possible to show how creatures like us acquire and employ a language with the properties that the semantic theory ascribes to it. It must be possible to show how the theoretical structures assumed in the semantic theory play a role in the actual process of language acquisition and use.... But in possible-worlds semantics the postulated semantic structure appears to be totally divorced from the psychological process of language acquisition and use. How do *we*, as finite creatures in *this* world, relate to entities (and sets of entities, and sets of sets of entities …) in *other* possible worlds? If anything, possible-world semantics makes it harder to connect linguistic theory with psychological and social theory than it was before. Possible-worlds semantics appears to lead away from, rather than toward, theoretical unification.

Friedman's objection is not that Lewisian possible worlds do not causally act on objects in the actual world. The objection concerns the puzzle of how what is the case at other possible worlds could be explanatorily relevant to what occurs at the actual world — for example, in our actual learning and use of language. Consequently, Friedman alleges that Lewis's theory disunifies our semantic and psychological theories.[4]

A more general worry about philosophical appeals to unification as explanation is that whereas every unification is a re-description of certain phenomena, not every re-description is a unification, and some re-descriptions may masquerade as unifications and not be genuinely explanatory (Kraut 2001, 155–56). Astrology says that every event that is fated has to happen, and it re-describes every event of every type as a fated event. Astrology is thereby a comprehensive theory, but it is a poor potential explanation of any event. So, if we preserve the link between unification and explanation, astrology is not a unifying theory.

The main reason why astrology is a poor potential explanation is that it has no predictive power whatever. In addition, it has no explanation of how the supposed causes (the movements of the stars) can produce the effects they are said to explain. Moreover, according to the scientific theories that we currently accept the distribution of planets and stars at a time has no explanatory relevance to the occurrence of (say) storms or lottery results. Proponents of modal realism claim that positing possible worlds offers a comprehensive way of describing different phenomena. But is it a good explanation of them? As noted, Friedman cannot see the relevance of the distribution of possible worlds to our acquisition or use of language. Proponents of mathematical Platonism claim that positing numbers offers a way of describing the conditions under which mathematical claims are true or false. According to mathematical Platonism, there are true mathematical claims and those claims are true because they describe a domain of abstract mathematical objects. But is mathematical Platonism a good explanation of the conditions under which mathematical claims are true? Some philosophers, such as van Fraassen, cannot see the relevance of such posits to our practices of counting and measuring. The issue, then, is how the theories of the modal realist or the mathematical realist are any better placed than astrology. If a given philosophical theory is a poor explanation, then applying it to many phenomena will not make it a better explanation. It will just be using the same poor explanation more widely. That is not shedding the light of explanation. It is spreading the muck of obscurity.

We might reasonably reject astrological explanations as poor explanations because "we need to appeal to objective nomic relations, causal relations, or other sorts of physical mechanisms if we are to provide adequate scientific explanations" (Salmon 1989, 145). But just as astrology does not meet this requirement on explanation, neither do modal realism

---

4   See Swoyer (1979) for a reply.

nor mathematical Platonism. Modal realism rightly does not claim that causal relations or laws of nature hold between Lewisian possible worlds where there are talking donkeys and people in the actual world thinking about talking donkeys. Likewise, mathematical Platonism rightly does not claim that such relations hold between numbers not located in space-time and what people count or measure in the actual world. At some times, there have been respectable scientific theories that have posited certain phenomena although they have not been able to specify the mechanisms supposedly responsible for these phenomena. For example, for some time after it was formulated genetic theory was unable to specify the mechanism whereby genes produce inherited characteristics. Nevertheless, there were good prospects for finding these mechanisms and the search for them has often turned out to be successful, as it was in the case of genetic theory. In the case of modal realism and mathematical Platonism, however, there is no prospect for finding a mechanism mediating between the modal or the mathematical and us, as modal realists and mathematical Platonists would themselves acknowledge.

5. Inference to the Best Philosophical Explanation

Many philosophers think that science extensively uses the inferential strategy known as abduction or inference to the best explanation (Harman 1965). Some of these philosophers further think that philosophy uses this strategy. But what exactly does this strategy involve?

Inference to the best explanation is a method for inferring to the likely truth of a certain hypothesis. Suppose that there is a phenomenon P that we wish to explain. Suppose too that there is a pool of pairwise incompatible hypotheses $H_1, H_2, \ldots, H_n$. (For the hypotheses in the series to be "pairwise incompatible" means that if you take any pair of these hypotheses, the two hypotheses selected are mutually incompatible.) Suppose that these hypotheses are such that, for each hypothesis H_i, were H_i true, it would explain P. Which of these hypotheses (if any) should be accepted as the explanation of P? It is natural to want to infer the hypothesis that is most likely. But which hypothesis is the most likely? We are no further forward, and it is not clear what resources are available to us to answer the question.

The method of inference to the best explanation reverses the order in which we answer these questions. Our first task is to select which hypothesis, if it were true, would best explain P. It is on that basis that we then say which hypothesis is the most likely to be true. The first task involves weighing up the explanatory credentials of each hypothesis. This is a comparative task: we compare the credentials of each of H_1, H_2, ... , H_n against its rivals. To do this we need to consider such factors as the internal consistency of the hypothesis, its scope, its fruitfulness, whether it is consistent with hypotheses that we already accept, the degree to which accepting it would increase our ontological and ideological (in Quine's sense) commitments, the degree to which it avoids raising intractable issues, and so on.[5] We also need to consider the difficult question of how these various factors should be weighed against each other. One hypothesis may have certain theoretical virtues to a greater degree than another, although the second hypothesis may have certain other theoretical virtues to a greater degree than the first. If we had to choose between the two hypotheses, which one should we choose? (See chapter 4, §6 and Lewis 1986, 133–34.)

To return to the main issue, suppose that a member of our pool of hypotheses can be selected as the best potential explanation of P. Suppose too that this hypothesis is a good enough potential explanation of P to be acceptable; that it meets some minimal requirement of explanatory power. We might also require that the hypothesis is significantly better than any nearest rival hypothesis (Dorr and Rosen 2001, §7). According to the strategy of inference to the best explanation, we are warranted to infer that that hypothesis is the (most likely) explanation of P. That is, we infer from the hypothesis that would best explain P, and that meets a suitable standard of explanatory power, to its being the hypothesis that most likely explains P. A hypothesis's explanatory potential provides a reason to believe that the hypothesis is likely to be true.

A hypothesis can have a low epistemic probability in absolute terms, but a higher epistemic probability than each of many rival hypotheses. A more cautious form of inference to the best explanation will not infer to a hypothesis's likely truth (its having a high epistemic probability in absolute terms), but only to its being more likely (its having a higher epistemic probability) than its rival hypotheses.[6]

Of the two inference strategies considered here — theoretical unification, and inference to the best explanation — the last is the most widely appealed to by philosophers. (It is not always distinguished from the first, however.) For example, Swoyer thinks that inferences to the best explanation from certain truths about mathematics, semantics, or the laws of nature warrant philosophical conclusions about the existence of properties, understood as universals or properties that are identical between their instances (Swoyer 1999, esp. §§5–7). Armstrong, Bigelow

5   Thagard (1976) and McAllister (1989) spell out some of these factors.
6   See Okasha (2000, 697–98).

and Pargetter also use this strategy to infer certain philosophical hypotheses (Armstrong 1997, 235, and Bigelow and Pargetter 1990, 344–45).

There are two main difficulties facing philosophers' appeal to inference to the best explanation. First, there are quite general questions about the justification, and even the rationality, of the strategy itself (van Fraassen 1989, ch. 6).[7] Second, there are specific worries about the use of the strategy in philosophy (van Fraassen 1995, §iv). We will concentrate on the second difficulty.

Inference to the best explanation involves taking a pool of potential explanations, and inferring the likely truth of the member of the pool that, if it were true, would provide the best explanation of some target phenomenon. Inferences to the best explanation can be inferences from things of one type to other things of the same type. Typically, such an inference is from a sample of Ks having a common feature, F, to the conclusion that every K has F, or that many unexamined Ks have F. For example, an inference might be from the fact that a planet's observed spatial locations form an ellipse to the conclusion that all of the planet's spatial positions — its orbit — form an ellipse. Such an inference is an inference from things of one type to things of the same type, but some important philosophical examples of inference to the best explanation are not instances of that type of inference. For example, neither the inference from sensory experiences to the existence of physical objects, nor the inference from modal phenomena to the existence of Lewisian possible worlds are of that type. These examples are better modelled as inferences from entities of one type to entities of another type. Inferences of this type in science include the inference from observations of the bending of light waves in deep space to the existence of black holes, and the inference from observations of Brownian motion to the existence of molecules. In these scientific cases, the inferred entities are causally efficacious, and the scientific hypotheses that infer them make novel predictions. In conjunction with auxiliary hypotheses not specifically about black holes, scientific hypotheses about black holes are sufficiently detailed to make novel predictions that can subsequently be confirmed or disconfirmed. A similar point holds with respect to scientific hypotheses about molecules. By contrast, philosophical hypotheses about the existence of the external world or the existence of possible worlds do not generate novel predictions. Consequently, philosophical hypotheses imperfectly emulate their scientific counterparts.

We have seen that inference to the best explanation licenses inferring the truth of a given hypothesis only if that hypothesis is a good

---

7   For replies, see Lipton (2004, 107–17, 151-63), Kvanvig (1994), and Okasha (2000).

enough potential explanation to be acceptable. In an inference to the best explanation, the pool of potential explanations may be "unfiltered" and include all possible candidate explanations, no matter how eccentric. Or it may be "filtered" and include only promising candidate explanations. Assuming that the pool is unfiltered would markedly deviate from theory selection in actual scientific practice. In the latter case we do not begin by considering all possible theories about some phenomenon because the pool would be too large to generate or handle (Lipton 2004, 119). But if the pool is filtered, so that only what are antecedently considered to be promising candidates are admitted, then certain familiar philosophical theories are in danger of being excluded at the outset.[8] For instance, the "incredulous stare" facing modal realism testifies to how implausible many philosophers find that theory (Lewis 1986, 133–35). Excluding modal realism from the pool for that reason would be to disqualify it as a candidate for explaining modal phenomena. The modal realist might take issue with a setting on the filter that excluded his theory from the pool. But if the argument between the modal realist and his opponents occurs at this early stage, it forestalls our going on to the next stage: of taking the pool of admitted candidates and inferring the best potential explanation of the phenomena to be explained. Accordingly, inference to the best explanation would have to wait upon a prior resolution of the dispute between the modal realist and his incredulous opponents, rather than provide that resolution itself. This would leave the role of inference to the best explanation in philosophy much less useful and interesting than it had promised to be. It would be a "bystander" to the crucial argument between Lewis and his opponents, and that argument would have to be conducted along independent lines.

What do these criticisms show? A friend of the use of inference to the best explanation may warn against conflating the *effectiveness* of this inferential method with its *legitimacy* (Vahid 2001, §5). To show that inference to the best explanation is legitimate is to show that it is truth-conducive: that following this method leads more often than not to true hypotheses. Following Sober, Vahid appeals to the role of background assumptions in guiding hypothesis choice. He claims that these assumptions justify describing a given hypothesis as the best of a number of hypotheses. Moreover, if these assumptions are reliable ones, if they are well-confirmed, "our grounds for choosing the best explanation would then be firmly anchored in truth." But to be an epistemically effective inferential method, the method cannot simply tell us which hypothesis is the best in an arbitrarily given pool. The hypothesis may merely be

---

8   This worry is shared by Nozick (1981, 12).

the best of a bad bunch. To be epistemically effective, then, the pool of hypotheses to which the method is applied needs to be suitably filtered. Vahid looks to a substantial theory of knowledge to provide this filter. As an illustration, he considers a relevant alternatives theory of knowledge, such as the one found in Dretske (1981). Applied to the case at issue, a relevant alternatives theory would say that to know that hypothesis H is true, one need not rule out every alternative to H. One need only rule out every relevant alternative to it. The pool of hypotheses from which H is selected includes only all relevant alternatives to H. Context (including shared presuppositions in our epistemic community and the objective likelihood of certain situations) settles which hypotheses are relevant.

Appealing to well-confirmed hypotheses as background hypotheses raises the question of what method is used to confirm those hypotheses. If the method of confirmation used is inference to the best explanation, then this defence of the legitimacy of inference to the best explanation is circular. We would be relying on certain hypotheses inferred by inference to the best explanation to defend the legitimacy of using inference to the best explanation to infer certain other hypotheses. Yet what is at issue is the legitimacy of the use of inference to the best explanation to infer *any* hypothesis. Some account of confirmation other than inference to the best explanation would need to be appealed to. And if an independent account is forthcoming, we would have to be told what the method of inference to the best explanation is then needed for.

Circularity also threatens the illustrative use of a relevant alternatives theory of hypothesis choice. This theory appeals to context to determine which hypotheses are relevant, and the context involves the objective likelihood of certain situations. Now making such a choice requires knowing what the context is. That will then require knowing the objective likelihood of the situations in question. But how is that to be done? It will not be done by inference to the best explanation, since the claims of objective likelihood need to be in place as part of the filter on potential hypotheses. (This, and the preceding, threat of circularity particularly face the views of Harman [1965] and Lycan [1998, 128] according to whom "all justified reasoning is fundamentally explanatory reasoning that aims at maximising the "explanatory coherence" of one's total belief system.") To avoid circularity, some other method has to be available for working out what the objective likelihood of various claims is. If such a method is forthcoming, we might wonder whether the method can be used more generally in working out the objective likelihood of hypotheses, and so we would have to be told why the method of inference to the best explanation is still needed.

In the next two sections we will consider two case studies of philosophical explanations: an inference to the best explanation for the mind-brain identity theory, and an inference to the best explanation to the postulation of the external world.

6. Case Study: The Mind-Brain Identity Theory

In chapter 4, §4 we examined the mind-brain identity theory. This theory claims that every mental property is identical to some physical property of the brain. Christopher Hill has appealed to the strategy of inference to the best explanation to infer to the likely truth of this theory. He argues as follows (Hill 1991, 23):

> (P1) *Inference to the best explanation*: "If a theory provides a good explanation of a set of facts, and the explanation is better than any explanation provided by a competing theory, then one has a good and sufficient reason to believe that the theory is true."
>
> (P2) *Explanatory adequacy claim*: The identity theory provides a good explanation of the one-to-one correlation between instances of mental properties and instances of some physical properties: namely, that the properties are identical.
>
> (P3) *Explanatory superiority claim*: The identity theory's explanation is superior to the explanations provided by all rival theories.
>
> (C) So there is good and sufficient reason to believe the mind-brain identity theory.

(P2) claims that the correlation between instances of a mental and a physical property is best explained by the hypothesis that the properties are the same. Somewhat similarly, the best explanation of why the Cincinnati Strangler's victims were invariably past girlfriends of Fred Jones is that the Cincinnati Strangler and Fred Jones are the same person. By contrast with the identity theory, Hill claims that "A dualistic 'explanation' of a psychophysical law is usually little more than a euphemistic way of confessing that the law has the status of an unexplained primitive" (Hill 1991, 25).

The dualist will make some of the same objections to Hill's argument from explanatory considerations as he made to the argument for the identity theory from Ockham's Razor. The identity theory is the best explanation of the correlations between instances of mental and physical properties only if it is possible that the theory is true. The dualist will raise the logically prior issue of whether it is possible for mental and physical properties to be identical, and typically he will argue that it is not possible. He will argue that mental properties have features, such as intrinsic intentionality or an experiential quality, that no physical property could have. If those arguments succeed, the identity theory cannot be the best explanation of the mental-physical correlations because that theory cannot be true.

Setting this response aside, we might wonder whether Hill's identity theorist faces a similar charge to the one he makes against the dualist. The dualist is charged with accepting certain unexplained primitives, namely, the mental-physical correlations in question. But the identity theorist faces a parallel charge of accepting certain unexplained primitives, namely, the identities between mental and physical properties. Either these identities lack an explanation or they have an explanation. If they lack an explanation, then the charge against the identity theorist sticks. If they have an explanation, then the charge of accepting certain unexplained primitives can be made with respect to their *explanans*, or with respect to whatever are the ultimate *explanans* that the identity theorist accepts. At some stage the identity theorist is going to run out of explanations and will have to accept certain unexplained primitives. Hill may reply that it matters how far you can extend a series of explanations. The dualist gives up too soon, and the identity theorist does better by taking explanation at least a stage further (Rey 1998, 5–6).

It is natural to think that the fact that H_1 explains more than H_2 is one factor in assessing its worth, and would contribute toward a conclusion that H_1 is a better theory than H_2 (where "better than" means *overall better than*, and not simply *better explainer than*). But it is not clear that scientific practice bears this out (van Fraassen 1980, 94–96). Newton deliberately declined to explain why gravity occurred. He also deliberately declined to explain why there were six planets (as he and his contemporaries thought that there were). Widely accepted versions of quantum theory do not explain why there are correlations in the behaviour of particles that have interacted in the past. Perhaps one reason why the task of explaining these phenomena was shirked was that the theories available that would have explained them would either not have made novel correct predictions (as in the Newtonian examples), or they would not have been as observationally accurate as the standard theories were (as in the quantum theory example). A hypothesis that explains just about everything might nevertheless be bad because empty: e.g., explaining whatever happens as the will of God. If philosophical theories are not in the business of making predictions, but can still be in the business of giving explanations, perhaps this constraint would not apply. If so, the methodological principle mentioned at the beginning of this paragraph can be straightforwardly applied to the dispute between the identity theory and dualism. A different view, however, is that explanation is a theoretical virtue because it is conducive to accurate and wide-ranging predictions (van Fraassen 1980, 92). That view is not a threat to the explanatory status of the identity theory. That theory predicts for example, the discovery of neurological correlates for mental states. The view does, however, confront the explanatory status of various other philosophical theories. Neither modal realism nor mathematical Platonism, for example, makes predictions. So those theories' claims to be explanatory conflict with van Fraassen's view.

To sum up, the argument from explanatory factors for the mind-brain identity theory faces some of the objections that face the argument from simplicity for that theory. Furthermore, the argument needs to address a general query about whether explanations that do not generate additional predictive power need to be accepted.

7. Case Study: The External World Hypothesis

Jonathan Vogel has argued that the strategy of inference to the best explanation can show that we have reason to believe that we are not brains in vats and that we have experience of a physical world (Vogel 1990).[9] Vogel presents the issue in terms of how to make a rational selection between two rival hypotheses. According to the external world hypothesis we have experience of a physical world and at least many of our common sense beliefs about what the physical world is like are true. According to the brain in a vat hypothesis, there exists only your brain and a computer feeding it data. All that you experience are the data, but the data deceive you by giving every appearance that you are experiencing a world of physical objects. For every physical object that the external world hypothesis posits, and for every observable property of such an object, the brain in a vat hypothesis posits a corresponding object with a corresponding property. The corresponding object will be a digital object: some information stored in the computer memory. For example, suppose that according to the external world hypothesis there is a frog in the garden pond. Then, according to the brain in a vat hypothesis, the computer programme will hold a file about a frog in the pond. Similarly, for every physical property the external world hypothesis attributes to the

---

9   See also Weintraub (1997, 116–20) and Feldman (2003, 148–52).

frog, the brain in a vat hypothesis will attribute a corresponding, though different, property to the file about the frog.

In this way, then, the two hypotheses cannot be distinguished by our experiences alone. But Vogel thinks that the hypotheses differ in their degree of complexity. He seeks to bring this out by focusing on the issue of location properties — the properties of being located in a certain place at a certain time. The external world hypothesis attributes locations in space and time to physical objects. Vogel, along with many other philosophers, think that physical objects are governed by the principle that non-identical physical objects are not located in the same place at the same time. The frog is in the pond. According to this principle, another frog cannot occupy the same place at the same time as the other frog. According to Vogel, the principle that physical objects of the same kind are not located at the same place at the same time is a necessary truth. "We do not need any empirical law or regularity to explain [the principle]; it is a necessary truth pertaining to the nature of physical objects that there cannot be two such objects in the same place at the same time" (Vogel 1990, 664). (Vogel's principle is controversial. Three-dimensional objects such as a statue and a lump of bronze can be located in the same place at the same time. Yet, it can be argued, the statue and the lump of bronze are non-identical because the bronze continues to exist even if the statue is melted down and the bronze is formed into a ball. Vogel would deny these objects belong to the same kind, but is that *ad hoc*?)

Now if the brain in a vat hypothesis is to match the external world hypothesis in explanatory power, the former has to have a corresponding principle. It needs to have a principle that says that non-identical digital objects are not represented as having the same spatial location at the same time. (The computer programme might represent where an object is located in space and time by assigning a string of co-ordinates in its file. Call this property the object's "pseudo location.") This principle, however, is not a necessary truth. Nothing in the nature of a digital object, or of a computer programme, excludes such a programme taking non-identical digital objects as having the same pseudo location. Therefore, Vogel says, the brain in a vat hypothesis has to take the principle to be "an extra empirical regularity, to which no regularity in the [external world hypothesis] corresponds" (Vogel 1990, 665). Consequently, by adding such an empirical regularity, the sceptical hypothesis is less simple than the external world hypothesis; and if it omits it, the sceptical hypothesis is less explanatory than its rival. Inference to the best explanation says that the hypothesis that is more explanatory than a rival is more likely to be the correct hypothesis. We are then licensed to infer that the external world hypothesis is the more likely hypothesis.

Ernest Sosa thinks that appeals to explanatory considerations to meet external world scepticism are flawed. Such appeals claim that we can know that there are external objects because it provides the best explanation of our sensory experiences. Consequently, it is further claimed that we know that we are not dreaming. Sosa asks "How plausible can it be that one could *discover* that one is not dreaming as a by-product of any such inference?" He offers the following analogy:

> Compare a case where one knows about one's current speed only by reading one's speedometer. And suppose this knowledge to depend entirely on an explanatory inference from the speedometer reading to the actual speed. Could one thereby *discover*, and come to know, that one's speedometer was properly connected so as to be sensitive to one's speed? If one asked oneself whether the speedometer was properly installed and operative, one could hardly settle the matter *exclusively* by inferring one's actual speed from the speedometer reading, as an explanatory inference, so as to draw the further inference that the instrument must indeed be properly installed and operative. (Sosa 2007, 59)

In this passage Sosa asks whether we could get to know whether the speedometer is reliable by having inferred that the speedometer's reading is explained by our current speed. He claims that we could not, but we need to tease out what his reason for claiming this is. He says that we could not know that the speedometer is reliable *exclusively* by having inferred that the speedometer's reading is explained by our current speed. This, however, is precisely what is at issue. Sosa thinks that an explanatory inference cannot provide knowledge in a case in which we have to rely exclusively on that inference. Sosa's opponents believe that explanatory inferences are a source of knowledge, and that, at least in some cases, those inferences provide us with knowledge (or at least justified belief) that we would otherwise lack. For instance, Vogel thinks that explanatory inference is a source of our knowledge of the external world, and that we have to rely exclusively on that inference to have that knowledge. That is, he thinks that our only source of the external world is an explanatory inference from our sensory experiences. So Sosa assumes the very point at issue in the debate with Vogel.

In assuming that an explanatory inference cannot provide knowledge in a case in which we have to rely exclusively on that inference, Sosa is apparently assuming that an explanatory inference provides knowledge that p only if there is some independent means of discovering whether p is true. We may make an explanatory inference from the speedometer read-ing to our current speed. Yet unless there is some way of telling what our current speed is independently of making this inference, we cannot know what our speed is, and we cannot know whether the speedometer is reli-able. Similarly, we may make an explanatory inference from our sensory experience to the existence of an external world. Yet unless there is some way of telling whether there is an external world independently of making this inference, we cannot know whether there is an external world.

There is reason to reject this assumption that there has to be an independent means of testing the explanatory inference. Philosophers of science have recognized that some explanations are self-evidencing (Hempel 1965, 370–74). In a **self-evidencing explanation**, a theory *T* explains a phenomenon *P* although *P* provides the only evidence for *T*. For example, the Doppler law links the recession of an object with the red-shift (a distinctive spectrum that is shifted towards the red). That law, in conjunction with the fact that a given galaxy is receding from us at a certain velocity, explains the fact that the galaxy exhibits the red-shift. Yet the only evidence that the galaxy is receding at that velocity is the fact that the galaxy is exhibiting the red-shift. It is standardly thought by philosophers of science that such a pattern of reasoning is neither worthless nor viciously circular. It is not viciously circular because one relation (the explanation relation) holds between the *explanans* and the *explanandum* (in that order), while a distinct relation (the confirmation relation) holds between the *explanandum* and the *explanans* (in that order). It is not worthless because the only way in which we can have knowledge of unobservable scientific entities is via an explanatory infer-ence from observed entities, and (scientific realists will claim) we do have some such knowledge.

It is open to Vogel to claim that the explanatory inference from our sensory experience to the existence of an external world is a self-evidenc-ing explanation, and that so too is the inference in Sosa's speedometer example. Those inferences are none the worse for that if, as seems to be the case, self-evidencing explanations are widely accepted in current sci-entific practice. Of course, Sosa might wish to take issue with this trend in science, but then he would need to say what is in general wrong with self-evidencing explanations.

It is also open to Vogel to claim that any persuasive power in Sosa's example of the speedometer does not lie in any supposed vicious circu-larity in the speed of the car explaining the speedometer's reading and the speedometer's reading being the only evidence for the speed of the car. Instead, given how minimally the example is described, that seems no reason to claim that the best explanation of the speedometer's reading is that it is reliably tracking the speed of the car. The example does not tell us anything about the workings of the speedometer — whether it is a standard model, whether it has been tampered with, and so on. Given this paucity of information, we may be disinclined to think that the reliability hypothesis is a much better hypothesis than its nearest rivals. In the case of the problem of the external world, however, we have seen that Vogel thinks that the external world hypothesis is markedly simpler than, and in at least that respect better than, the sceptical hypothesis. (Curiously, Vogel had already devised an example similar to Sosa's and directed it against reliabilism in epistemology [Vogel 2000, 613]. Sosa's example might then serve as an *ad hominem*.)

What is crucial to Vogel's argument is the claim that the sceptical hypothesis is less simple than the external world hypothesis. Vogel's reason for making this claim is that the sceptical hypothesis posits an empirical regularity although the external world hypothesis posits no corresponding hypothesis. Whether this shows that the sceptical hypothesis is less simple is debatable for two reasons. First, according to Vogel, the external world hypothesis posits a necessary truth — namely, that non-identical physical objects of the same kind do not occupy the same space-time location — although the sceptical hypothesis posits no corresponding necessary truth. So the situation seems to be that the sceptical hypothesis posits an empirical regularity to which the external world hypothesis posits no corresponding empirical regularity, and that the external world hypothesis posits a necessary truth to which the sceptical hypothesis posits no corresponding necessary truth. But then it no longer seems that the sceptical hypothesis is a less simple hypothesis than the external world hypothesis; they seem to be equally simple (equally complicated) hypotheses. Second, we should re-consider the assumption that the external world hypothesis does not posit an empirical regularity corresponding to the sceptical hypothesis's empirical regularity. According to Vogel, it is a necessary truth that non-identical physical objects of the same kind do not occupy the same space-time location. But that (alleged) necessary truth entails the empirical generalization that non-identical physical objects of the same kind do not occupy the same space-time location. If it is a necessary truth about the nature of physical objects that physical objects of the same kind do not occupy the same location in space and time, then it is an observationally discoverable general fact that physical objects of the same kind do not occupy the same location in space and time. So it is not the case that the external world hypothesis lacks an empirical regularity corresponding to the sceptical hypothesis's empirical regularity that non-identical digital objects do not have the same pseudo-location. Vogel's case for claiming that the external world hypothesis is more simple than the sceptical hypothesis seems to be mistaken.

Furthermore, since the external world hypothesis posits a *necessary truth* while the sceptical hypothesis does not posit a corresponding necessary truth, it seems that the external world hypothesis is less simple than the sceptical hypothesis. One version of Ockham's Razor says that necessities are not to be multiplied beyond necessity. (Forrest [2001, 93] calls this "Hume's Razor.") The external world hypothesis posits a necessity that the sceptical hypothesis does not. Still, even if Vogel were to concede this, he might reply that even what the external world hypothesis loses in simplicity, it gains in explanatory power. For the hypothesis can explain the empirical regularity that no non-identical physical objects of the same kind are in the same location in space and time. It is explained by the necessary truth that no non-identical physical objects of the same kind are in the same location in space and time. Since the sceptical hypothesis does not posit a corresponding necessary truth, it cannot explain in this way its corresponding empirical regularity. And none of the other empirical regularities that the hypothesis posits seem able to explain the empirical regularity in question. So the sceptical hypothesis cannot explain the regularity at all.

Which (if either) hypothesis should we accept? The hypothesis that explains more by being less simple, or the hypothesis that is more simple by explaining less? The strategy of inference to the best explanation needs to be supplemented not only by detailed accounts of each of the theoretical virtues, but also by a detailed account of how to make a rational theory choice in cases such as the above.[10]

8. Conclusion

Philosophers who have thought that there was such a thing as philosophical explanation have tended simply to assume that there was such a thing. They have not thought that their assumption needed to be argued. Even Kant, who billed himself as a critic of rationalist metaphysics and its explanatory pretensions, seemed to have thought that he was stating the proper way of giving philosophical explanations: we perceive the world as a world containing *F*s (causes and effects, substances in space and time, ...) because our minds structure our perceptions that way. For Kant, there is no question that philosophy is in the business of explanation. His chief difference with his rationalist opponents is that he takes

---

10 For further criticism of the use of this strategy to solve sceptical problems, see Wright (1985, 68–71), Fumerton (1992), and Vahid (2001, §2).

the locus of this explanation to lie in special powers of the mind. Kant did not think that these powers were to be discovered by empirical psychology. They were the special domain of synthetic *a priori* knowledge.

Serious challenges to the idea of philosophical explanation emerged only in the work of Hume, Mach and the logical positivists. The challenges were obscured by more prominent ideas in their work — Hume and Mach's stringent empiricism and logical positivism's verificationist theory of meaning. But simply rebutting these views does not meet the challenge about explanation. Grant (against the logical positivists) that talk about unobservable things can be meaningful. Grant too (against Hume and Mach) that there can be epistemic reason to believe talk about such things. There remains, though, the challenge of how philosophy's positing such things is supposed to explain anything. What kind of explanation is involved? How does it work? This was the point of departure for the present chapter.

In closing, three very recent approaches to philosophical explanation are worth noting.

FUNCTIONALISM ABOUT EXPLANATION AND EXPLANATIONISM
For many kinds of thing, a distinction can be drawn between the role of a thing of a given kind and what realizes that role in a given case. For example, the role of a lock is to secure something against unwanted opening. In different cases, different things may realize the role of a lock. On a tool-shed door, the role of a lock may be realized by a peg pushed through a hasp. By contrast, on a money-safe, the role of a lock may be realized by a combination dial and a mechanism of tumblers.

A philosophical view known as functionalism about explanation distinguishes between the role of explanation and what realizes it.[11] The view makes two principal claims. First, the role of explanations has to do with answering why-questions. Second, the role can be realized by various different non-inferential consequence relations. The first claim says that the role of an explanation is to give understanding, to give knowledge of why, or how, it is true that p rather than that it is true that q, given that it is true that r. The second claim says that in different cases, this role can be occupied or realized by different relations. These relations include logical consequence, nomic consequence, probabilistic consequence, mathematical consequence, and other such "non-inferential consequence relations."

Functionalism about explanation can then be combined with an independent view that Carrie Jenkins calls "explanationism": the view that

---

11 The view builds on ideas found in Jenkins (2006, 2008) and is the subject of a future monograph by her.

a philosophical account of any topic should take the notion of explanation to have a central role in the account. Call this combined view "the project." The project need not be taken as an across the board strategy. For Jenkins, the project is often a promising strategy to try in areas where causal theories or modal theories (for example) have been offered but were not successful.

CONCEPTUAL ANALYSIS

Another approach to philosophical explanation looks to conceptual analysis. On this approach, a philosophical explanation is given by a description of conceptual connections between the *explanandum* and *explanans* concepts. Take some examples:

> Abe's action is good because it maximizes happiness.

> Beth believes that it's going to rain because she is in a certain functional state.

> It is possible for Chuck to count to ten because there is an (accessible) possible world at which Chuck counts to ten.

(We will assume that examples are correct. Nothing turns on these particular examples. They are used only for illustrative purposes.) It is because of the concepts involved in Abe's act being good and in Abe's act maximizing happiness that Abe's act is good and that it is good because Abe's act maximizes happiness. In general, on this approach, a philosophical explanation is a (partial or complete) conceptual analysis (Schnieder 2006, 32–33).

METAPHYSICAL GROUNDING

A third approach looks to ontology. On this approach, philosophical explanations involve a primitive notion of metaphysical grounding. Grounding is a relation that holds between different kinds of thing. It is irreflexive, asymmetric and transitive. More fundamental kinds of thing ground less fundamental kinds of thing (Schaffer 2009). Notice that this approach and the conceptual analysis approach do not give the same results. Consider the following three examples:

> Gromit is a dog because he is a beagle.
> Chris is Suzie's uncle because he is a brother of Suzie's mother.
> Jack was in front of Ginger because Ginger stepped behind him.

Let's grant that these sentences are true at least partly because of conceptual connections between the concepts involved in the *explanandum* and *explanans*. Yet presumably in none of the sentences the *explanans* describes a more fundamental kind of thing than the *explanandum* does. This should make us wonder whether philosophers are operating with a single notion of philosophical explanation and that they are engaged in different attempts to capture it.

Questions for Discussion

1. In §2 we saw that Nozick claimed that philosophical problems have the following contrastive form:

> Given that *r*, how is it possible that *p* rather than that *q*?

Is there any way of arguing for Nozick's claim? Are there any counter-examples to his claim?

2. §3 emphasized certain differences between scientific and philosophical explanation. How telling are those differences? We already know that there are some differences between science and philosophy (whether they are of kind or of degree). So did listing those differences between scientific and philosophical explanation add anything? In particular, did they really do anything to discredit the idea that there are philosophical explanations?

3. Is there a single notion of philosophical explanation? Does the conclusion provide much of a case for thinking that different philosophers are working with different notions of philosophical explanation? Would it matter if they do?

Core Reading for Chapter 5

Armstrong, D.M. (1978) *Nominalism and Realism: Universals and Scientific Realism* Vol. I ch. 12.

Friedman, Michael (1981) "Theoretical Explanation".

Harman, Gilbert (1965) "The Inference to the Best Explanation."

Kraut, Robert (2001) "Metaphysical Explanation and the Philosophy of Mathematics: Reflections on Jerrold Katz's *Realistic Rationalism*."

Nozick, Robert (1981) *Philosophical Explanations* ch. 1.

Oddie, Graham (1982) "Armstrong on the Eleatic Principle and Abstract Entities."

Swoyer, Chris (1999) "How Ontology Might Be Possible: Explanation and Inference in Metaphysics."

Thagard, Paul R. (1976) "The Best Explanation: Criteria for Theory Choice."

Vahid, Hamid (2001) "Realism and the Epistemological Significance of Inference to the Best Explanation."

Vogel, Jonathan (1990) "Cartesian Skepticism and Inference to the Best Explanation."

SIX Science

1. Introduction

In chapter 1 we considered the role of common sense in philosophy since common sense is a source of a great deal of information. Now science is also a source of a great deal of information. Like common sense, it uses our senses and powers of reasoning to provide information. It also uses specialized techniques of observation, reasoning and theorizing to provide striking information. These considerations raise the following three questions:

> (Q1) How are science and philosophy related?
> (Q2) Can scientific evidence support, or undermine, philosophical claims?
> (Q3) Can philosophical problems be resolved by scientific theories?

Answers to these questions will overlap. (Q1) is the most general of the questions. All parties agree that science and philosophy are not one and the same discipline. (Q1) asks what more can be said about them. Do science and philosophy differ in kind, or do they differ only in degree? Do they fundamentally differ in their methods and goals, or do they share them? Now science uses observation and experiment. (Q2) asks whether evidence gathered by those means can provide evidence for, or against, philosophical theories. Philosophical theories seek to solve philosophical problems. (Q3) asks whether scientific theories, theories supported by observation and experiment and designed to solve empirical problems, can solve philosophical problems.

Two quite different views may be prompted by (Q1–3). As we will see, these two views stand at opposite points on a spectrum of possible views.

It is worth considering these extreme views first because they help frame the debate and because they have had some notable defenders.

Suppose we think that philosophy addresses problems fundamentally unlike those pursued by science, and that it uses uniquely philosophical methods and principles to resolve those problems. If we take such a view of philosophy, we would be likely to think that there are no interesting points of contact between science and philosophy. We would think that scientific findings have no bearing on any philosophical theory, and that there is no prospect of any scientific theory informing, let alone replacing, any philosophical theory. According to such a view, philosophy is autonomous from science: it has methods, standards and goals that it does not share with science. Call this "the Autonomy view." Quine calls it "First Philosophy" as the view takes philosophy to be prior to, and more fundamental than, science (Quine 1981b, 72). Quine takes the phrase "First Philosophy" from Aristotle's *Metaphysics* Book Γ, where Aristotle says that First Philosophy should identify the most fundamental principles that are used in all reasoning.

The Autonomy view has had a number of proponents besides Aristotle. In the opening paragraph of his *Meditations*, Descartes indicated that his philosophical method of doubt was designed to provide foundations for scientific knowledge:

> I was convinced that I must once for all seriously undertake to rid myself of all the opinions which I had formerly accepted, and commence to build anew from the foundation, if I wanted to establish any firm and permanent structure in the sciences. (Descartes 1641 Meditation 1)

Descartes goes on to argue that the foundation consists in truths that are immune to doubt and self-evident to the intellect, notably the *Cogito*: "I think, therefore I am."

Wittgenstein (1922) makes the following stark claims:

4.111   Philosophy is not one of the natural sciences.

4.112   Philosophy aims at the logical clarification of thoughts …

4.1121 Psychology is no more closely related to philosophy than any other natural science....

4.1122 Darwin's theory has no more to do with philosophy than any other hypothesis in natural science.

At one stage in his career Russell echoed such sentiments:

> [Philosophical propositions] are true of any possible world, independently of such facts as can only be discovered by our senses.

> [Philosophical propositions] must be *a priori*. A philosophical proposition must be such as can be neither proved nor disproved by empirical evidence. Too often we find in philosophical books arguments based upon the course of history, or the convolutions of the brain, or the eyes of shell-fish. Special and accidental facts of this kind are irrelevant to philosophy, which must make only such assertions as would be equally true however the actual world were constituted. (Russell 1918, 107)

One of the reasons that Russell took philosophy to be a source of *a priori* knowledge was that he required philosophical claims to provide a sufficiently secure and independent standpoint from which to evaluate non-philosophical claims, and in particular scientific claims. For instance, Russell took it to be a philosophical task to establish whether matter exists and, if it does, what its nature is (Russell 1911, chs. 2 and 3). He also thought that scientific theorizing assumes that there are regularities in nature, and that philosophy is needed to justify that assumption (Russell 1911, ch. 6). In general, at this stage of his philosophical career, Russell required philosophy to be independent of, and epistemically prior to, science.[1]

In contrast, suppose we think that science and philosophy are closely related. We might think that they share various methods and principles, and that the problems that they each pursue differ only in degree of generality. This opens up the prospect that scientific findings are relevant to the testing of philosophical theories, and that some of the issues previously addressed by philosophical theories are better addressed by scientific theories. Later in his philosophical career Russell took exactly this view. Commenting on Ryle's book *The Concept of Mind* (Ryle 1949), Russell wrote that

> Professor Ryle's attitude to science is curious. He no doubt knows that scientists say things which they believe to be relevant to the problems he is discussing, but he is quite persuaded that the philosopher need pay no attention to science. He

---

1   A recent defender of a very similar view is Bealer (1987), (1992), (1996).

seems to believe that a philosopher need not know anything scientific beyond what was known in the time of our ancestors when they dyed themselves with woad. It is this attitude that enables him to think that the philosopher should pay attention to the way in which uneducated people speak and should treat with contempt the sophisticated language of the learned.... A great many philosophical problems are, in fact, scientific questions with which science is not yet ready to deal. Both sensation and perception were in this class of problems, but are now, so I should contend, amenable to scientific treatment and not capable of being fruitfully handled by anyone who chooses to ignore what science has to say about them. (Russell 1958, 8–9)

Here are two other illustrations of the kind of philosophy that Russell is inveighing against. First, the psychology of animals. Some philosophers make claims about animals without any empirical evidence. For instance, Davidson notoriously argued that animals lack beliefs or desires, while apparently utterly ignoring any psychological literature on the matter (Davidson 1975). Second, moral psychology. Some philosophers claim that, necessarily, any fully rational person will be moral. Empirical evidence that some psychopaths are fully rational but indifferent to morality has an obvious bearing on this thesis (Nichols 2002). (Recall the discussion of experimental philosophy in chapter 3, §6.)

The view that scientific methods and results are valuable, or even indispensable, to philosophy is known as naturalism. In the late twentieth century W.V.O. Quine notably championed naturalism, and the view continues to attract many adherents in analytic philosophy. In this chapter we will consider what the view involves and some of the arguments for, or against, it. To this end the next section will discuss Quine's naturalism. We will then take naturalism in epistemology (or "naturalized epistemology" as it is known) as a case study (§§3 and 4). The three sections that follow this case study (§§5–7) will pose various problems for naturalism and assess how well the naturalist can tackle them.

Before closing this section, two points should be noted. First, no single view can be identified with naturalism. In the following sections we will consider a number of views that are standardly classified as statements of naturalism. Although these views differ in content, they are typically associated with certain pro- and anti-attitudes. Each of the views is associated with an attitude of deference towards the claims of science, and a suspicion of purely philosophical sources of information, such as the *a priori*. Second, and to repeat a point, the Autonomy thesis and naturalism are not the only answers that can be given to (Q1-3). Intermediate views are available on the roles of science and philosophy, and we will consider some of the most promising of these views later in the chapter.

2. Quine's Naturalism

Quine's naturalism has two major components. We might call these (1) metaphysical naturalism and (2) methodological naturalism.

(1) Metaphysical naturalism is a view about what kinds of entity exist. The view is that the only entities that exist are natural entities. A natural entity is either an entity that can be studied by the natural sciences (such as physics, chemistry and biology) or an entity whose existence and behaviour are determined by entities that can be studied by the natural sciences. So, for example, electrons, acids, and solar systems are natural entities because they can each be studied by the natural sciences. And so too are tables and weather systems because whether tables and weather systems exist, and how they behave, is determined by the behaviour of entities that can be studied by the natural sciences. Accounts vary on what the determination relation is. Hellman and Thompson (1975) take it to be the relation of composition: the relation that holds between various components and the thing that they compose. Others take it to be a supervenience relation (Papineau 1993, ch. 1). For Quine's own view, see Quine (1977). There is also an issue of how the natural sciences are to be characterized. Here the natural sciences have simply been listed. But how are the sciences on the list themselves to be characterized? If the term "physics," for instance, is taken to apply only to present physics, it will not count many past or any future stages as physics. It seems better, then, to take "physics" to apply to some suitably idealized version of present physics (Papineau 1993, ch. 1, §10). Similar points apply to each of the other sciences listed as natural sciences.

(2) Quine's methodological naturalism consists of three theses. These are:

(2a) the No First Philosophy thesis,
(2b) the Continuity thesis, and
(2c) the No *A Priori* thesis. (This reading of Quine follows Colyvan [2001, 23–24])

(2a), the No First Philosophy thesis, says that we should abandon First Philosophy and look to science to answers for questions about the world. "[Naturalism is] the recognition that it is within science itself, and not in some prior philosophy, that reality is to be identified and described" (Quine 1981, 21).

(2b), the Continuity thesis, says that science and philosophy are continuous and that philosophy is part of the scientific enterprise.

Quine's case for these two theses stems from a third thesis, (2c), the No *A Priori* Truth thesis. This thesis says that no statements are justified *a priori*. One of Quine's arguments for the No *A Priori* Truth thesis is an argument from the history of science (Quine 1951, §6). According to Quine, the history of science shows that at least some statements that have been taken to express necessary truths (specifically, analytic truths or "truths in virtue of meaning") were subsequently rejected because of empirical considerations.

Even more importantly, Quine offers an account of science's rationale in making such revisions. Our beliefs form an interconnected system, a "web of belief." Experience impinges directly only on the beliefs at the edge of this web. But no belief is in principle "immune from revision." When an experience conflicts with our belief system, we have some latitude about which beliefs to revise in order to resolve the conflict. Such revisions are governed by twin constraints of conservatism and simplicity. Conservatism means that, given new evidence, we should revise as few beliefs as possible, and that the more strongly a belief is supported by our total evidence, the more reluctant we should be to revise that belief. Simplicity means that our set of beliefs should be as simple as possible.

What has this got to do with the No *A Priori* Truth thesis? Quine assumes that if a statement is justified on *a priori* grounds, then no experience could diminish that justification. The history of science and Quine's accompanying account of it together show that no statement is immune to revision on empirical grounds. Quine concludes that no statements are justified *a priori*. The Autonomy view says that philosophy does not use the empirical methods of science and that philosophy justifies claims on *a priori* grounds. But since no statements are justified *a priori*, the Autonomy view is mistaken. This establishes (2a), the No First Philosophy thesis. And since no statements are justified *a priori*, the data and methods used by philosophy do not differ in kind from those used by science. This establishes (2b), the Continuity thesis, the thesis that knowledge is seamless (Hylton 2007, 11).

Consequently, Quine and his followers make claims such as the following:

> [K]nowledge, mind, and meaning are part of the same world
> that they have to do with, and ... are to be studied in the same
> empirical spirit that animates natural science. There is no place
> for *a priori* philosophy. (Quine 1969a, 26)

Proper philosophical method is scientific method applied self-consciously to problems more general than those ordinarily considered within a particular science. [Philosophy is] self-conscious science. (Harman 1967, 343)

[Metaphysics] is largely an activity of conceptual clarification in the service of attaining the most plausible view of the universe in the light of a synthesis of the various sciences. Plausibility in the light of total science is the ontologist's touchstone. On this view there is of course no sharp line between science and metaphysics. Metaphysics is the most conjectural and conceptually interesting end of total science.... Its ontological claims must be tested by general scientific plausibility. Plausibility is largely a matter of maximal coherence of our beliefs in the light of often recalcitrant experience: in other words not only must theoretical beliefs cohere with one another, but they must cohere with beliefs derived from observation and experience. (Smart 1989, 50–51)

Quine's No First Philosophy and Continuity theses are important claims about what philosophy is and about how it should be done. To understand them better, and to test them, it helps to consider how those theses would apply to a particular area of philosophy and to the problems found in that area. Quine himself pioneered an application of his metaphysical and methodological naturalism to epistemology. He called the resulting view "naturalized epistemology." Other epistemologists have followed Quine's lead and developed accounts of naturalized epistemology of their own. Goldman (1986) and Kornblith (2002b) are two book-length accounts. The topic of naturalized epistemology then serves as a case study of naturalism. This case study will be the focus of the next section.

3. Case Study: Epistemology

Traditionally epistemology sets itself a number of tasks. It seeks to specify principles of epistemic justification, and to justify those principles. Given that those principles are justified, it further seeks to establish what kinds of claims we can know or justifiably believe. This last task traditionally involves addressing sceptical challenges to our possession of knowledge or justified belief. When evaluating an account of naturalized epistemology, we need to consider which (if any) of these tasks it undertakes and in what form it undertakes the task.

Quine's project of naturalized epistemology has a negative and a positive component. The negative component is about how epistemology has been done to date. The positive component is about how epistemology should instead be done. Take these components in turn.

As Quine sees it, traditional epistemology requires that knowledge had foundations. These foundations are supposed to be beliefs that are justified but which are not justified by other beliefs. Traditional epistemology explores which beliefs are foundational in this sense. Suggestions about which beliefs count as foundational beliefs include certain perceptual beliefs and beliefs about one's current experiences. Traditional epistemology also requires that there are certain epistemic principles that show how justification can be transmitted from foundational beliefs to other beliefs. Non-foundational beliefs are to be justified by being derived from the foundational beliefs via these epistemic principles. Traditional epistemology then seeks to show how all and only justified beliefs belong to a structure as so described. These beliefs would either be foundational beliefs, or beliefs suitably related by the epistemic principles to foundational beliefs. The goals of traditional epistemology are to show what a justified belief is, which beliefs count as justified because of their place in a foundational structure, and how to improve our set of beliefs — which beliefs to retain and which to revise. A particular challenge to the traditional epistemologist's project is posed by scepticism about justification: the view that few, if any, of our beliefs are justified. Traditional epistemology seeks to rebut this scepticism. Quine takes the project of traditional epistemology to run from Descartes (1641) to at least Carnap (1928). (We should not overlook, though, the major differences between the epistemologies of philosophers such as Descartes and Carnap. Carnap took perceptual experiences to be among the foundations of knowledge. Descartes did not. As noted above, his foundations consisted only in what he took to be truths that are immune to doubt and self-evident to the intellect.)

The negative component of Quine's naturalized epistemology is the claim that traditional epistemology is a failed research programme. No beliefs qualify as foundational in the requisite sense, and no epistemic principles show how all of our other justified beliefs could be derived from the usual candidates for foundational beliefs. Quine does not offer supporting arguments for those claims. At the time of writing he may have thought that they did not need to be given and that the anti-foundationalist lessons had already been learnt by philosophers. Whatever Quine's thinking, the foundationalist project should not be lightly dismissed. A foundational belief need only be a justified belief that is not justified by other beliefs; it need not be indubitable (immune to doubt) or incorrigible (immune to error). Criticisms of foundationalism on the grounds that no beliefs have the latter features are misguided (Alston 1976). Furthermore, foundationalism need not require that non-foundational beliefs are justified only if they can be derived from foundational beliefs. It is open to foundationalism to allow weaker evidential relations to hold between foundational and non-foundational beliefs.

Our chief concern, however, is with the positive component of Quine's naturalized epistemology. Let's turn to that. This component consists in an alternative to the foundationalist project. Having renounced the goal of providing foundations for science and common sense, Quine writes that:

> ... epistemology still goes on, though in a new setting and a clarified status. Epistemology, or something like it, simply falls into place as a chapter of psychology and hence of natural science. It studies a natural phenomenon, viz., a physical human subject. This human subject is accorded a certain experimentally controlled input-certain patterns of irradiation in assorted frequencies, for instance, and in the fullness of time the subject delivers as output a description of the three-dimensional external world and its history. The relation between the meagre input and the torrential output is a relation that we are prompted to study for somewhat the same reasons that always prompted epistemology; namely, in order to see how evidence related to theory, and in what ways one's theory of nature transcends any available evidence. (Quine 1969b, 82–83)

In the above passage Quine is making a recommendation about the direction that epistemology should take. But exactly what Quine is recommending is a matter of debate. One prevalent reading takes him to be recommending the replacement of epistemology by psychology. In particular, he is taken to be recommending that we study the psychological processes underlying how our experiences cause our beliefs, and that we ignore evaluative issues about whether these experiences provide evidence for those beliefs. Instead of studying whether our experiences support our beliefs, we study only how our experiences bring about our beliefs. Traditional epistemological issues about rationality and justification are thereby shelved.[2] Nevertheless, it is doubtful whether this is an accurate reading of Quine's views. Quine himself rejects the reading (Quine 1990, 19–21), and at about the same time that he was writing his paper "Epistemology

---

2   This reading is endorsed by Stroud (1984, ch. 6), Kim (1988, 390), Kitcher (1992), and Feldman (1998, 4–5, 23) among others.

Naturalized" Quine was co-authoring a book that was explicitly a book on normative epistemology (Quine and Ullian 1970).[3]

Instead of taking Quine to be advocating the thesis that psychology should replace epistemology, we might more fruitfully take him to be advocating the relevance of psychology to epistemology. The positive component of Quine's naturalized epistemology involves two features. First, there is the claim that epistemology can and should use the empirical results of our best scientific theories, and, in particular, what psychological theories have to tell us about how our beliefs are caused. As Alvin Goldman puts it:

> In studying and criticizing our cognitive procedures, we should use whatever powers and procedures we antecedently have and accept. There is no "starting from scratch." ... (Goldman 1978, 522)

The second feature of the positive component of Quine's naturalized epistemology is that sceptical problems arise from within science:

> ... the skeptical challenge springs from science itself, and that in coping with it we are free to use scientific knowledge. (Quine 1974, 3)

Kornblith agrees:

> It is because science shows us how various aspects of our common-sense view of the world may be mistaken that we come to raise the question of whether we might be entirely mistaken in the way we view the world. But because this question arises from within science, it is perfectly appropriate to draw on the resources (e.g.) of science to answer it. (Kornblith 1995, 240-41)

We will examine these two features of Quine's positive component in the next two sections.

4. Psychological Theory and Epistemology

According to Quine, epistemology "studies a natural phenomenon," i.e., our knowledge, and any facts or methods of science that seem relevant

---

3   For more on how best to read Quine's work on naturalized epistemology and the place of normativity in it, see Haack (1993), Foley (1994), Roth (1999), Hylton (2007, 84), and Gregory (2008).

to its study can be appealed to (Quine 1969b, 82). Similarly, according to Kornblith, knowledge is a natural kind, and, like other natural kinds, we should investigate it using empirical methods (Kornblith 1994b, 48-49). Other philosophers express similar sentiments:

> How could our psychological and biological capacities and limitations fail to be relevant to the study of human knowledge? (Kitcher 1992, 58)

> Thus, a mix of philosophy and psychology is needed to produce acceptable principles of justifiedness. (Goldman 1994b, 314)

Two views can be distinguished. One view might be called psychologism. It is the view that epistemological theories should, amongst other things, be concerned with the psychological processes that cause our beliefs. In particular, the view claims that beliefs are justified in virtue of the psychological processes that produce them. The other view is naturalized epistemology, the view that it is appropriate or advisable to use the methods of the natural sciences in epistemology. It is tempting to think that psychologism implies naturalized epistemology, but that inference is questionable. Psychologism does not seem to imply that empirical psychological data can or must be used to support epistemological theories. A *fortiori*, psychologism seems consistent with the view that those processes should be investigated by *a priori* methods. On the latter view, how people acquire, integrate and retain knowledge has to be investigated by using *a priori* methods. This combination of psychologism and *a priorism* is defended by Anne Bezuidenhout:

> Even if our epistemological investigations must focus on psychological processes, there may be no interesting or *substantive* sense in which the investigation of these processes is constrained by *empirical* psychological investigations of such processes. (Bezuidenhout 1996, 753)

A point about terminology: The view here called "psychologism" — the study of the psychological processes that cause beliefs — Goldman calls "substantive naturalism," and he distinguishes it from methodological naturalism (Goldman 1994b, 302). On Goldman's choice of terminology, Bezuidenhout's overall view accepts substantive naturalism while rejecting methodological naturalism.

It is tempting to think that empirical psychology should play a role in epistemology because it is important for epistemologists to know the psychological abilities and limitations of human beings. That, however, is dubious reasoning. By the same token, it should be important for epistemologists to know the physical abilities and limitations of human beings — how much sleep or food they can survive without. Yet that seems little reason to think that medical science should play a substantive role in epistemology (Bezuidenhout 1996, 754).

The view that psychological processes could be investigated by *a priori* methods might seem a non-starter. Hasn't Quine shown that no beliefs are immune from revision on empirical grounds? There are two ways of justifying a belief. One way is holistic: it appeals to an entire system of beliefs, and to the simplicity and explanatory power of that system. Another way is local: it appeals to a proper sub-set of our beliefs and specific inferential practices. Quine writes as though justification is always holistic:

> our beliefs confront the tribunal of experience only as a corporate body. (Quine 1951b, 41)

Local and holistic methods of justification, however, do not exclude one another. So Quine's claim that beliefs are tested by experience only as a corporate body is unfounded (Rey 2004, 228). In addition, the holistic method of justification might show that the most confirmed theory is one that says that among the local forms of justification is a form of *a priori* justification. Given the holistic justification of the claim that there is *a priori* justification, we could then set about identifying which specific claims are justified *a priori* (Rey 2004, 237).

Furthermore, suppose that Quine has shown that no beliefs are immune to revision on empirical grounds. That result would show that no beliefs are justified *a priori* only on the assumption that a belief's being justified *a priori* would make it immune to empirical counter-evidence. Some defenders of the *a priori* reject that assumption.[4] Furthermore, some philosophers have put forward theories of *a priori* justification that are intended to make it naturalistically acceptable.[5] According to an epistemological view known as reliabilism, whether a certain way of forming beliefs makes those beliefs justified depends on whether that way is reliable, whether it tends to produce more true beliefs than false ones. Rey, Goldman, and Antony each suggest that beliefs are justified *a priori* if the way in which they are formed is both reliable and does not have any input from the senses. Suppose, for example, that our minds have a reasoning module that makes us believe theorems of the propositional

---

4   Rey (1998, 39), and Casullo (2003, chs. 2 and 5).
5   Rey (1996, §6), (1998), (2004, 238–39); Goldman (1999), and Antony (2004).

calculus without needing any input from the senses. Our belief in such theorems would be justified because they were produced by a reliable process, and they would be justified *a priori* because the senses were not involved in producing them.

Rey thinks that, on the above view, someone could know *a priori* that *p* without knowing that they know *a priori* that *p* (Rey 1994, 92; 1998, 36; and 2004, 237–38). Whether someone knows *a priori* that *p* depends upon the reliability of the process that produced their belief and upon that process not needing any data from the senses in producing that belief. The person in question need not have any beliefs, and *a fortiori* any knowledge, about whether those conditions are met. Rey and Kornblith each think that it follows from this that:

> whether or not there is *a priori* knowledge is an empirical issue. (Rey 1998, 25)

> … the claim that we have such *a priori* knowledge is itself an empirical claim. Whether we should believe that this kind of *a priori* knowledge genuinely exists thus needs to be determined by experimental research. (Kornblith 2007, §5)

I doubt whether these claims do follow. Rey's original point is that:

(1) *x*'s knowing *a priori* that *p*

does not entail that:

(2) *x* knows that *x* knows *a priori* that *p*.

Rey's original point, however, does not entail that:

(3) *x*'s knowing *a priori* that *p*

entails that:

(4) *x* does not know *a priori* that *x* knows *a priori* that *p*.

Rey's original point leaves it open whether anyone knows *a priori* that they know *a priori* that a certain proposition is true. On his account of *a priori* justification, *x* knows *a priori* that *p* if *x*'s belief that *p* is produced by a reliable method and no input from the senses was needed for that belief to be produced. This account allows that someone can know *a priori* that they know a certain proposition *a priori* provided that the process by which they formed the belief that they know a certain proposition *a priori* is both reliable and did not need input from the senses to produce that belief. Since the account allows that people can have such higher-order *a priori* knowledge, the account is not committed to claiming that the existence of *a priori* knowledge "needs to be determined by experimental research." (Rey [2005b, 480] grants that his account allows such higher-order *a priori* knowledge. His key point is that *x*'s knowing *a priori* that *p* is compatible with its being knowable only *a posteriori* that *x* knows *a priori* that *p*.)

Rey takes his naturalistic account of the *a priori* to challenge the assumption that "if there is to be *a priori* knowledge, its existence as *a priori* knowledge should be readily to hand, establishable either by introspection or behavioural tests." He attributes this assumption to "both Quine and his traditional Rationalist opponents" (Rey 2004, 228). Here Rey assumes that, if anything is a case of *a priori* knowledge, its being a case of *a priori* knowledge can be readily established by introspection or by behavioural tests. Yet it is very doubtful whether anyone has made the assumption. Rationalists such as Leibniz and Spinoza thought that some propositions that they knew *a priori* — that the fundamental entities are simple mental substances (Leibniz), or that God and nature are identical (Spinoza) — are anything but easily established. Critics of Leibniz and Spinoza did not reject their claims of *a priori* knowledge on the basis of (in Rey's phrase) "the introspective or behavioural surfaces of our lives." Kant thought that nothing less than the 600 pages of his *Critique of Pure Reason* were needed to set them straight.

One interesting consequence of the above naturalistic account of the *a priori* is that there can be cases of *a priori* knowledge of contingent truths. It is contingent that you exist. So it is contingent that you exist and know anything. Suppose that you know *a priori* that *p*. If you had not existed, you would not know *a priori* that *p*. It follows that it is contingent that you know *a priori* that *p*. (What may be necessary is that if you know that *p*, you know *a priori* that *p*.) The above account allows that it is possible for you to know *a priori* that you know *a priori* that *p*. If that is possible, it follows that it is possible for you to know *a priori* a contingent truth.

To sum up, Bezuidenhout's view that epistemology can investigate psychological processes by using only *a priori* methods seems tenable. It follows that the claim that epistemological theories should be concerned with the psychological processes that cause our beliefs does not imply naturalized epistemology's claim that it is appropriate or advisable to use the methods of the natural sciences in epistemology.

Here is another reason for querying whether there is such an implication. The discussion so far has talked of empirical information and scientific information as though the terms used were interchangeable. They are not. Scientific information is a specialized, technical kind of empirical information, and there is another kind of empirical information that is non-specialized and non-technical. This is common sense empirical information. This information is freely available to philosophers to inform their epistemological theories. It is then unclear whether the specialized empirical information of psychological theories is needed in epistemology. To take just one example, Goldman appeals to empirical results from experiments in psychology that show that visual object recognition is more reliable in some circumstances than others (Goldman 1994b, 304–06). But the same conclusion has already been drawn by common sense. Common sense says that we see things better in some conditions than others — we see well in broad daylight and poorly in the dark. Again, common sense tells us that people sometimes reason on the basis of too small a sample, that their reasoning is open to bias and wishful thinking, and so on. Citing the results from cognitive psychology only tells us something that we already knew, at least in broad outline (Feldman 1998, 16-18 and 2002, 175–76). What cognitive psychology tells us is how extensive such bad reasoning is, what forms of it we are particularly prone to, and why.[6]

The above objection to naturalized epistemology concerned the relevance of scientific information to epistemology. This objection lends strength to the following dilemma for naturalized epistemology (Feldman 1998, 8-10 and 2002, 171–72). The dilemma is that either naturalized epistemology is true but trivial, or it is non-trivial but apparently false. The dilemma is generated by posing the following question: How broadly should epistemology be understood?

Suppose that it is understood broadly, so that epistemology is understood as the study of human knowledge. Such a study would be very broad. It would include "historical studies of what people knew, when and how knowledge has grown (or been lost) over time, studies in neuroscience concerning the ways the brain processes information, psychological studies of the cognitive processes involved in belief formation, sociological studies about the ways knowledge is transmitted in societies, and so on" (Feldman 1998, 8). Now, if that is how epistemology is understood, scientific and other empirical information is relevant to epistemology. Indeed, such information would be essential to it, and presumably no one would argue otherwise. But if this is the understanding

---

6   See the empirical results collected in Kahneman, Slovic and Tversky (1982).

of epistemology that naturalized epistemology works with, than the latter is uncontentious and trivially true.

Alternatively, if epistemology is understood more narrowly, so that it is concerned with only philosophical questions about knowledge and justification, then epistemology has a smaller scope than the study of human knowledge. But then the claim that scientific information is relevant to epistemology so understood is far from obvious.

5. Science and Scepticism

At the end of §3 we identified two features of the positive component of Quine's naturalized epistemology. One feature was the relevance of psychological data to epistemology. We examined that claim in the previous section. The other feature was the claim that sceptical problems arise from within science. To quote Kornblith again:

> It is because science shows us how various aspects of our com-
> mon-sense view of the world may be mistaken that we come
> to raise the question of whether we might be entirely mistaken
> in the way we view the world. But because this question arises
> from within science, it is perfectly appropriate to draw on the
> resources (e.g.) of science to answer it. (Kornblith 1995, 240–41)

Mark Colyvan echoes this view:

> If scepticism originates within science, it is only reasonable
> that epistemologists are justified in using whatever portion of
> science they require to combat scepticism. (Colyvan 2001, 26)

The current section will examine this second feature of Quine's positive contribution to epistemology.

Quine seems to be right about the starting point for philosophy. We come to philosophy with a wealth of beliefs. At any given time only some of those beliefs can be evaluated and revised. The evaluation and revision of some beliefs requires that other beliefs are used in making the evaluation and the revision. During that process of evaluation, the latter beliefs will not themselves be under evaluation. Quine appeals to Neurath's metaphor of our beliefs being like planks making up a boat (Quine 1960, 3). While at sea, while using our beliefs to navigate around the world, we cannot replace all of those planks at once. But we can replace them in a piecemeal fashion and thereby gradually improve the seaworthiness of our boat. Furthermore, among these beliefs are our beliefs about epistemology. These include our beliefs about what it is for a belief to be justified or knowledge, and about which of our beliefs have this status.

On this basis Quine rejects the traditional epistemological project of providing a justification for science from a vantage point outside of science. He claims that any justification for science must be given from within science (Quine 1960, 275). It is not clear, however, whether these further claims of Quine's are warranted.

Let's grant that there is no vantage point outside of our *entire belief system* with which that system can be evaluated. It does not follow that there is no vantage point outside of *science* with which it can be evaluated (Siegel 1995, 50–51). Quine frequently equivocates between two senses of "science" (Haack 1993, 339). In a narrow sense, "science" includes only the natural sciences. In a broader sense, science includes our ordinary, non-specialist beliefs and our mathematical, logical and philosophical beliefs, as well as more narrowly scientific beliefs. The broad sense of science is at work in the following passage:

> [S]cience is self-conscious common sense. And philosophy, in turn, as an effort to get clear on things, is not to be distinguished in essential points of method or purpose from good or bad science. (Quine 1960, 3–4)[7]

The narrow sense is at work in this next passage:

> Science, after all, differs from common sense only in degree of methodological sophistication. (Quine 1969c, 129)

And both senses are found in this last passage:

> [T]his structure of interconnected sentences is a single connected science including all sciences, and indeed anything we ever say about the world. (Quine 1960, 67–68)

Part of the plausibility of the claim that epistemology is continuous with science lies in construing science in the broad sense. But, in conflating both senses of "science," the claim that epistemology is continuous with science in the narrow sense of the word is given specious plausibility.

What about the claim that sceptical problems arise within science and so it is appropriate to appeal to science to resolve those problems? Quine, Colyvan and Kornblith presumably have in mind the sceptical problem

---

7   See also Quine (1960, 22), and Hylton (2007, 2, 8, 11, and 15).

of the external world: the problem of how to justify the belief that what causes our sensory experiences are external objects. Science tells us much about the physics and physiology of perception. In explaining how the senses work, science also explains to us how the senses can be deceived and how the causes of our experiences can appear to be other than they are. Because of false perspective, distance, tiredness or hallucinogens, science explains how we can misperceive our environment. So it seems that not only does science show that we can be in error about what we perceive, but it can also tell us in what situations we are in error. It might then seem that science can solve the problem of the external world by identifying the conditions in which we perceive veridically and those conditions in which we do not.

Two replies to this. First, science is not needed to generate the sceptical problem of the external world. Descartes's thought experiment that he is dreaming and not perceiving an external world does not rely on anything that science has told us. Yet his thought experiment is enough to generate the sceptical problem of how we can know that we are awake and perceiving rather than asleep and dreaming.

Second, even if sceptical problems arise within science, it does not follow that science can solve them. A discipline or theory can generate a problem but it does not follow that its resources are sufficient to solve that problem. Here are two examples. Consider Newtonian mechanics. This is a theory of the behaviour of matter. One problem arising within the theory was the effect of electromagnetism on matter. Newtonian mechanics was unable to explain this effect. Next, consider theology. Sceptical problems arise within theology. One of them is the problem of evil. This is the problem that evil acts occur and yet if God is all-powerful, all-knowing, and morally perfect, he has the power, knowledge and motivation to prevent any evil occurring. It remains debatable whether theology can solve this problem. Returning to the case of science, everything that science tells us assumes that we often perceive the world reliably. Since the sceptical problem of the external world raises the problem of how that assumption can be justified, it seems illegitimately circular to appeal to any scientific claim to justify that assumption. The situation here seems to be essentially the same as the one in the discussion of Moore's proof of an external world (chapter 1, §6). Science and common sense each assume that we perceive the world reliably. Scepticism about the external world calls that assumption into question. It seems illegitimate to appeal to what science or common sense says to defend that assumption. This charge of circularity, however, is one that Quine and other naturalized epistemologists are aware of. They have sought to address it in several ways. We will consider some of them in the next section.

6. The Problem of Circularity

Not only does Quine reject the traditional claim that epistemology should provide a foundation for scientific and common sense beliefs, he also thinks that science can evaluate its own claims and methods of inquiry. As others put it:

> [Naturalism seeks] to derive the reliability of our methods from our psychological and physical theories, our theories about how the mind arrives at beliefs through interaction with its environment. (Friedman 1979, 370)[8]

> ... where scientific reasons give out, reasons give out altogether ... And where science is satisfied in the absence of further reasons, the skeptical demand for further reasons is simply illegitimate. (Rosen 1999, 467. Rosen should not be taken as endorsing this view; he is only reporting it here)

Notice that Quine's view that science does not require extra-scientific warrant from First Philosophy does not entail his further view that the only reasons supporting scientific claims are themselves scientific claims. What is the argument for Quine's further view? It would be using a false dichotomy to argue that since First Philosophy cannot justify scientific claims, then science can justify its own claims. This overlooks the sceptical option that scientific claims lack justification altogether. Moreover, the sceptic can object that science cannot justify its own claims without vicious circularity. After all, numerology (for example) cannot justify its own claims without vicious circularity, and it would be special pleading to say that science can justify its claims without vicious circularity.

Quine replies to the charge of circularity by saying that:

> such scruples against circularity have little point once we have stopped dreaming of deducing science from observations. If we are out simply to understand the link between observation and science, we are well advised to use any available information, including that provided by the very science whose link with observation we are seeking to understand. (Quine 1969b, 76–77)

The problem of circularity arises, however, whatever kind of justification is at issue — whether it is deductive or non-deductive. It would still be

8   See also Hylton (2007, 17–18).

viciously circular to argue that it is even probable that science is true because science says so. Even if the kind of justification that Quine has in mind is non-deductive, and he rejects the dream of "deducing science from observations," the problem of circularity remains (Teller 1971, 379 and Hylton 1994, 269–70).

A distinction is often drawn between virtuous and viciously circular arguments or methods.[9] Whereas a viciously circular argument is bad, a virtuously circular argument is not. How to classify circular arguments as virtuous or vicious, though, remains difficult and contentious. We have seen how Quine compares the piecemeal revision of our beliefs with sailors rebuilding their ship at sea plank by plank. But, although such belief revision is reasonable, it is not clear that this is a case of self-authentication — a case where a given method, or a given set of claims, shows that that method is a reasonable one, or that those very claims are reasonably held. It seems reasonable to use one claim to justify another claim to show that the latter claim is justified if the former is. But justifying a set of claims, S, by means of S amounts only to showing that the members of S are justified if the members of S are justified. If it is circular for science to evaluate science, then any evaluation of science — traditionally, a task of First Philosophy — needs to be sufficiently independent of science. Quine apparently thinks that this would require First Philosophy to be better justified than science (Quine 1960, 235). But being sufficiently independent of science to criticize it does not require having more justification than science (Siegel 1995, 51–52).

Peter Hylton offers the following reconstruction of Quine's thinking:

> Quine's naturalism [claims that] there is no perspective, no standpoint, except that of some theory, from which our theory can be judged to conform or not to conform to reality. We can now reformulate this idea. To speak a language at all — and hence, at least on Quine's view, to think thoughts of any significant complexity — is to accept a large though ill-defined body of judgments. In particular, it is to accept the reality of at least some of the objects that our theory of the world talks about. Hence there is no coherent position from which the reality of all such objects — or the truth of all such judgments — can be denied: the attempted denial undercuts the language in which it is made, and hence leaves us with no coherent statement at all. (Hylton 1994, 275)

---

9   E.g., Goodman (1955, 63–64) and Haack (1993, 352).

It is doubtful whether the above line of argument is valid. Suppose that to speak a language (which, for Quine, is equivalent to holding a theory) involves accepting some body of claims. It is consistent with this that people speaking different languages thereby accept different bodies of claims — even disjoint bodies of claims. It is then possible for a speaker of language L_1 to deny all of the claims associated with another language L_2. Speakers of L_2 can follow this reasoning, and so come to understand that there *is* a coherent position from which the reality of all the objects that they posit — or of the truth of all the judgements that they make — can be denied. It is the position of a speaker of L_2. The argument that Hylton reconstructs from Quine needs further work to make it valid.[10]

Hylton thinks that it is significant that the above quotation from Quine talks of understanding, and not justification. Hylton claims that "if our aim is one of understanding, however, rather than justification, then this circularity is in no way vicious" (Hylton 2007, 83). Yet shifting the issue from justification to understanding seems to make no substantive difference. If scientific information helps us to understand our scientific theories, that information has to be reliable: it has to confer genuine understanding rather than the illusion of understanding. But then why think that that information is reliable? Suppose that the only reason is that our scientific theories say that it is. That raises the question: why think that those theories are themselves reliable? Suppose that the only reason for thinking so is that the information says that they are. That would be to argue in a circle — a circle that does not appreciably differ from the circle that results when the issue is put in terms of justification. Consequently, if the circle of justification is vicious, it is not clear how the viciousness is dispelled through recasting the issue in terms of understanding.

Hylton anticipates something like the above objection. He replies that:

> In Quine's view, [the objection] is making an impossible, per-
> haps incoherent, demand. That demand could only be satis-
> fied by a source of knowledge altogether different in kind from
> ordinary theoretical knowledge, independent and prior, which
> would thus afford us a perspective from which all our ordinary
> knowledge could be critically evaluated. Quine derogatively
> calls this idea "First Philosophy," and rejects it completely.
> (Hylton 2007, 90)

Hylton's reply is a restatement of Quine's naturalism. Yet Quine's naturalism was precisely what was at issue. So it is not clear how the reply

---

10   For Hylton's own criticism of the argument, see Hylton (1994, 276–78).

advances the debate. The fact (if it is one) that the objection makes an impossible demand does not automatically count against the objection unless we are assuming at the outset that Quine's view is right. To assume that Quine's view is right, however, is to beg the question. As an analogy, consider the problem of induction. The inductivist makes inductive inferences: inferences from the observed to the unobserved. The problem of induction places a demand on the inductivist; namely, to justify inductive inferences. If inductive inferences cannot be justified, the demand is an impossible one. The fact (if it is one) that the problem of induction makes an impossible demand on the inductivist does not automatically count against the problem and warrant our "rejecting it completely." (The analogy with the problem of induction is particularly apt, as Quine regards the problem of induction as a genuine one and concedes to Hume that inductive inferences cannot be justified. See Quine 1969b, 72 and Hylton 2007, 83.)

Naturalized epistemologists other than Quine have tried to show that it is virtuously circular to use science's methods and claims to justify those same methods and claims.[11] Kornblith argues that the circularity is virtuous because there is no guarantee that scientific investigation will confirm the overall reliability of our mechanisms of belief production:

> While it is certainly true that this investigation is itself carried out by using the very mechanisms of belief production whose reliability is in question, this does not assure that the investigation will confirm the overall reliability of our methods of belief production. (Kornblith 1995, 246)[12]

Kornblith's thinking seems to be as follows. A viciously circular argument includes its conclusion as a member of its premise-set. A viciously circular argument is thereby also a valid argument. A valid argument guarantees its conclusion in the sense that, necessarily, if all of its premises are true, its conclusion is true. A viciously circular argument, then, will guarantee its conclusion. By **contraposition**, an argument that does not guarantee its conclusion is not viciously circular. Now there is no guarantee that scientific investigation will confirm scientific claims. So it is not viciously circular to argue that scientific investigation confirms current scientific claims.

A weakness in Kornblith's line of argument is that it is open to the same criticism that faces Quine's response to the problem of circularity.

---

11 For example, Friedman (1979, 370–73) and Kitcher (1992, 90–93). See Tiel (1999, 315–18) for some replies.

12 See also Friedman (1979, 371).

As noted, the problem arises whatever kind of justification is in question. Granted there is no guarantee that scientific investigation will confirm current scientific claims. That leaves open the issue whether it does confirm them. It would still seem viciously circular to argue "Scientific claims and methods are largely correct because scientific claims and methods (i.e., scientific investigation) says they are." Here is an analogy. Is Richie Nix a liar? There is no guarantee that if we asked him whether he is a liar, he would lie to us. Perhaps he is not an inveterate liar and would give us an honest answer on this occasion. Nevertheless, it would still seem viciously circular to argue in the following way: "Richie Nix is not a liar because he told me that he is not."

7. The Problem of Epistemic Authority

The previous section discussed one problem facing naturalism. It was the problem of the apparently vicious circularity of using scientific methods to justify naturalist claims. This section will discuss a closely related problem. This problem is not confined to naturalism about epistemology. It is a problem about what epistemic authority a subject can have, given that we are naturalists about that subject.

The problem of epistemic authority for naturalism about science is generated by two claims that naturalists characteristically make. Claim (1): science is our best source of information (Kornblith 1994b, 40; Colyvan 2001, 23; Ladyman and Ross 2007, ch. 1). Claim (2): there is no perspective outside of science from which to judge science. In the previous section we saw that Quine takes claim (2) to be a consequence of the rejection of First Philosophy. The naturalized epistemologist

> no longer dreams of a first philosophy, firmer than science, on which science can be based; he is out to defend science from within, against its self-doubts. (Quine 1974, 3)

Now what are the reasons for making claim (1), the claim that science is our best source of information? Given claim (2), claim (1) has to be asserted from the perspective of science. But then claim (1) amounts to this: From the perspective of science, science is the best source of information. That claim may be true, but it is not equivalent to the claim that science is the best source of information. It may be that, from the perspective of my guru, my guru is the best source of information about the world. But even though that may be true, it does not entail that my guru is the best source of information. The naturalized epistemologist needs to say what is special about the perspective of science. What gives it a privileged epistemic status that my guru lacks? Unfortunately, there seems no way for the naturalized epistemologist to answer this. Claim (2) denies that there is any neutral, non-scientific perspective with which to make the comparison between the perspective of science and the perspective of my guru.

That, then, is the problem of epistemic authority. Claim (1) says that science is epistemically superior to other disciplines. Claim (2) says that science cannot be compared with other disciplines in neutral terms. Either claim (1) collapses into the uninteresting claim that science says that science is best, or the comparison that claim (1) needs to make cannot be made.

Let's explore this problem in another setting — that of naturalism about mathematics. Cognitive practices have goals. Science is such a practice. One of its goals is to predict and explain the behaviour of natural phenomena. According to Quine's naturalism, if accepting a certain scientific sentence S would help science reach that goal, and if reaching that goal could not be done as simply if S were not accepted, then S is acceptable. No further justification of S's acceptability is needed or even available. Our use of set theory is also a cognitive practice. One of the goals of this practice is to provide a framework that models all of classical mathematics. According to Penelope Maddy's mathematical naturalism, if accepting a certain mathematical sentence M would help set theory reach that goal, and if reaching that goal could not be done without accepting M, then M is acceptable. No further justification of M's acceptability is needed or even available. Naturalism, according to Maddy, is the view that

> a successful enterprise, be it science or mathematics ... should not be subject to criticism from, and does not stand in need of support from, some external supposedly higher point of view. (Maddy 1997, 184)

Quine and Maddy's naturalism take science and mathematics respectively to be autonomous in the sense that claims and methods that do not belong to these practices are irrelevant to the justification of claims made, and methods used, within the practices. More generally, naturalism about a given cognitive practice renders that practice immune from outside criticism. Any practitioners will find this a desirable feature. So unless science and mathematics are privileged, however, naturalism about each and every other cognitive practice is an open option that its practitioners can take up.

For example, astrology is a cognitive practice. One of its goals is to discover mystical relations between planets and people's lives. Let astrological naturalism be the thesis that if accepting a certain astrological sentence A would help astrology achieve that goal, and if reaching that goal could not be done without accepting A, then A is acceptable. No further justification of A's acceptability is needed or even available. That is, astrology's claim that A is not open to external criticism.

Examples such as this one of astrological naturalism pose a challenge to Quine and Maddy. The challenge is for them to provide a principle that endorses naturalism about science, or about mathematics, but not about astrology and other pseudo-sciences (Rosen 1999, 471). In the above quotation Maddy talked of naturalism about a "successful enterprise." But according to which standards is naturalism successful? Although mathematics is successful according to its own standards, presumably astrology is successful according to its own standards. It is true that some mathematics is successfully used in its application to empirical phenomena. Yet not all of mathematics has empirical application. So this route would support mathematical naturalism at most with respect to some branches of mathematics, not all.

Nevertheless, Maddy seems to take this route in meeting the problem. She says that mathematics is indispensable to scientific practice whereas astrology is not (Maddy 1997, 204–05). But, if this is her chosen reply, it does not sit well with her claim that mathematics is autonomous and "not answerable to any extra-mathematical reality tribunal" (Maddy 1997, 184).[13] Furthermore, what was wanted was something more general than a defence of mathematical naturalism. What was wanted was a principle that separated science and mathematics from the rest. If naturalism about science is legitimate, then Maddy's appeal to indispensability considerations shows that mathematics (or at least applied mathematics) can be legitimized too. But this does nothing to show that naturalism about science is legitimate although naturalism about astrology is not. Maddy's response is incomplete.[14]

8. Conclusion

This chapter has a mixed message. Philosophers have tended to overrestimate how much they could establish without appealing to empirical information. Nevertheless, it would be an exaggeration to suppose that empirical information without philosophical reflection can resolve any

---

13   For this criticism, see Dieterle (1999), Rosen (1999, 472), and Roland (2007, 435–36).
14   For further discussion, see Roland (2009).

philosophical problems. The chapter began by distinguishing between metaphysical and methodological naturalism. Metaphysical naturalism says that all entities are natural entities. A natural entity is an entity that can be studied by the natural sciences. The natural sciences are themselves to be characterized as suitably idealized versions of today's natural sciences.

Turning to methodological naturalism, there is a question about how it is best understood. Suppose that it is taken to say that empirical information can confirm or disconfirm philosophical theories. Suppose that epistemology advances hypotheses about what people justifiably believe or know, and at least some of this justification is supposed to be empirical. Empirical information can then be used to test whether people have the alleged justification, and so test whether those hypotheses are true.

Alternatively, suppose that methodological naturalism is taken to say that empirical information is needed to confirm, or disconfirm, certain philosophical theories, and that only science can supply this information. The issue is then whether that claim is justifiable.

How plausible are either of these options? There are two kinds of case to consider. First, there are cases where empirical evidence is supposed to be indispensable to confirming or disconfirming a philosophical theory. Now evidence of the senses is needed to support the hypothesis that there is an external world. Evidence that there is evil is needed to support the hypothesis that there is a problem of evil for theism. Evidence that other human bodies behave as your body does is needed to support the hypothesis that there are other minds. And so on. But in none of these cases does the empirical evidence have to be provided by science. In each case it can be provided by common sense observation without the aid of scientific instruments or theories.

The second kind of case concerns cases where methodological naturalists might argue that scientific evidence can confirm or disconfirm a philosophical theory, even if it is not indispensable evidence. Examples are controversial, but here are two candidates. First, the fossil record and other evidence for the theory of evolution is evidence against the argument from design. Second, evidence for the theory of relativity is evidence against Kant's claim that necessarily the geometry of space is Euclidean. But, the challenge goes, although this scientific evidence counts against these theories, the evidence is not indispensable. There are sufficient non-scientific reasons to reject the theories. Hume's philosophical criticisms of the argument of design are sufficiently telling to justify rejecting the argument. The same mathematical methods that show the consistency of non-Euclidean geometries also refute Kant's claim that necessarily the geometry of space is Euclidean. More generally, in any case where scientific evidence can confirm or disconfirm a philosophical theory, that evidence is dispensable because non-scientific reasons can confer at least the same degree of support.

In sum, the challenge says that either the empirical evidence that bears on a philosophical theory is not dispensable, but the evidence need not be scientific; or the empirical evidence is scientific, but the evidence is dispensable. In no case is the empirical evidence both scientific and required to confirm, or disconfirm, a philosophical theory.

Naturalists will not let the challenge go unanswered. First, the application of scientific methods to philosophical theories does not require that those theories can be directly tested empirically — that is, by observing the subject matter of such a theory. After all, the subject matter of many scientific theories cannot be tested directly because that subject matter is too small or too distant, but (at least many scientists and philosophers of science think) that does not prevent such theories from receiving empirical support. Second, given the sheer range of subject matters of philosophical theories, it would be surprising if none of them were open to empirical testing. For example, philosophy of physics seems hardly distinguishable from advanced theoretical physics. These disciplines (or this discipline?) are principally concerned with how best to formulate and understand current physics. The distinction between the theoretical physicist and the philosopher of physics might be only administrative and not substantive. Similar observations apply to the distinctions between linguistics and philosophy of language, or cognitive psychology and philosophy of mind (Cooper 2005, 329). And if scientific findings bear on such theories, those findings are not obviously duplicated by untutored common sense observation. Other branches of philosophy might seem less obviously sensitive to empirical results. Philosophers of logic concerned with working out the nature of logical consequence seem to be engaged in work far removed from any empirical observations. In response, Quineans tend to emphasize the picture of "the web of belief" (as discussed in §2 above). Empirical observations can have ramifications at the centre of the web where our beliefs about logic and mathematics are located. Considerations of explanatory power and simplicity can, in principle, even warrant the revision of such core beliefs. Whether this Quinean picture of the structure of our beliefs should be accepted, however, is challenged by defenders of the Autonomy view (Bonjour 1998, 74–76).[15]

---

15   But see Kornblith (2000).

Questions for Discussion

1. One formulation of naturalism involves deference to the epistemic authority of the natural sciences. Is there any justification for privileging the natural sciences over the other sciences? Another formulation involves deference to the epistemic authority of the sciences more generally. What counts as a science? What distinguishes the sciences from the non-sciences?

2. In §4 we considered the claim that cognitive science and psychology have nothing of relevance to say to philosophy that common sense does not already say. How plausible is that claim? Does work in experimental philosophy (chapter 3, §6) tend to support it or to undermine it?

3. Suppose Eric believes that p. If it is true that p, evidence that implies that p is false is misleading evidence. So Eric should believe that any evidence that implies that p is false to be misleading evidence. So Eric should not revise his belief that p irrespective of what evidence to the contrary he receives. Now, if p is true, evidence that p is true need not be misleading evidence. So Eric's belief that p can be supported by evidence, and so his degree of belief that p can increase. Ginger believes that p is false. If p is false, evidence that implies that p is misleading evidence, whereas evidence that implies that p is false need not be misleading evidence. By parallel reasoning, Ginger's belief that p is false can be supported by evidence, and his degree of belief that p is false can increase.

　Why is the case of Eric and Ginger paradoxical? How should the paradox be solved? (The paradox is Kripke's: see Harman 1973, 148–49.)

Core Reading for Chapter 6

Feldman, Richard (2002) "Methodological Naturalism in Epistemology."
Foley, Richard (1994) "Quine and Naturalized Epistemology."
Hylton, Peter (2007) *Quine* chs. 1 and 4.
Kim, Jaegwon (1988) "What is Naturalized Epistemology?"
Knobe, Joshua and Shaun Nichols (2008) (eds.) *Experimental Philosophy*.
Kornblith, Hilary (2002a) "In Defense of Naturalized Epistemology."
Quine, W.V.O (1969b) "Epistemology Naturalised."

Conclusion

We will close by reviewing three questions: What data and methods should we use in philosophy? How should we justify selecting those data and methods? And, given a selection of data and assumptions, how should we then proceed?

What data and methods should we use in philosophy? What kinds of data and principles are admissible in philosophy is itself open to philosophical debate. There is nothing untoward in this. By the same token, we should not expect to advance philosophical programmes without making debatable assumptions (Nozick 1981, 19). If we were to take as assumptions only those assumptions that all philosophers agreed on, the set of assumptions would either be too anaemic or empty to found a substantive philosophical programme on. Making contentious assumptions leaves us open to charges of bias or of parochialism. The charge of bias is best met by showing the benefits of hypotheses founded on the alleged biases. The charge of parochialism applies to insular views, and the remedy to that is to be responsive to developments in, and criticisms from, other philosophical programmes.

There are some straightforwardly philosophical assumptions. In the introduction we saw that what philosophical methods people are prepared to use will partly depend upon their view of philosophy and of the nature of philosophical problems (their "metaphilosophy"). But assumptions about what the world is like are also made:

> In philosophy, no less than in science, methodological practice presupposes substantive theoretical commitment; in order for a given methodological practice to be appropriate, whether in science or philosophy, the world has to cooperate by being a certain way. (Melnyck 2008a, 267–68)

How should we justify selecting those data and methods? It is tempting to try to dodge the difficult question of justifying the selection and use of certain data or principles by claiming that it is a brute epistemic truth that they are epistemically privileged, that they should be so selected and used. Well, perhaps there are certain brute epistemic truths, but conceding this does not license our admitting as brute epistemic truths that our preferred data and principles are privileged. We should minimize the number of epistemic truths we take as basic:

> In our ordinary doings, we legitimately reject hypotheses as, *inter alia*, unduly complex, *ad hoc*, or as simply not supported by the data. Various properties — complexity, being *ad hoc*, being unsupported by the data — are thus taken to have something in common, namely that they are bases of epistemic disconfirmation. However, the positing of additional, widely disparate grounds for rejecting hypotheses makes it more difficult to see them all as aspects of one single thing. (Vogel 1993, 243–44, his italics)

Given a selection of data and assumptions, how should we proceed? One method that suggests itself is the method of "cost-benefit analysis" (Lewis 1983a, and Armstrong 1989, 19–20). To reach a solution to a given philosophical problem, we consider the arguments for, and the arguments against, each theory that proposes to solve the problem. We then draw up a "balance sheet." The balance sheet records the strengths and weaknesses of each theory — how simple it is, how explanatory it is, how well it coheres with already accepted theories, which intuitions it is consistent with, which it is inconsistent with, and so on. We weight the costs of each theory against its benefits, forming a ranking of theories. The theory at the top of the ranking, the theory that provides the most benefits for the least costs, is the theory we should tentatively accept.

It might be thought wrong-headed to apply this method of assessment to philosophy. Here are four comments in its defence. First, the method is appealing to something familiar and sensible: when working out what to believe, we should work out where the balance of evidence lies. That is what being rational involves. In every other area of cognitive life, we should try to find out where the balance of evidence lies. It would be very curious if this were not the right way to do philosophy (DePaul 1998). The cost-benefit method also subsumes the method of reflective equilibrium described in chapter 2, §3. Narrow reflective equilibrium seeks to make philosophical theories cohere with intuitions by making judicious revisions of one or the other. Wide reflective equilibrium seeks to make philosophical theories cohere with a broader range of data: intuitions, observations, and other relevant theories (Daniels 1980). Reflective equilibrium can be reached in many ways, depending on which theories or which pieces of data are revised or sacrificed. The different results then need to be critically compared to establish which (if any) is the best way of reaching reflective equilibrium. The cost-benefit method promises to give us the answer to this.

Second, the cost-benefit model might be criticized on the ground that the costs and benefits considered are merely pragmatic ones. The criticism is that although the model may give us reason to believe that a particular theory is the best to use, it does not give us reason to believe that that theory is true (Rosen 1990, 338, fn. 18.) This criticism, however, seems properly directed not so much against the cost-benefit model itself, as against certain of the kinds of costs and benefits that are selected. Moreover, the criticism has ramifications far beyond the cost-benefit model. The general criticism is that theoretical virtues as simplicity, explanatory power or fruitfulness are only pragmatic considerations, and that the fact that a theory has such features is no reason to believe it. (We saw this criticism being made of considerations of simplicity in chapter 4, §6.) This criticism faces theory-choice both in science and philosophy (van Fraassen 1980, 87–89).

Third, it might be complained that the cost-benefit model is flawed because of its bad results. For example, David Lewis championed the use of this model in making his case for modal realism (Lewis 1986, 3–5.) But, the complaint says, the model has the bad result of claiming that modal realism is the correct theory of modality, and that discredits the model. The model has this result, however, only given the particular weightings that Lewis gave each of the costs (such as its ontological diseconomy) and benefits (such as the range of phenomena it applies to), and the calculation he made on that basis. Lewis's weightings are open to dispute. For example, we saw in chapter 4, §5 that some philosophers argue that Lewis put insufficient stress on the ontological diseconomy of modal realism. Perhaps he also underestimated the difficulties facing an epistemology of Lewisian possible worlds. If these criticisms and similar ones are correct, then the balance sheet for modal realism is quite different from what Lewis took it to be. Consequently, the cost-benefit model does not support modal realism and so cannot be discredited on those grounds.

Fourth, some would-be critics of the method may not so much reject the method as reject the weighting given to various costs and benefits. In particular, the critics may assign more weighting to philosophical theories that do not markedly differ from the philosophical views implicit in common sense and our ordinary literal ways of talking about things.

Here epistemic conservatism (accepting theories only if they are consistent with our prior beliefs, especially our folk philosophical beliefs) is assigned strong weighting. (Recall the discussion of common sense and conservatism in chapter 1, §4.) Philosophers who appear to be critics of the cost-benefit method may in fact accept the method. Their opposition may instead be to other philosophers giving weaker weighting to epistemic conservatism as compared to such factors as simplicity or explanatory power. The culprits here notably include revisionary metaphysicians. A revisionary metaphysics conflicts to a greater or less extent with folk or descriptive metaphysics, and advocates revising the latter accordingly (Strawson 1959, ch. 1). The locus of the debate between the friends of folk metaphysics and the revisionary metaphysicians will then not be over the appropriateness of the cost-benefit method. It will be over which factors are costs, which are benefits, and what weightings to give them. We can also compare the long-term results reached by each of these different weightings, and form an informed judgement about which weightings are the most fruitful ones.

Further Reading

Maddy, Penelope (2007) *Second Philosophy: A Naturalistic Method.*
Williamson, Timothy (2007) *The Philosophy of Philosophy.*
Wilson, Mark (2006) *Wandering Significance: An Essay on Conceptual Behaviour.*

Glossary

A *posteriori* knowledge
Propositional knowledge acquired through sense experience.
Contrast with ***a priori* knowledge**.

A *priori* knowledge Propositional knowledge that is acquired solely through understanding propositions and reasoning, and independently of sense experience. Contrast with ***a posteriori* knowledge**.

Abstract object An object that is not located in space or time. Examples include numbers, propositions, and types. Contrast with **concrete object**.

Ad hoc An ad hoc adjustment to a theory modifies it to accommodate contrary evidence in a way unsupported otherwise; this empty sort of modification is bad theoretic practice.

Analysis Philosophical analysis seeks a deeper understanding of a claim by identifying more clear or fundamental claims that are involved in it.

Analytic truth A sentence that expresses a conceptual truth. Contrast with **synthetic truth**.

Begging the question An argument begs the question if its premise set assumes the argument's conclusion.

Certainty A belief can be held more or less strongly. We have degrees of belief, or degrees of certainty. We are more confident, or more certain, that some of our beliefs are true rather than others. For example, Moore was more certain that he had hands than that there were any good arguments for the claim that he didn't have hands.

Common sense What is commonly, spontaneously and strongly accepted by a community.

Concept A mental way of representing something. The concept RAT, for instance, represents all and only rats. Concepts are often also taken to be the meanings of words, so that the concept RAT is the meaning of the English word "rat," the German word "ratte," and so on.

Conceptual analysis Philosophical analysis understood as specifying the meanings of words and sentences, the concepts involved in an assertion.

Conceptual truth A proposition is a conceptual truth if and only if it is true in virtue of the content of the concepts it involves. Example: the proposition *that all cats are felines.*

Concrete object An object that is located in space or time. Examples include trees, inscriptions of words and sentences, the experiences you are now having, and your belief that you are currently reading. (Since those inscriptions are inscriptions at particular places, they are located in space. Since those experiences and that belief are ones that you have at one time, but not at a later time, they are located in time.) Contrast with **abstract object**.

Contingent truth A truth that is not a necessary truth.

Contraposition The contraposition of the proposition *that all Fs are Gs* is the proposition *that all non-Gs are non-Fs*. For example, the contraposition of the proposition *that all dogs bark* is the proposition *that all things that do not bark are not dogs*. A proposition and its contraposition are logically equivalent.

Domain of quantification A theory's domain of quantification consists in what entities have to exist in order for the theory to be true.

Epistemic conservatism The position that your already believing *p* constitutes a reason for you now to believe that *p*.

Epistemic priority We know that some propositions are true only because we know that certain others are true. The latter propositions are epistemically prior to the former propositions. Propositions in set *S* are *epistemically prior* to propositions in set *S** if and only if it is possible to know all the propositions in set *S* without knowing any propositions in set *S**, but not conversely.

Equivalence Two propositions are equivalent if and only if they are either both true or both false.

Experimental philosophy
Philosophy that draws on empirical data, such as the results of surveys of non-philosophers' opinions.

Explanation by unification To explain disparate kinds of phenomena by classifying them as belonging to a smaller number of more fundamental kinds.

Explication The replacement of a vague, inexact term with a more clear and exact term.

Family resemblance The things to which a family resemblance term applies have no feature in common; any pair of those things resemble each other in ways that another pair of those things need not.

Idealism The view that reality is fundamentally mental.

Ideological simplicity The ideological simplicity of a theory is a measure of the number of primitive non-logical terms it uses.

Inference to the best explanation
Inferring that a certain hypothesis is the correct explanation of some phenomenon because it provides the best potential explanation of that phenomenon.

Intuition An inclination to believe a claim based solely on an understanding of that claim.

Logically equivalent Two propositions are logically equivalent if and only if they have the same truth value in every possible situation. For example, the proposition *that all beagles are dogs* is logically equivalent to the proposition *that it is not the case that some beagle is not a dog.*

Mind-brain identity theory
Mental properties are identical with physical properties of the brain.

Modal knowledge Knowledge of what is possible or of what is necessary.

Modal realism Talk of possibility and necessity is to be understood as talk of possible worlds, where other possible worlds are things of the same kind as the actual world.

Naturalism Methodological naturalism says that philosophy should adopt scientific methods of investigation and should use scientific results. Metaphysical naturalism says that philosophy should posit the existence of all and only entities recognized by the sciences.

Necessary truth A proposition is necessarily true if and only if it is true in every possible situation. Contrast with **contingent truth**.

Ockham's razor The principle that a theory should not be more complicated than it needs to be, and it should not posit more entities than it needs to.

Ontological commitment The ontological commitments of a theory are the entities that have to exist if the theory is true. A person's ontological commitments are the entities that have to exist if the theories he or she believes are true.

Ontological simplicity The ontological simplicity of a theory is a measure of the number of entities the theory posits. Ontological simplicity can be further distinguished in terms of the number of kinds of entity the theory posits (qualitative simplicity) or the number of instances of kinds of entity the theory posits (quantitative simplicity).

Open question argument Terms "F" and "G" differ in meaning if it is possible for a conceptually competent person to doubt that an F is a G.

Paradox of analysis An analysis is true only if it is uninteresting, and it is interesting only if it is false.

Paraphrase To use another form of words to convey what a sentence says more clearly or succinctly.

Phenomenalism A view about the analysis of statements about physical objects. Every statement about a physical object can be analysed as a conjunction of statements about actual and possible experiences. Talk about physical objects turns out to be talk about what kinds of experience we can and do have.

Premise set The premise set of an argument is the set of all the premises in the argument.

Problem of multiple analyses Equally good analyses of the same concept need not have the same meaning.

Properly basic A given belief of a person is properly basic if it is reasonable for that person to hold that belief although the belief is not justified by any other belief that that person has.

Proposition The piece of information a sentence expresses (often relative to a context).

Reflective equilibrium A coherent integration of theories and intuitions. This may be achieved by modification in either or both areas.

Self-evidencing explanation An explanation the only support of which is the phenomenon that it is explaining. For example, you might explain certain tracks in the snow by the hypothesis that someone in snowshoes passed by, although the only evidence that someone in snowshoes passed by consists in the tracks in the snow.

Synthetic truth A proposition whose truth is not merely a matter of the nature of the concepts involved. Contrast with **analytic truth**.

Thought experiment An experiment carried out in imagination.

References

Where a paper has been noted as reprinted, all page references are to the reprinted version.

Ackerman, D.F. (1981) "The Informativeness of Philosophical Analysis" *Midwest Studies in Philosophy* volume VI: 313–20.

Ackerman, D.F. (1990) "Analysis, Language, and Concepts: The Second Paradox of Analysis" *Philosophical Perspectives 4, 1990, Action Theory and Philosophy of Mind*: 535–43.

Alexander, Joshua and Jonathan M. Weinberg (2007) "Analytic Epistemology and Experimental Philosophy" *Philosophy Compass* 2: 56–80.

Alston, William P. (1958) "Ontological Commitments" *Philosophical Studies* 9: 8–17.

Alston, William P. (1976) "Two Types of Foundationalism" *Journal of Philosophy* 73: 165–85.

Anderson, C. Anthony (1987) "Bealer's *Quality and Concept*" *Journal of Philosophical Logic* 16: 115–64.

Anderson, C. Anthony (1990) "Logical Analysis and Natural Language: The Problem of Multiple Analyses" in Peter Klein (ed.) *Praktische Logik* (Göttingen: Vandenhoeck and Ruprecht): 169–79.

Anderson, C. Anthony (1993) "Analyzing Analysis" *Philosophical Studies* 72: 199–222.

Anderson, C. Anthony (1998) "Alonzo Church's Contributions to Philosophy and Intensional Logic" *The Bulletin of Symbolic Logic* 4: 129–71.

Antony, Louise (2004) "A Naturalised Approach to the *A Priori*" *Philosophical Issues* 14: 1–17.

Aristotle, *Metaphysics*, W.D. Ross (trans. and ed.) (1924) (Oxford: Oxford University Press).

Aristotle, *De Caelo*, J.L. Stocks (trans.) in W.D. Ross (ed.) (1930) *The Works of Aristotle* volume 2 (Oxford: Clarendon Press).

Armstrong, D.M. (1978) *Nominalism and Realism: Universals and Scientific Realism* volume 1 (Cambridge: Cambridge University Press).

Armstrong, D.M. (1989) *Universals: An Opinionated Introduction* (Boulder, CO: Westview Press).

Armstrong, D.M. (1997) *A World of States of Affairs* (Cambridge: Cambridge University Press).

Armstrong, D.M. (2006) "The Scope and Limits of Human Knowledge" *Australasian Journal of Philosophy* 84: 159–66.

Armstrong, Sharon L., Lila R. Gleitman, and Henry Gleitman (1980) "What Some Concepts Might Not Be" *Cognition* 13: 263–308.

Austin, J.L. (1962) *Sense and Sensibilia* (Oxford: Clarendon Press).

Ayer, A.J. (1936) *Language, Truth and Logic* (London: Victor Gollancz).

Baker, Alan (2003) "Quantitative Parsimony and Explanatory Power" *British Journal for the Philosophy of Science* 54: 245–59.

Baker, Gordon and P.M.S. Hacker (1992) *An Analytical Commentary on Wittgenstein's Philosophical Investigations* volume 1 (Oxford: Blackwell).

Balaguer, Mark (2009) "The Metaphysical Irrelevance of the Compatibilism Debate (and, More Generally, of Conceptual Analysis")" *Southern Journal of Philosophy* 48: 1–24.

Baldwin, Thomas (1990) *G.E. Moore* (London: Routledge).

Baldwin, Thomas (2003) "The Indefinability of Good" *Journal of Value Inquiry* 37: 313–28.

Ball, Stephen W. (1988) "Reductionism in Ethics and Science: A Contemporary Look at G.E. Moore's Open-Question Argument" *American Philosophical Quarterly* 25 (3): 197–213.

Ball, Stephen W. (1991) "Linguistic Intuitions and Varieties of Ethical Naturalism" *Philosophy and Phenomenological Research* 51: 1–38.

Bangu, Sorin (2005) "Later Wittgenstein on Essentialism, Family Resemblance and Philosophical Method" *Metaphysica* 6: 53–73.

Barber, Alex (2007) "Review of Noah Lemos, *Common Sense: A Contemporary Defense*" *Philosophical Books* 48: 177–80.

Barnes, E.C. (2000) "Ockham's Razor and the Anti-Superfluity Principle" *Erkenntnis* 53: 353–74.

Barnes, Eric (1992) "Explanatory Unification and Scientific Understanding" *Philosophy of Science Association 1992* volume 1: 3–12.

Bealer, George (1987) "The Philosophical Limits of Scientific Essentialism" *Philosophical Perspectives 1, Metaphysics*: 289–365.

Bealer, George (1992) "The Incoherence of Empiricism" *Proceedings of the Aristotelian Society* supplementary volume 66: 99–138.

Bealer, George (1996) "A Priori Knowledge and the Scope of Philosophy" *Philosophical Studies* 81: 121–42.

Beaney, Michael (2001) "From Conceptual Analysis to Serious Metaphysics" *International Journal of Philosophical Studies* 9: 521–42.

Beaney, Michael (2006) "Appreciating the Varieties of Analysis: a Reply to Ongley" *The Bertrand Russell Society Quarterly* 128–29: 42–9.

Beaney, Michael (2007) "Analysis" Stanford Encyclopedia of Philosophy <http://plato.stanford.edu/entries/analysis/index.html>.

Beebee, Helen (2001) "Transfer of Warrant, Begging the Question, and Semantic Externalism" *Philosophical Quarterly* 51: 356–74.

Bezuidenhout, Anne (1996) "Resisting the Step Toward Naturalism" *Philosophy and Phenomenological Research* 56: 743–70.

Bigelow, John and Robert Pargetter (1990) *Science and Necessity* (Cambridge: Cambridge University Press).

Bishop, Michael (1992) "Theory-ladenness of Perception Arguments" *Philosophy of Science Association 1992* volume 1: 287–99.

Bishop, Michael (1999) "Why Thought Experiments Are Not Arguments" *Philosophy of Science* 66: 534–41.

Blackburn, Simon (1973) *Reason and Prediction* (Cambridge: Cambridge University Press).

Blanchette, Patricia (2007) "Frege on Consistency and Conceptual Analysis" *Philosophia Mathematica* 15: 321–46.

Block, Ned and Robert Stalnaker (1999) "Conceptual Analysis, Dualism, and the Explanatory Gap" *Philosophical Review* 108: 1–46.

Bokulich, Alisa (2001) "Rethinking Thought Experiments" *Perspectives on Science* 9: 285–307.

Bonjour, Laurence (1998) *In Defense of Pure Reason* (Cambridge: Cambridge University Press).

Braddon-Mitchell, David and Robert Nola (2009) (eds.) *Conceptual Analysis and Philosophical Naturalism* (Cambridge, MA: MIT Press).

Brock, Stuart and Edwin Mares (2007) *Realism and Anti-Realism* (Chesham: Acumen).

Brown, James Robert (1991a) "Thought Experiments: A Platonic Account" in Tamara Horowitz and Gerald Massey (eds.) *Thought Experiments in Science and Philosophy* (Savage, MD: Rowman and Littlefield): 119–28.

Brown, James Robert (1991b) *The Laboratory of the Mind: Thought Experiments in the Natural Sciences* (London: Routledge).

Brown, James Robert (2004a) "Peeking into Plato's Heaven" *Philosophy of Science* 71: 1126–38.

Brown, James Robert (2004b) "Why Thought Experiments Transcend Experience" in Christopher Hitchcock (ed.) *Contemporary Debates in Philosophy of Science* (London: Routledge): 23–43.

Brown, James Robert (2007a) "Counter Thought Experiments" in Anthony O'Hear (ed.) *Philosophy of Science* (Cambridge: Cambridge University Press): 155–77.

Brown, James Robert (2007b) "Thought Experiments in Science, Philosophy, and Mathematics," *Croatian Journal of Philosophy* 10: 3–27.

Burgess, John P. (1983) "Why I Am Not a Nominalist" *Notre Dame of Formal Logic* 24: 93–105.

Burgess, John P. (1998) "Occam's Razor and Scientific Method" in Matthias Schirn (ed.) *Philosophy of Mathematics Today* (Oxford: Oxford University Press): 195–214.

Burgess, John P. and Gideon Rosen (1997) *A Subject with No Object: Strategies for Nominalistic Interpretation of Mathematics* (Oxford: Oxford University Press).

Byrne, Alex and Ned Hall (2004) "Necessary Truths: Scott Soames's *Philosophical Analysis in the Twentieth Century*" *Boston Review* October/November 2004: 34–36.

Campbell, Keith (1988) "Philosophy and Common Sense" *Philosophy* 63: 161–74.

Carnap, Rudolf (1928) *Der logische Aufbau der Welt* (Berlin: Weltkreis-Verlag).

Carnap, Rudolf (1950) *Logical Foundations of Probability* (Chicago: University of Chicago Press).

Carroll, John W. (1994) *Laws of Nature* (Cambridge: Cambridge University Press).

Casullo, Albert (2003) *A Priori Justification* (Oxford: Oxford University Press).

Chalmers, David (1996) *The Conscious Mind* (Oxford: Oxford University Press).

Cherniss, H.F. (1936) "The Philosophical Economy of Plato's Theory of Ideas" *American Journal of Philology* 57: 445–56. Reprinted in H.F. Cherniss (1977) *Selected Papers*, L. Tarán (ed.) (Leiden: E.J. Brill): 121–32.

Chisholm, Roderick M. (1959) *Perceiving* (Ithaca: Cornell University Press).

Chisholm, Roderick M. (1966) *Theory of Knowledge* (2nd edition; Englewood Cliffs, NJ: Prentice-Hall).

Chisholm, Roderick M. (1982) *The Foundations of Knowing* (Brighton: The Harvester Press).

Christensen, David (1994) "Conservatism in Epistemology" *Noûs* 28: 69–89.

Churchland, Paul M. (1988) "Perceptual Plasticity and Theoretical Neutrality: A Reply to Fodor" *Philosophy of Science* 55: 167–87.

Coady, C.A.J. (2007) "Moore's Common Sense" in Susana Nuccetelli and Gary Seay (eds.) *Themes from G.E. Moore: New Essays in Epistemology and Ethics* (Oxford: Oxford University Press): 100–18.

Cohnitz, Daniel (2003) "Personal Identity and the Methodology of Imaginary Cases" in Klaus Petrus (ed.) *On Human Persons* (Frankfurt: Ontos Verlag): 145–81.

Cohnitz, Daniel (2006) "Poor Thought Experiments?" *Journal for General Philosophy of Science* 37: 373–92.

Coleman, Stephen (2000) "Thought Experiments and Personal Identity" *Philosophical Studies* 98: 53–69.

Colyvan, Mark (2001) *The Indispensability of Mathematics* (Oxford: Oxford University Press).

Conee, Earl (1996) "Why Solve the Gettier Problem?" in Paul Moser (ed.) *Empirical Knowledge: Readings in Contemporary Epistemology* (2nd edition; Lanham, MD: Rowman and Littlefield): 261–65.

Conee, Earl (2001) "Comments on Bill Lycan's Moore Against the New Sceptics" *Philosophical Studies* 103: 55–59.

Cooper, Rachel (2005) "Thought Experiments" *Metaphilosophy* 36: 328–47.

Craig, Edward (1990) *Knowledge and the State of Nature: An Essay in Conceptual Synthesis* (Oxford: Oxford University Press).

Cummins, Robert (1998) "Reflections on Reflective Equilibrium" In Michael DePaul and William Ramsey (eds.) *Rethinking Intuition: The Psychology of Intuition and Its Role in Philosophical Inquiry* (Lanham, MD: Rowman and Littlefield): 113–28.

Daniels, Norman (1980) "Reflective Equilibrium and Archimedean Points" *Canadian Journal of Philosophy* 10: 83–103.

Darwell, Stephen, Allan Gibbard, and Peter Railton (1992) "Towards *Fin de Siécle* Ethics: Some Trends" *Philosophical Review* 101: 115–89.

Davidson, Donald (1975) "Thought and Talk" in Samuel Guttenplan (ed.) *Mind and Language* (Oxford: Oxford University Press): 7–24. Reprinted in Donald Davidson (2001) *Inquiries into Truth and Interpretation* (2nd edition; Oxford: Oxford University Press): 155–71.

Davies, Martin (2000) "Externalism and Armchair Knowledge" in Paul Boghossian and Christopher Peacocke (eds.) *New Essays on the A Priori* (Oxford: Oxford University Press): 384–414.

Davies, Martin (2003) "The Problem of Armchair Knowledge" in Susanna Nuccetelli (ed.) *New Essays on Semantic Externalism and Self-Knowledge* (Cambridge, MA: MIT Press): 25–55.

DePaul, Michael R. (1998) "Why Bother With Reflective Equilibrium?" in Michael R. DePaul and William Ramsey (eds.) *Rethinking Intuition: The Psychology of Intuition and Its Role in Philosophical Inquiry* (Lanham, MD: Rowman and Littlefield): 293–309.

Descartes, René (1641) *Meditations on First Philosophy*, Donald A. Cress (trans.) (1993) (3rd edition; Indianapolis: Hackett Press).

Deutsch, Max (2009) "Experimental Philosophy and the Theory of Reference" *Mind and Language* 24: 445–466.

Dieterle, J.M. (1999) "Mathematical, Astrological, and Theological Naturalism" *Philosophia Mathematica* 7: 129–35.

Dieterle, J.M. (2001) "Ockham's Razor, Encounterability, and Ontological Naturalism" *Erkenntnis* 55: 51–72.

Divers, John (1994) "On The Prohibitive Cost of Indiscernible Concrete Worlds" *Australasian Journal of Philosophy* 72: 384–89.

Dorr, Cian and Gideon Rosen (2001) "Composition as a Fiction" in Richard Gale (ed.) *Blackwell's Guide to Metaphysics* (Oxford: Blackwell): 151–74.

Došen, Kosta (1994) "Logical Constants as Punctuation Marks" in Dov M. Gabbay (ed.) *What Is A Logical System?* (Oxford: Oxford University Press): 273–96.

Dretske, Fred (1981) "The Pragmatic Dimension of Knowledge" *Philosophical Studies* 40: 363–78.

Dretske, Fred (1988) *Explaining Behaviour: Reasons in A World of Causes* (Cambridge, MA: MIT Press).

Dretske, Fred (2003) "Skepticism: What Perception Teaches" in Steven Luper (ed.) *The Skeptics: Contemporary Essays* (Aldershot, Hampshire: Ashgate): 105–18.

Duhem, Pierre (1914) *The Aim and Structure of Physical Theory*, Philip P. Wiener (trans.) (1952) (2nd edition; Princeton: Princeton University Press).

Dummett, Michael (1979) "Common Sense and Physics" in G.F. Macdonald (ed.) *Perception and Identity: Essays Presented to A.J. Ayer with his Replies to Them* (London: Macmillan): 1–40.

Dummett, Michael (1991) *The Seas of Language* (Oxford: Oxford University Press).

Einstein, Albert (1949) "Autobiographical Notes" in Paul A. Schilpp (ed.) *Albert Einstein: Philosopher–Scientist* (La Salle, IL: Open Court): 665–88.

Euclid, *The Thirteen Books of the Elements, Volume 1: Books 1 and 2*, Thomas Heath (trans. and ed.) (2000) (2nd edition; London: Dover Publications).

Feldman, Richard (1998) "Naturalism in Epistemology" *EurAmerica* 28: 1–39.

Feldman, Richard (2001) "Naturalized Epistemology" *Stanford Encyclopedia of Philosophy*. <http://www.seop.leeds.ac.uk/entries/epistemology-naturalized/>.

Feldman, Richard (2002) "Methodological Naturalism in Epistemology" in John Greco and Ernest Sosa (eds.) *The Blackwell Guide to Epistemology*: 170–86.

Feldman, Richard (2003) *Epistemology* (Upper Saddle River, NJ: Prentice Hall).

Feltz, Adam (2008) "Problems with the Appeal to Intuition in Epistemology" *Philosophical Explorations* 11: 131–41.

Field, Hartry H. (1981) "Mental Representation" (and Postscript) in Ned Block (ed.) *Readings in the Philosophy of Psychology* volume II (Cambridge, MA: Harvard University Press): 78–114.

Field, Hartry (2005) "Recent Debates about the *A Priori*" in Tamar Gendler and John Hawthorne (eds.) *Oxford Studies in Epistemology* (Oxford: Oxford University Press): 69–88.

Fodor, Jerry (1984) "Observation Reconsidered" *Philosophy of Science* 51: 23–43.

Fodor, Jerry (1998) *Concepts: Where Cognitive Science Went Wrong* (Oxford: Oxford University Press).

Fodor, Jerry and Ernest Lepore (1994) "The Red Herring and The Pet Fish: Why Concepts Still Can't Be Prototypes" *Cognition* 58: 253–70.

Foley, Richard (1993) "What's to Be Said for Simplicity?" *Philosophical Issues, Volume 3, Science and Knowledge*: 209–24.

Foley, Richard (1994) "Quine and Naturalized Epistemology" *Midwest Studies in Philosophy* volume XIX: 243–60.

Forrest, Peter (1982) "Occam's Razor and Possible Worlds" *The Monist* 65: 456–64.

Forrest, Peter (2001) "Counting the Cost of Modal Realism" in Gerhard Preyer and Frank Siebelt (eds.) *Reality and Humean Supervenience: Essays on the Philosophy of David Lewis* (Lanham, MD: Rowman and Littlefield): 93–103.

Forster, Michael and Elliott Sober (2004) "How to Tell When Simpler, More Unified, or Less *Ad Hoc* Theories Will Provide More Accurate Predictions" *British Journal for the Philosophy of Science* 45: 1–36.

Frankena, W.K. (1939) "The Naturalistic Fallacy" *Mind* 48: 464–77.

Frege, Gottlob (1879) *Begriffschrift*. Preface translated in Michael Beaney (ed.) (1997) *The Frege Reader* (Oxford: Blackwell): 48–52.

Friedman, Michael (1979) "Truth and Confirmation" *Journal of Philosophy* 76: 361–82.

Friedman, Michael (1981) "Theoretical Explanation" in R. Healey (ed.) *Reduction, Time and Reality* (Cambridge: Cambridge University Press): 1–16.

Fumerton, Richard (1992) "Skepticism and Reasoning to the Best Explanation" in Enrique Villaneuva (ed.) *Philosophical Issues Volume 2: Rationality in Epistemology* (Atascadero, CA: Ridgeview Publishing): 149–69.

Fumerton, Richard (2007) "Open Questions and the Nature of Philosophical Analysis" in Susana Nuccetelli and Gary Seay (eds.) *Themes from G.E. Moore: New Essays in Epistemology and Ethics* (Oxford: Oxford University Press): 237–43.

Galilei, Galileo (1638) *Dialogues Concerning Two New Sciences* (1991) (Buffalo: Prometheus Books).

Geach, P.T. (1972) *Logic Matters* (Oxford: Blackwell).

Gendler, Tamar Szabó (1998) "Galileo and the Indispensability of Scientific Thought Experiments" *British Journal for the Philosophy of Science* 49: 397–424.

Gendler, Tamar Szabó (2000) *Thought Experiment: On the Powers and Limits of Imaginary Cases* (New York: Garland/Routledge).

Gendler, Tamar Szabó (2004) "Thought Experiments Rethought — and Reperceived" *Philosophy of Science* 71: 1152–63.

Gendler, Tamar Szabó and John Hawthorne (2002) (eds.) *Conceivability and Possibility* (Oxford: Oxford University Press).

Gettier, Edmund (1963) "Is Justified True Belief Knowledge?" *Analysis* 23: 121–23.

Goldman, Alvin I. (1978) "Epistemics: The Regulative Theory of Cognition" *Journal of Philosophy* 75: 509–23.

Goldman, Alvin I. (1986) *Epistemology and Cognition* (Harvard: Harvard University Press).

Goldman, Alvin I. (1994a) "Epistemic Folkways and Scientific Epistemology" in Hilary Kornblith (ed.) *Naturalizing Epistemology* (2nd edition; Cambridge, MA: MIT Press): 291–315.

Goldman, Alvin I. (1994b) "Naturalistic Epistemology and Reliabilism" *Midwest Studies in Philosophy* volume XIX: 301–20.

Goldman, Alvin I. (1999) "*A Priori* Warrant and Naturalistic Epistemology" *Philosophical Issues* 13: 1–28.

Goldman, Alvin I. (2007) "Philosophical Intuitions: Their Target, Their Source, and Their Epistemic Status" *Grazer Philosophische Studien* 74: 1–26.

Gooding, David (1990) *Experiment and the Making of Meaning: Human Agency in Scientific Observation and Experiment* (Dordrecht: Kluwer Academic Press).

Goodman, Nelson (1951) *The Structure of Appearance* (Harvard: Harvard University Press).

Goodman, Nelson (1955) *Fact, Fiction and Forecast* (Cambridge, MA: Harvard University Press).

Goodman, Nelson (1963) "The Significance of *Der Logische Aufbau der Welt*" in P.A. Schilpp (ed.) *The Philosophy of Rudolf Carnap* (La Salle, IL: Open Court): 545–58.

Govier, Trudy (1992) *A Practical Study of Argument* (3rd edition; Belmont: Wadsworth).

Gregory, Paul A. (2008) *Quine's Naturalism: Language, Theory, and the Knowing Subject* (London: Continuum Press).

Grim, Patrick, Gary Mar, and Paul St. Denis (1998) (eds.) *The Philosophical Computer: Exploratory Essays in Philosophical Computer Modelling* (Cambridge, MA: MIT Press).

Gunner, D.L. (1967) "Comments on Professor Smart's 'Sensations and Brain Processes'" in C.F. Presley (ed.) *The Identity Theory of Mind* (St. Lucia: Queensland University Press): 1–20.

Gupta, Anil and Nuel Belnap (1993) *The Revision Theory of Truth* (Cambridge, MA: MIT Press).

Gustafsson, Martin (2006) "Quine on Explication and Elimination" *Canadian Journal of Philosophy* 36: 57–70.

Haack, Susan (1993) "The Two Faces of Quine's Naturalism" *Synthese* 94: 335–56.

Häggqvist, Sören (1996) *Thought Experiments in Philosophy* (Stockholm: Almqvist and Wiksell International).

Häggqvist, Sören (2007) "The *A Priori* Thesis: A Critical Assessment" *Croatian Journal of Philosophy* 19: 47–61.

Häggqvist, Sören (2009) "A Model for Thought Experiments" *Canadian Journal of Philosophy* 39: 55–76.

Hales, Stephen D. (1997) "Ockham's Disposable Razor" in Paul Weingartner, Gerhard Schurz, and Georg Dorn (eds.) *The Role of Pragmatics in Contemporary Philosophy: Contributions of the Austrian Ludwig Wittgenstein Society* (Vienna: Hölder-Pichler-Tempsky): 356–61.

Hales, Stephen D. (2006) *Relativism and the Foundations of Philosophy* (Cambridge, MA: MIT Press).

Hanna, Joseph F. (1968) "An Explication of 'Explication'" *Philosophy of Science* 35: 28–44.

Hanna, Robert (2006) *Rationality and Logic* (Cambridge, MA: MIT Press).

Harman, Gilbert (1965) "The Inference to the Best Explanation" *Philosophical Review* 74: 88–95.

Harman, Gilbert (1967) "Quine on Meaning and Existence: II" *Review of Metaphysics* 21: 343–67.

Harman, Gilbert (1973) *Thought* (Princeton: Princeton University Press).

Hellman, Geoffrey and Frank Wilson Thompson (1975) "Physicalism: Ontology, Determination and Reduction" *Journal of Philosophy* 72: 551–64.

Hempel, Carl G. (1965) *Aspects of Scientific Explanation and Other Essays in the Philosophy of Science* (New York: Free Press).

Hempel, Carl G. (1966) *Philosophy of Natural Science* (Englewood Cliffs, NJ: Prentice–Hall).

Henderson, David and Terry Horgan (2000) "What Is A Priori, and What Is It Good For?" *Southern Journal of Philosophy* supplementary volume 38: 51–86.

Hetherington, Stephen (2001) *Good Knowledge, Bad Knowledge: On Two Dogmas of Epistemology* (Oxford: Oxford University Press).

Hill, Christopher S. (1991) *Sensations: A Defense of Type Materialism* (Cambridge: Cambridge University Press).

Hintikka, Jaakko (1999) "The Emperor's New Intuitions" *Journal of Philosophy* 96: 127–47.

Hirsch, Eli (2002) "Quantifier Variance and Realism" in Enrique Villaneuva (ed.) *Philosophical Issues, 12, Realism and Relativism, 2002* (Atascadero, CA: Ridgeview Publishing): 51–73.

Horty, John F. (2008) *Frege on Definition: A Case Study of Semantic Content* (Oxford: Oxford University Press).

Horwich, Paul (1998) *Truth* (2nd edition; Oxford: Oxford University Press).

Huemer, Michael (2008) "When is Parsimony a Virtue?" *Philosophical Quarterly* 59: 216–36.

Humberstone, I.L. (1997) "Two Types of Circularity" *Philosophy and Phenomenological Research* 57: 249–80.

Hume, David (1739–40) *A Treatise on Human Nature*, David Fate Norton and Mary J. Norton (eds.) (2000) (Oxford: Oxford University Press).

Humphreys, Paul (1984) "Explanation in Philosophy and in Science" in James H. Fetzer (ed.) *Principles of Philosophical Reasoning* (Lanham, MD: Rowman and Littlefield): 172–89.

Humphreys, Paul (1993) "Greater Unification equals Greater Understanding?" *Analysis* 53: 183–88.

Hylton, Peter (1994) "Quine's Naturalism" *Midwest Studies in Philosophy* volume XIX: 261–82.

Hylton, Peter (2007) *Quine* (London: Routledge).

Ichikawa, Jonathan (2009) "Knowing the Intuition and Knowing the Counterfactual" *Philosophical Studies* 145: 435–43.

Jackson, Frank (1977) "Statements about Universals" *Mind* 86: 427–29.

Jackson, Frank (1982) "Epiphenomenal Qualia" *Philosophical Quarterly* 32: 127–36.

Jackson, Frank (1987) *Conditionals* (Oxford: Blackwell).

Jackson, Frank (1994) "Metaphysics by Possible Cases" *The Monist* 77: 93–110.

Jackson, Frank (1998) *From Metaphysics to Ethics: A Defence of Conceptual Analysis* (Oxford: Oxford University Press).

Jackson, Frank (2008) "Review of Joshua Knobe and Shaun Nichols (eds.) *Experimental Philosophy*" *Notre Dame Philosophical Reviews*, December 2008. <http://ndpr.nd.edu/review.cfm?id=14828>.

Jackson, Frank (2009) "Thought Experiments and Possibilities" *Analysis Reviews* 69: 100–09.

Jackson, Frank and David Braddon-Mitchell (1996) *Philosophy of Mind and Cognition* (Oxford: Blackwell).

Jenkins, Carrie (2006) "Knowledge and Explanation" *Canadian Journal of Philosophy* 36: 137–64.

Jenkins, Carrie (2008) "Romeo, René, and The Reasons Why: What Explanation Is" *Proceedings of the Aristotelian Society* 108: 61–84.

Johnston, Mark (1987) "Human Beings" *Journal of Philosophy* 84: 59–83.

Joyce, Richard (2002) "Theistic Ethics and the Euthyphro Dilemma" *Journal of Religious Ethics* 30: 49–75.

Jubien, Michael (1988) "Problems with Possible Worlds" in D.F. Austin (ed.) *Philosophical Analysis* (Kluwer: Kluwer Academic Press): 299–322.

Kahneman, David, Paul Slovic, and Amos Tversky (1982) *Reasoning Under Uncertainty: Heuristics and Biases* (Cambridge: Cambridge University Press).

Kalderon, Mark Eli (2004) "Open Questions and the Manifest Image" *Philosophy and Phenomenological Research* 68: 251–89.

Kauppinen, Antti (2007) "The Rise and Fall of Experimental Philosophy" *Philosophical Explorations* 10: 95–118.

Keefe, Rosanna (2002) "When Does Circularity Matter?" *Proceedings of the Aristotelian Society* 102: 275–92.

Keil, Frank (1989) *Concepts, Kinds, and Cognitive Development* (Cambridge, MA: MIT Press).

Kelly, Thomas (2008) "Common Sense as Evidence: Against Revisionary Ontology and Skepticism" *Midwest Studies in Philosophy* 32: 53–78.

Kim, Jaegwon (1988) "What is Naturalized Epistemology?" *Philosophical Perspectives, 2, 1988, Epistemology*: 381–405.

King, Jeffrey C. (2007) *The Nature and Structure of Content* (Oxford: Oxford University Press).

Kitcher, Patricia (1978) "On Appealing to the Extraordinary" *Metaphilosophy* 9: 99–107.

Kitcher, Philip (1992) "The Naturalists Return" *Philosophical Review* 101: 53–114.

Knobe, Joshua and Shaun Nichols (2008) (eds.) *Experimental Philosophy* (Oxford: Oxford University Press).

Kornblith, Hilary (1994a) "Introduction: What is Naturalized Epistemology?" in *Naturalizing Epistemology* (2nd edition; Cambridge, MA: MIT Press): 1–14.

Kornblith, Hilary (1994b) "Naturalism: Both Metaphysical and Epistemological" *Midwest Studies in Philosophy* volume XIX: 39–52.

Kornblith, Hilary (1995) "Naturalistic Epistemology and its Critics" *Philosophical Topics* 23: 237–55.

Kornblith, Hilary (2000) "The Impurity of Reason" *Pacific Philosophical Quarterly* 81: 67–89.

Kornblith, Hilary (2002a) "In Defense of Naturalized Epistemology" in John Greco and Ernest Sosa (eds.) *The Blackwell Guide to Epistemology*: 158–69.

Kornblith, Hilary (2002b) *Knowledge and Its Place in Nature* (Oxford: Oxford University Press).

Kornblith, Hilary (2006) "Appeals to Intuition and the Ambitions of Epistemology" in Stephen Cade Hetherington (ed.) *Epistemology Futures* (Oxford: Oxford University Press): 10–25.

Kornblith, Hilary (2007) "The Naturalistic Project in Epistemology: Where Do We Go From Here?" in Chienkuo Mi and Ruey-lin Chen (eds.) *Naturalized Epistemology and Philosophy of Science* (Amsterdam: Rodopi Press): 39–59.

Kraut, Robert (2001) "Metaphysical Explanation and the Philosophy of Mathematics: Reflections on Jerrold Katz's *Realistic Rationalism*" *Philosophia Mathematica* 9: 154–83.

Kripke, Saul (1971) "Identity and Necessity" in Milton K. Munitz (ed.) *Identity and Individuation* (New York: New York University Press): 135–64. Reprinted in A.P. Martinich and David Sosa (eds.) (2001) *Analytic Philosophy: An Anthology* (Oxford: Blackwell): 72–89.

Kripke, Saul (1972) "Naming and Necessity" in Gilbert Harman and Donald Davidson (eds.) *Semantics of Natural Language* (Reidel: D. Dordrecht): 253–355, 763–69. Reprinted as Saul Kripke (1980) *Naming and Necessity* (Oxford: Blackwell).

Kuhn, Thomas S. (1964) "A Function for Thought Experiments" in *L'Aventure de la science, Mélanges Alexandre Koyré* 2: 307–34. Reprinted in *The Essential Tension* (Chicago: University of Chicago Press): 240–65.

Kvanvig, Jonathan L. (1994) "A Critique of van Fraassen's Voluntaristic Epistemology" *Synthese* 98: 325–48.

Ladyman, James and Don Ross with David Spurrett and John Collier (2007) *Every Thing Must Go: Metaphysics Naturalized* (Oxford: Oxford University Press).

Lance, Mark Norris and John O'Leary-Hawthorne (1997) *The Grammar of Meaning: Normativity and Semantic Discourse* (Cambridge: Cambridge University Press).

Langford, C.H. (1942) "The Notion of Analysis in Moore's Philosophy" in P.A. Schilpp (ed.) *The Philosophy of G.E. Moore* (La Salle, IL: Open Court): 321–42.

Laurence, Stephen and Eric Margolis (2003) "Concepts and Conceptual Analysis" *Philosophy and Phenomenological Research* 67: 253–82.

Leibniz, Gottfried (1679) "On Universal Synthesis and Analysis, or the Art of Discovery and Judgment" in Leroy E. Loemker (trans. and ed.) (1956) *Philosophical Papers and Letters* volume 1 (Chicago: Chicago University Press): 229–34.

Leibniz, Gottfried (1715–16) *The Leibniz-Clarke Correspondence*, H.G. Alexander (ed.) (1956) (Manchester: Manchester University Press).

Lemos, Noah (2004) *Common Sense: A Contemporary Defense* (Cambridge: Cambridge University Press).

Levin, Janet (2004) "The Evidential Status of Philosophical Intuitions" *Philosophical Studies* 121: 193–224.

Lewis, David (1973) *Counterfactuals* (Oxford: Blackwell).

Lewis, David (1983a) "Introduction" in *Philosophical Papers* volume 1 (Oxford: Oxford University Press): i–xiii.

Lewis, David (1983b) "New Work For A Theory of Universals" *Australasian Journal of Philosophy* 61: 343–77. Reprinted in David Lewis (1999) *Papers in Metaphysics and Epistemology* (Cambridge: Cambridge University Press): 8–55.

Lewis, David (1986) *On The Plurality of Worlds* (Oxford: Blackwell).

Lewis, David (1988) "What Experience Teaches" *Proceedings of the Russellian Society* 13: 29–57. Reprinted in David Lewis (1999) *Papers in Metaphysics and Epistemology* (Cambridge: Cambridge University Press): 262–90.

Lewis, David (1989) "Dispositional Theories of Value" *Proceedings of the Aristotelian Society* supplementary volume 63: 113–37. Reprinted in David Lewis (2000) *Papers in Ethics and Social Philosophy* (Cambridge: Cambridge University Press): 68–94.

Lewis, David (1991) *Parts of Classes* (Oxford: Blackwell).

Lewis, David (1994) "Reduction of Mind" in Samuel Guttenplan (ed.) *A Companion to the Philosophy of Mind* (Oxford: Blackwell): 412–31. Reprinted in David Lewis (1999) *Papers in Metaphysics and Epistemology* (Cambridge: Cambridge University Press): 291–324.

Lewis, David (1996) "Desire as Belief II" *Mind* 105: 303–13. Reprinted in David Lewis (2000) *Papers in Ethics and Social Philosophy* (Cambridge: Cambridge University Press): 55–67.

Lewis, David (1997) "Naming the Colours" *Australasian Journal of Philosophy* 75: 325–42. Reprinted in David Lewis (1999) *Papers in*

Metaphysics and Epistemology (Cambridge: Cambridge University Press): 332–58.

Lewy, Casimir (1964) "G.E. Moore on the Naturalistic Fallacy" *Proceedings of the British Academy* 50: 251–62. Reprinted in Alice Ambrose and Morris Lazerowitz (eds.) (1970) *G.E. Moore: Essays in Retrospect* (London: George Allen and Unwin): 292–303.

Liao, S. Matthew (2008) "A Defense of Intuitions" *Philosophical Studies* 140: 247–62.

Linsky, Bernard and Edward N. Zalta (1995) "Naturalized Platonism Versus Platonized Naturalism" *Journal of Philosophy* 92: 525–555.

Lipton, Peter (2004) *Inference to the Best Explanation* (2nd edition; London: Routledge).

Locke, John (1694) *An Essay Concerning Human Understanding*, Peter H. Nidditch (ed.) (1975) (Oxford: Oxford University Press).

Lucretius, Titus *The Poem on Nature: De Rerum Natura*, C.H. Sissons (trans.) (2003) (London: Routledge).

Lycan, William G. (1998) *Judgement and Justification* (Cambridge: Cambridge University Press).

Lycan, William G. (2001) "Moore Against the New Skeptics" *Philosophical Studies* 103: 35–53.

Lycan, William G. (2003) "Free Will and the Burden of Proof" in Anthony O'Hear (ed.) *Minds and Persons* (Cambridge: Cambridge University Press): 107–22.

Lycan, William G. (2007) "Moore's Anti-skeptical Strategies" in Susana Nuccetelli and Gary Seay (eds.) *Themes from G.E. Moore: New Essays in Epistemology and Ethics* (Oxford: Oxford University Press): 84–99.

Lynch, Michael (2006) "Trusting Intuitions" in Patrick Greenough and Michael P. Lynch (eds.) *Truth and Realism* (Oxford: Oxford University Press): 227–38.

McAllister, James W. (1989) "Truth and Beauty in Scientific Reason" *Synthese* 78: 25–51.

McCloskey, Michael (1983) "Intuitive Physics" *Scientific American* 248: 122–30.

McGrew, Tim and Lydia McGrew (1998) "Psychology for Armchair Philosophers" *Idealistic Studies* 28: 147–57.

Machery, Edouard, Ron Mallon, Shaun Nichols, and Stephen P. Stich (2004) "Semantics, Cross-Cultural Style" *Cognition* 92: B1–B12.

Maddy, Penelope (1997) *Naturalism in Mathematics* (Oxford: Oxford University Press).

Maddy, Penelope (2007) *Second Philosophy: A Naturalistic Method* (Oxford: Oxford University Press).

Madell, Geoffrey (1991) "Personal Identity and the Idea of a Human Being" in David Cockburn (ed.) *Human Beings* (Cambridge: Cambridge University Press): 127–42.

Margolis, Eric and Stephen Laurence (2003) "Should We Trust Our Intuitions? Deflationary Accounts of the Analytic Data" *Proceedings of the Aristotelian Society* volume 103: 299–323.

Martí, Genoveva (2009) "Against Semantic Multi-Culturalism" *Analysis* 69: 42–48.

Maudlin, Tim (2007) *The Metaphysics Within Physics* (Oxford: Oxford University Press).

Melia, Joseph (1992) "A Note on Lewis's Ontology" *Analysis* 52: 191–92.

Melia, Joseph (2003) *Modality* (Chesham, Buckinghamshire: Acumen Press).

Melnyck, Andrew (2008a) "Conceptual and Linguistic Analysis: A Two-Step Program" *Noûs* 42: 267–91.

Melnyck, Andrew (2008b) "Philosophy and The Study of Its History" *Metaphilosophy* 39: 203–19.

Miščević, Nenad (1992) "Mental Models and Thought Experiments" *International Studies in the Philosophy of Science* 6: 215–26.

Miščević, Nenad (2001) "Science, Commonsense, and Continuity: A Defense of Continuity (A Critique of 'Network Apriorism')" *International Studies in the Philosophy of Science* 15: 19–31.

Miščević, Nenad (2004) "The Explainability of Intuitions" *Dialectica* 58: 43–70.

Miščević, Nenad (2005) "Rescuing Conceptual Analysis" *Croatian Journal of Philosophy* 15: 47–63.

Moore, A.W. (2009) "Not to be Taken at Face Value" *Analysis Reviews* 69: 116–24.

Moore, G.E. (1903) *Principia Ethica* (revised edition, 1993; Cambridge: Cambridge University Press).

Moore, G.E. (1925) "A Defence of Common Sense" in J.H. Muirhead (ed.) *Contemporary British Philosophy, second series* (London: George Allen and Unwin): 193–223. Reprinted in G.E. Moore (1959) *Philosophical Papers* (London: George Allen and Unwin Limited): 32–59.

Moore, G.E. (1939) "Proof of an External World" *Proceedings of the British Academy* 25: 273–300. Reprinted in G.E. Moore (1959) *Philosophical Papers* (London: George Allen and Unwin): 127–50.

Moore, G.E. (1942) "A Reply to My Critics" in Paul Arthur Schillp (ed.) *The Philosophy of G.E. Moore* (Evanston and Chicago: Northwestern University Press): 535–677.

Moore, G.E. (1953) *Some Main Problems of Philosophy* (London: George Allen and Unwin).

Moore, G.E. (1959) *Philosophical Papers* (London: George Allen and Unwin).

Mucciolo, Laurence F. (1974) "The Identity Theory and Neuropsychology" *Noûs* 8: 327–42.

Nernessian, Nancy J. (1991) "Why Do Thought Experiments Work?" *Proceedings of the Cognitive Science Society* volume 13 (Hillsdale, NJ: Lawrence Erlbaun): 430–38.

Nernessian, Nancy J. (1993) "In The Theoretician's Laboratory: Thought Experiments as Mental Modelling" in D. Hull, M. Forbes and K. Okruhlik (eds.) *Proceedings of the 1992 Biennial Meeting of the Philosophy of Science Association* volume 2 (Michigan: Philosophy of Science Association): 291–301.

Neta, Ram (2007) "Fixing the Transmission: The New Mooreans" in Susana Nuccetelli and Gary Seay (eds.) *Themes from G.E. Moore: New Essays in Epistemology and Ethics* (Oxford: Oxford University Press): 62–83.

Newton, Isaac (1686) *Philosophiæ Naturalis Principia Mathematica*, Andrew Motte's 1729 translation into English, revised by Florian Cajori (1966) (Berkeley: University of California Press).

Newton-Smith, W.H. (1981) *The Rationality of Science* (London: Routledge and Kegan Paul).

Nichols, Shaun (2002) "How Psychopaths Threaten Moral Rationalism, or Is It Irrational to Be Amoral?" *The Monist* 85: 285–304.

Nichols, Shaun, Stephen Stich, and Jonathan M. Weinberg (2003) "Metaskepticism: Meditations in Ethno-Epistemology" in Stephen Luper (ed.) *The Skeptics: Contemporary Essays* (Aldershot: Ashgate Press): 227–47.

Nolan, Daniel (1997) "Quantitative Parsimony" *British Journal for the Philosophy of Science* 48: 329–43.

Nolan, Daniel (2001) "What's Wrong with Infinite Regresses?" *Metaphilosophy* 32: 523–38.

Nolan, Daniel (2005) *David Lewis* (Chesham, Buckinghamshire: Acumen Publishing).

Norton, John D. (1991) "Thought Experiments in Einstein's Work" in Tamara Horowitz and Gerald J. Massey (eds.) *Thought Experiments in Science and Philosophy* (Lanham, MD: Rowman and Littlefield): 129–48.

Norton, John D. (1993) "Seeing the Laws of Nature" *Metascience* 3: 33–38.

Norton, John D. (1996) "Are Thought Experiments Just What You Thought?" *Canadian Journal of Philosophy* 26: 333–66.

Norton, John D. (2004a) "On Thought Experiments: Is There More to the Argument?" *Proceedings of the 2002 Biennial Meeting of the Philosophy of Science Association, Philosophy of Science* 71: 1139–51.

Norton, John D. (2004b) "Why Thought Experiments Do Not Transcend Experience" in Christopher Hitchcock (ed.) *Contemporary Debates in Philosophy of Science* (London: Routledge): 44–66.

Nozick, Robert (1974) *Anarchy, State and Utopia* (New York: Basic Books).

Nozick, Robert (1981) *Philosophical Explanations* (Cambridge, MA: Harvard University Press).

Nuccetelli, Susana and Gary Seay (2007) "What's Right with the Open Question Argument" in Susana Nuccetelli and Gary Seay (eds.) *Themes from G.E. Moore: New Essays in Epistemology and Ethics* (Oxford: Oxford University Press): 261–82.

Oddie, Graham (1982) "Armstrong on the Eleatic Principle and Abstract Entities" *Philosophical Studies* 41: 285–95.

Okasha, Samir (2000) "Van Fraassen's Critique of Inference to the Best Explanation" *Studies in the History and Philosophy of Science* 31: 691–710.

Oliver, Alex (1996) "The Metaphysics of Properties" *Mind* 105: 1–80.

Pap, Arthur (1959) "Nominalism, Empiricism and Universals — 1" *Philosophical Quarterly* 9: 330–40.

Papineau, David (1993) *Philosophical Naturalism* (Oxford: Blackwell).

Parfit, Derek (1984) *Reasons and Persons* (Oxford: Oxford University Press).

Peijeneburg, Jeanne and David Atkinson (2003) "When Are Thought Experiments Poor Ones?" *Journal for General Philosophy of Science* 35: 304–22.

Peijeneburg, Jeanne and David Atkinson (2006) "On Poor and Not So Poor Thought Experiments, A Reply to Daniel Cohnitz" *Journal for General Philosophy of Science* 38: 159–61.

Petersen, Stephen (2008) "Analysis, Schmanalysis" *Canadian Journal of Philosophy* 38: 289–300.

Pigden, Charles R. (2007) "Desiring to Desire: Russell, Lewis, and G.E. Moore" in Susana Nuccetelli and Gary Seay (eds.) *Themes from G.E. Moore: New Essays in Epistemology and Ethics* (Oxford: Oxford University Press): 244–60.

Plantinga, Alvin (1981) "Is Belief in God Properly Basic?" *Noûs* 15: 41–51.

Plato, *Euthyphro*, Chris Emlyn-Jones (trans.) (1988) (London: Bristol Classical Press).

Poincaré, Henri (1952) *Science and Hypothesis*, William Greenstreet (trans.) (New York: Dover Books).

Polger, Thomas (2008) "H_2O, 'Water', and Transparent Reduction" *Erkenntnis* 69: 109–30.

Pryor, James (2000) "The Skeptic and the Dogmatist" *Noûs* 34: 517–49.

Pryor, James (2004) "What is Wrong with Moore's Argument?" *Philosophical Issues* 14: 349–78.

Pust, Joel (2000a) "Against Explanationist Skepticism Regarding Philosophical Intuitions" *Philosophical Studies* 106: 227–58.

Pust, Joel (2000b) *Intuitions as Evidence* (New York: Garland Press).

Putnam, Hilary (1975) "The Meaning of 'Meaning'" in his *Mind, Language and Reality: Philosophical Papers* volume 2 (Cambridge: Cambridge Philosophical Press): 215–71.

Quine, W.V.O. (1951a) "Ontology and Ideology" *Philosophical Studies* 2: 11–15.

Quine, W.V.O. (1951b) "Two Dogmas of Empiricism" *Philosophical Review* 60: 20–43.

Quine, W.V.O. (1960) *Word and Object* (Cambridge, Massachusetts: MIT Press).

Quine, W.V.O. (1969a) "Ontological Relativity" in *Epistemology Naturalised and Other Essays* (Columbia: Columbia University Press): 26–68.

Quine, W.V.O. (1969b) "Epistemology Naturalised" in *Epistemology Naturalised and Other Essays* (Columbia: Columbia University Press): 69–90.

Quine, W.V.O. (1969c) "Natural Kinds" in *Epistemology Naturalised and Other Essays* (Columbia: Columbia University Press): 114–38.

Quine, W.V.O. (1972) "Review of Milton K. Munitz (ed.) *Identity and Individuation*" *Journal of Philosophy* 69: 488–97.

Quine, W.V.O. (1974) *The Roots of Reference* (La Salle, IL: Open Court Press).

Quine, W.V.O. (1977) "Facts of the Matter" in Robert W. Shahan (ed.) *American Philosophy from Edwards to Quine* (Norman: University of Oklahoma Press): 176–96.

Quine, W.V.O. (1981a) "Things and Their Place in Theories" in *Theories and Things* (Cambridge, MA: Harvard University Press): 1–23.

Quine, W.V.O. (1981b) "Five Milestones of Empiricism" in *Theories and Things* (Cambridge, MA: Harvard University Press): 67–72.

Quine, W.V.O. (1981c) "Success and Limits of Mathematization" in *Theories and Things* (Cambridge, MA: Harvard University Press): 148–55.

Quine, W.V.O. (1990) *Pursuit of Truth* (Cambridge, MA: Harvard University Press).

Quine, W.V.O. and J.S. Ullian (1970) *The Web of Belief* (New York: McGraw-Hill Humanities).

Quinton, Anthony (1962) "Spaces and Times" *Philosophy* 37: 130–47.

Ramsey, William (1992) "Prototypes and Conceptual Analysis" *Topoi* 11: 59–70.

Rawls, John (1971) "A Theory of Justice" (Cambridge, MA: Harvard University Press).

Reid, Thomas (1764) *An Inquiry Into the Human Mind on the Principles of Common Sense*, Derek R. Brookes (ed.) (1997) (Pennsylvania: Pennsylvania State University Press).

Rey, Georges (1983) "Concepts and Stereotypes" *Cognition* 15: 237–62.

Rey, Georges (1985) "Concepts and Conceptions" *Cognition* 19: 297–303.

Rey, Georges (1994) "The Unavailability of What We Mean: A Reply to Quine, Fodor and Lepore" *Grazer Philosophisce Studien* 46: 61–101.

Rey, Georges (1997) *Contemporary Philosophy of Mind* (Oxford: Blackwell).

Rey, Georges (1998) "A Naturalistic *A Priori*" *Philosophical Studies* 92: 25–43.

Rey, Georges (2004) "The Rashness of Traditional Rationalism and Empiricism" in Maite Ezcurdia, Robert Stainton, and Christopher Viger (ed.) *New Essays in the Philosophy of Language and Mind, Canadian Journal of Philosophy* supplementary volume 30: 227–58.

Rey, Georges (2005a) "Philosophical Analysis as Cognitive Psychology: the Case of Empty Concepts" in Henri Cohen and Claire Leferbvre (eds.) *Handbook of Categorization in Cognitive Science* (Dordrecht: Elsevier): 71–89.

Rey, Georges (2005b) "Replies to Critics" *Croatian Journal of Philosophy* 15: 465–80.

Rey, Georges (2006) "Does Anyone Really Believe in God?" in Daniel Kolak and Raymond Martin (eds.) *The Experience of Philosophy* (6th edition; Oxford: Oxford University Press): 335–53.

Rey, Georges (2007) "Meta-atheism: Religious Avowal as Self-Deception" in Louise M. Antony (ed.) *Philosophers without Gods: Meditations on Atheism and on the Secular Life* (Oxford: Oxford University Press): 243–65.

Richard, Mark (2001) "Analysis, Synonymy and Sense" in C. Anthony Anderson and Michael Zeleny (eds.) *Logic, Meaning and Computation: Essays in Memory of Alonzo Church* (Dordrecht, Reidel: Kluwer University Press): 545–71.

Rieber, S.D. (1994) "The Paradoxes of Analysis and Synonymy" *Erkenntnis* 41: 103–16.

Rieber, Steven (1992) "Understanding Synonyms without Knowing That They Are Synonyms" *Analysis* 52: 224–28.

Roland, Jeffrey W. (2007) "Maddy and Mathematics: Naturalism or Not" *British Journal for the Philosophy of Science* 58: 423–50.

Roland, Jeffrey W. (2009) "On Naturalizing the Epistemology of Mathematics" *Pacific Philosophical Quarterly* 90: 63–97.

Rosch, Eleanor (1987) "Wittgenstein and Categorization Research in Cognitive Psychology" in Michael Chapman and Roger A. Dixon (eds.)

Meaning and Growth of Understanding: Wittgenstein's Significance for Developmental Psychology (Berlin: Springer): 151–66.

Rosch, Eleanor and C.B. Mervis (1975) "Family Resemblances: Studies in the Internal Structure of Categories" *Cognitive Psychology* 7: 573–605.

Rosen, Gideon (1990) "Modal Fictionalism" *Mind* 99: 327–54.

Rosen, Gideon (1999) "Review of Penelope Maddy, *Naturalism in Mathematics*" *British Journal for the Philosophy of Science* 50: 467–74.

Rosen, Gideon (2006) "The Limits of Contingency" in Fraser MacBride (ed.) *Identity and Modality* (Oxford: Oxford University Press): 13–39.

Roth, Paul (1999) "The Epistemology of 'Epistemology Naturalized'" *Dialectica* 53: 87–109.

Russell, Bertrand (1897) "Is Ethics a Branch of Empirical Psychology?", paper read to the Apostles society, Cambridge University. Reprinted in Kenneth Blackwell, Andrew Brink, and Nicholas Griffin (eds.) (1983) *The Collected Papers of Bertrand Russell, Volume 1, Cambridge Essays, 1888–1899* (London: George Allen and Unwin): 100–04.

Russell, Bertrand (1905) "On Denoting" *Mind* 14: 479–93. Reprinted in Robert C. Marsh (ed.) (1956) *Logic and Knowledge: Essays 1901–1950* (London: George Allen and Unwin): 41–56.

Russell, Bertrand (1911) *The Problems of Philosophy* (Oxford: Oxford University Press).

Russell, Bertrand (1914) *Our Knowledge of the External World as a Field for Scientific Method in Philosophy* (London: Routledge).

Russell, Bertrand (1918) "On Scientific Method in Philosophy" (Oxford: Oxford University Press). Reprinted in Bertrand Russell (1954) *Mysticism and Logic and Other Essays* (Harmondsworth: Penguin Books): 95–119.

Russell, Bertrand (1919) *Introduction to Mathematical Philosophy* (London: George Allen and Unwin).

Russell, Bertrand (1958) "What is Mind?" *Journal of Philosophy* 58: 5–12.

Ryle, Gilbert (1949) *The Concept of Mind* (London: Hutchinson Press).

Salmon, Nathan (1989) "Illogical Belief" *Philosophical Perspectives* 3, 1989, *Action Theory and Philosophy of Mind*: 243–85.

Salmon, Wesley C. (1957) "Should We Attempt to Justify Induction?" *Philosophical Studies* 8: 33–48.

Salmon, Wesley C. (1989) *Four Decades of Scientific Explanation* (Minneapolis: University of Minnesota Press).

Salmon, Wesley C. (1990) "Rationality and Objectivity in Science *or* Tom Kuhn Meets Tom Bayes" in C. Wade Savage (ed.) *Scientific Theories, Volume 14, Minnesota Studies in the Philosophy of Science* (Minneapolis: University of Minnesota Press): 175–204. Reprinted in Martin Curd and

J.A. Cover (eds.) *Philosophy of Science: The Central Issues* (London: W.W. Norton and Company): 551–83.

Schaffer, Jonathan (2009) "On What Grounds What" in David J. Chalmers, David Manley and Ryan Wasserman (eds.) *Metametaphysics* (Oxford: Oxford University Press): 347–83.

Schlesinger, G. (1963) *Method in the Physical Sciences* (London: Routledge and Kegan Paul).

Schlesinger, George N. (1983) *Metaphysics: Methods and Problems* (Oxford: Basil Blackwell).

Schnieder, Benjamin (2006) "Truth-making without Truth-makers" *Synthese* 152: 21–46.

Schroeter, Laura (2006) "Against *A Priori* Reductions" *Philosophical Quarterly* 56: 562–86.

Searle, John (1969) *Speech Acts* (Cambridge: Cambridge University Press).

Searle, John (1980) "Minds, Brains and Programs" *Behavioral and Brain Sciences* 13: 585–642.

Shafer-Landau, Russ (2003) *Moral Realism: A Defense* (Oxford: Oxford University Press).

Shoemaker, Sydney (1984) "Causality and Properties" in *Identity, Cause and Mind: Philosophical Essays* (Cambridge: Cambridge University): 206–33.

Sider, Theodore (2001) *Four-Dimensionalism: An Ontology of Persistence and Time* (Oxford: Oxford University Press).

Siegel, Harvey (1995) "Naturalised Epistemology and 'First Philosophy'" *Metaphilosophy* 26: 46–62.

Skyrms, Brian (1966) *Choice and Chance* (Belmont, CA: Dickenson).

Smart, J.J.C. (1959) "Sensations and Brain Processes" *Philosophical Review* 68: 141–56.

Smart, J.J.C. (1966) "Philosophy and Scientific Plausibility" in Paul Feyerabend and Wilfrid Sellars (eds.) *Mind, Matter and Method: Essays in Philosophy and Science in Honor of Herbert Feigl* (Minnesota: University of Minnesota Press): 377–90.

Smart, J.J.C. (1984) "Ockham's Razor" in James H. Fetzer (ed.) *Principles of Philosophical Reasoning* (Lanham, MD: Rowman and Littlefield): 118–28.

Smart, J.J.C. (1989) "Methodology and Ontology" in Kostas Gavroglu, Yorgos Goudaroulis, Pantelis Nicolacopoulos (eds.) *Imre Lakatos and Theories of Scientific Change* (Dordrecht: Kluwer Academic Press): 47–57.

Smith, Edward E. and Douglas L. Medin (1981) Categories and Concepts (Cambridge, Massachusetts: Harvard University Press).

Snowdon, P.F. (1991) "Personal Identity and Brain Transplants" in David Cockburn (ed.) *Human Beings* (Cambridge: Cambridge University Press): 109–26.

Soames, Scott (2003) *Philosophical Analysis in the Twentieth Century, Volume 1, The Dawn of Analysis* (Princeton: Princeton University Press).

Sober, Elliott (1981) "The Principle of Parsimony" *British Journal for the Philosophy of Science* 32: 145–56.

Sober, Elliott (1990) "Let's Razor Ockham's Razor" in Dudley Knowles (ed.) *Explanation and Its Limits* (Cambridge: Cambridge University Press): 73–94.

Sober, Elliott (1996) "Parsimony and Predictive Equivalence" *Erkenntnis* 44: 167–97.

Sorensen, Roy (1992a) *Thought Experiments* (Oxford: Oxford University Press).

Sorensen, Roy (1992b) "Review of James Robert Brown *The Laboratory of the Mind: Thought Experiments in the Natural Sciences*" *Foundations of Physics* 22: 1103–09.

Sorensen, Roy (1992c) "Thought Experiments and the Epistemology of Laws" *Canadian Journal of Philosophy* 22: 15–44.

Sosa, David (2006) "Skepticism about Intuition" *Philosophy* 81: 633–48.

Sosa, Ernest (2007) "Moore's Proof" in Susana Nuccetelli and Gary Seay (eds.) *Themes from G.E. Moore: New Essays in Epistemology and Ethics* (Oxford: Oxford University Press): 49–61.

Sosa, Ernest (2008) "Experimental Philosophy and Philosophical Intuition" in Joshua Knobe and Shaun Nichols (eds.) *Experimental Philosophy* (Oxford: Oxford University): 231–40.

Stalnaker, Robert (1984) *Inquiry* (Cambridge, MA: MIT Press).

Stalnaker, Robert (2000) "Metaphysics without Conceptual Analysis" *Philosophy and Phenomenological Research* 62: 631–36.

Stampe, Dennis (1977) "Towards A Causal Theory of Linguistic Representation" *Midwest Studies in Philosophy* volume II: 42–63.

Steinhart, Eric (2009) *More Precisely: The Math You Need to Do Philosophy* (Peterborough, ON: Broadview Press).

Stern, Cindy D. (1989) "Paraphrase and Parsimony" *Metaphilosophy* 20: 34–42.

Stich, Stephen (1978) "Beliefs and Sub-Doxastic States" *Philosophy of Science* 45: 499–518.

Stich, Stephen (1992) "What is a Theory of Mental Representation?" *Mind* 101: 243–61.

Strandberg, Caj (2004) "In Defence of the Open Question Argument" *Journal of Ethics* 8: 179–96.

Strawson, P.F. (1959) *Individuals: An Essay in Descriptive Metaphysics* (London: Methuen Press).

Strawson, P.F. (1966) *The Bounds of Sense: An Essay on Kant's Critique of Pure Reason* (London: Methuen Press).

Strawson, P.F. (1992) *Analysis and Metaphysics: An Introduction to Philosophy* (Oxford: Oxford University Press).

Stroud, Barry (1977) *Hume* (London: Routledge).

Stroud, Barry (1984) *The Significance of Philosophical Scepticism* (Oxford: Oxford University Press).

Suppes, Patrick (1968) "The Desirability of Formalization in Science" *Journal of Philosophy* 65: 651–64.

Swain, Stacy, Joshua Alexander, and Jonathan Weinberg (2008) "The Instability of Philosophical Intuitions: Running Hot and Cold on Truetemp" *Philosophy and Phenomenological Research* 76: 138–55.

Swinburne, Richard (2001) *Epistemic Justification* (Oxford: Oxford University Press).

Swoyer, Chris (1979) "Sense and Nonsense" *Canadian Journal of Philosophy* 9: 685–700.

Swoyer, Chris (1982) "The Nature of Natural Laws" *Australasian Journal of Philosophy* 60: 203–32.

Swoyer, Chris (1999) "How Ontology Might Be Possible: Explanation and Inference in Metaphysics" *Midwest Studies in Philosophy* volume XXIII: 100–31.

Taylor, Richard (1968) "Dare to be Wise" *Review of Metaphysics* 21: 615–29.

Teller, Paul (1971) "Review of W.V.O. Quine, *Ontological Relativity and Other Essays*" *British Journal for the Philosophy of Science* 22: 378–82.

Thagard, Paul R. (1976) "The Best Explanation: Criteria for Theory Choice" *Journal of Philosophy* 75: 76–92.

Thomson, Judith Jarvis (1971) "A Defence of Abortion" *Philosophy and Public Affairs* 1: 47–66.

Tidman, Paul (1994) "Logic and Modal Intuitions" *The Monist* 77: 389–98.

Tidman, Paul (1996) "The Justification of *A Priori* Intuitions" *Philosophy and Phenomenological Research* 56: 161–71.

Tiel, Jeffrey R. (1999) "The Dogma of Kornblith's Empiricism" *Synthese* 120: 311–24.

Vahid, Hamid (2001) "Realism and the Epistemological Significance of Inference to the Best Explanation" *Dialogue* 40: 487–507.

Vahid, Hamid (2004) "Varieties of Epistemic Conservatism" *Synthese* 141: 97–122.

van Fraassen, Bas C. (1975) "Platonism's Pyrrhic Victory" in A.L. Anderson, R.B. Marcus, and R.M. Martin (eds.) *The Logical Enterprise* (New Haven: Yale University Press): 39–50.

van Fraassen, Bas C. (1980) *The Scientific Image* (Oxford: Oxford University Press).

van Fraassen, Bas C. (1989) *Laws and Symmetry* (Oxford: Oxford University Press).

van Fraassen, Bas C. (1995) "'World' Is Not a Count Noun" *Noûs* 29: 139–57.

van Fraassen, Bas C. (2002) *The Empiricist Stance* (New Haven: Yale University Press).

van Inwagen, Peter (1991) "Searle on Ontological Commitment" in Ernest Lepore (ed.) *John Searle and His Critics* (Oxford: Blackwell): 345–58.

van Inwagen, Peter (1996) "It Is Wrong, Everywhere, Always, and for Anyone, to Believe Anything upon Insufficient Evidence" in Jeff Jordan and Daniel Howard-Snyder (eds.) *Faith, Freedom, and Rationality: Philosophy of Religion Today* (Lanham, MD: Rowman and Littlefield): 137–54.

van Inwagen, Peter (1997) "Materialism and the Psychological-Continuity Account of Personal Identity" *Philosophical Perspectives, 11, Mind, Causation and World*: 305–19.

Vogel, Jonathan (1990) "Cartesian Skepticism and Inference to the Best Explanation" *Journal of Philosophy* 87: 658–66.

Vogel, Jonathan (1993) "Dismissing Sceptical Possibilities" *Philosophical Studies* 70: 235–50.

Vogel, Jonathan (2000) "Reliabilism Leveled" *Journal of Philosophy* 97: 602–23.

Walsh, Dorothy (1979) "Occam's Razor: A Principle of Intellectual Elegance" *American Philosophical Quarterly* 16: 241–44.

Walton, Douglas (1989) *Informal Logic: A Handbook for Critical Argumentation* (Cambridge: Cambridge University Press).

Ward, David E. (1995) "Imaginary Scenarios, Black Boxes and Philosophical Method" *Erkenntnis* 43: 181–98.

Weinberg, Jonathan M. (2007) "How To Challenge Intuitions Empirically Without Risking Skepticism" *Midwest Studies in Philosophy* volume XXXI: 318–43.

Weinberg, Jonathan M., Shaun Nichols and Stephen P. Stich (2008) "Normativity and Epistemic Intuitions" in Joshua Knobe and Shaun Nichols (eds.) *Experimental Philosophy* (Oxford: Oxford University): 17–45.

Weintraub, Ruth (1997) *The Sceptical Challenge* (London: Routledge).

White, Roger (2005) "Why Favour Simplicity?" *Analysis* 65: 205–10.

Wilkes, Kathleen V. (1988) *Real People: Personal Identity without Thought Experiments* (Oxford: Oxford University Press).

Williamson, Timothy (2007) *The Philosophy of Philosophy* (Oxford: Blackwell).

Williamson, Timothy (2009) "Replies to Kornblith, Jackson and Moore" *Analysis Reviews* 69: 125–35.

Wilson, Mark (2006) *Wandering Significance: An Essay on Conceptual Behaviour* (Oxford: Oxford University Press).

Wisdom, John (1934) "Is Analysis a Useful Method in Philosophy?"
Proceedings of the Aristotelian Society supplementary volume 13: 65–89.

Wittgenstein, Ludwig (1922) *Tractatus Logico-Philosophicus* (London:
Routledge).

Wittgenstein, Ludwig (1953) *Philosophical Investigations* (Oxford:
Blackwell).

Wittgenstein, Ludwig (1964) *The Blue and Brown Books* (2nd edition;
Oxford: Blackwell).

Wolpert, Lewis (2000) *The Unnatural Nature of Science* (Harvard: Harvard
University Press).

Wright, Crispin (1985) "Facts and Certainty" *Proceedings of the British
Academy* 71: 429–72. Reprinted in Thomas Baldwin and Timothy Smiley
(eds.) (2004) *Studies in the Philosophy of Logic and Knowledge* (Oxford:
Oxford University Press): 51–94.

Wright, Crispin (2002) "(Anti-)sceptics simple and subtle: Moore and
McDowell" *Philosophy and Phenomenological Research* 65: 330–48.

Wright, Crispin (2007) "The Perils of Dogmatism" in Susana Nuccetelli and
Gary Seay (eds.) *Themes from G.E. Moore: New Essays in Epistemology
and Ethics* (Oxford: Oxford University Press): 25–48.

Yablo, Stephen (2000) "Textbook Kripkeanism and the Open Texture of
Concepts" *Pacific Philosophical Quarterly* 81: 98–122.

Index

The interior of this book is printed on 100% recycled paper.